Last Press Bus Out of Middletown

LAST PRESS BUS
Out of Middletown

A Memoir

Bob Hammel

This book is a publication of

Indiana University Press
Office of Scholarly Publishing
Herman B Wells Library 350
1320 East 10th Street
Bloomington, Indiana 47405 USA

iupress.indiana.edu

ISBN 978-0-253-04467-9 (hardback)
ISBN 978-0-253-04469-3 (web PDF)

1 2 3 4 5 23   23 22 21 20 19

Contents

Preface

MICHAEL KORYTA

BOB HAMMEL, WHO IS AMONG THE MOST-HONORED SPORTS-writers of the last 50 years, was stubbornly reluctant to write this book. I say that assuredly, because over a lot of years I spent many a lunch, along with the late esteemed Indiana University history professor George Juergens, urging him to do it. But Bob was a journalist's journalist: he enjoyed telling other people's stories but did not see anything special about his own.

I am so glad he finally changed his mind.

What he has delivered here would have delighted George, and it certainly delights me. It's a wonderful, witty, and insightful insider's account of a golden age of sportswriting, but there's a lot more than sports here, too. A lot more. Even so, Bob leaves out a few crucial details that should be noted. Since he made the mistake of giving me the opportunity to write his preface, I'll take the liberty of telling you what Bob won't. He won't indicate just how many hours of his life went into perfecting his craft. He won't talk of late nights and early mornings spent in pursuit of the right words, of the diligence to make the extra phone call or the extra stop by practice, whatever it took to give his readers the best possible coverage, and the best possible writing. He won't tell you that he outworked every one of his competitors. He'll talk only about the rewards the newspaper brought to him, and how fortunate he was to be there. I'm here to say that he brought a lot of rewards to his readers, too, and how fortunate we were to have him there.

I began to work with Bob shortly after he'd retired as sports editor of the Bloomington *Herald-Times*. My neighbor, Michael Hefron (like Bob, a mentor who has turned into a dear friend), was the newspaper's general manager. I was in my early teens, but Mike knew I wanted to be a writer. He encouraged me to meet with Bob to talk about writing, if indeed I was actually serious about that as a career. I said something like, "But I don't want to be a sportswriter; I want to write books." The air around us turned a little blue, and I was left with the firm—and accurate—understanding that good writing is good writing, and I'd better figure that out real fast.

So, I found myself in Bob's basement lair at the *Herald-Times*. ("Lair" is a much more accurate description than "office" for the converted section of a basement storeroom with which Bob took few issues despite a year-round damp chill, a few leaky overhead pipes, and the tendency for people to accidentally turn off the storeroom lights and leave him in blackness.) It was a room that had an immediate appeal to me and remains in mind as an all-time cherished spot. So many books! Shelves and shelves of books, from sports to politics to the writer's art. Oh, how I loved that room—until the day I helped him move out of it. Then his decision to archive approximately 40 years' worth of *Swimming World* magazine seemed a lot less impressive.

Later in these pages, you'll get Bob's version of our first encounter. His may be more accurate, because he has a truly superior memory, but there's an advantage to writing the introduction—I get to tell it first. You'd have thought a breaking-news veteran like Bob wouldn't have made such a fundamental mistake.

As Bob will tell it, when I left his office that day, he didn't expect to see me again. As I recall it, I left with the notion that Bob didn't really wish to see *me* again. He'd sent me on my way with a collection of essays by Montaigne, promising that our study of the writing craft would begin there, in the French Renaissance of the 1500s. Catching up with Stephen King—or even Mark Twain—suddenly seemed a long way

0.1. With Michael Koryta—celebrating 20-year-old Michael's first book, in a familiar "lair" (Bloomington *Herald-Times* photo by David Snodgress).

off. To this day, I assert that nobody ever handed a 15-year-old kid the essays of Montaigne if he had a true desire to see that kid darken his doorstep again.

Even safe bets don't always come through. Sorry, Bob (fig. 0.1).

By the time I left that first meeting in the basement office where I would have so many wonderful talks over the years to come and learn so much, two things had become crystal clear:

1. Bob Hammel knew one heck of a lot about the craft of writing.
2. My writing was going to need to get one heck of a lot better, fast.

When I returned, I received the first of what Bob called, somehow with a straight face, "a little bit of editing" to my story. There was so much red ink on the pages I thought he'd surely nicked an artery with his letter opener. When I dropped off the story, I had placed a thank-you note on top of the manuscript, and I now observed, with an uneasy sense of what was to come, that Bob had edited even *that*. Bob doesn't remember doing this, but I have the evidence to prove it, because that initial edit and lesson in writing meant so much to me that I saved the story—*and* the thank-you note. Red ink on all of it.

He walked me through the massacre like an evidence technician recreating a crime scene, explaining what each blood splatter meant, how so many of the blood splatters shared fundamental root causes, how the blood splatters built upon one another to create a real mess, and how adherence to some basic principles could avert such bloodshed in the future.

Then he told me he thought it was a very good piece of work—a fairly bewildering summation considering he'd found only a few pronouns that didn't demand a swift strike of the red pen.

And so I left Session Two with revised but still-vivid impressions:

1. I was getting a free master's class on the craft of writing, and I ought not to waste it.
2. There probably weren't too many people among Bob's legions of loyal readers who understood just how damn hard he worked.

That last point matters a great deal to me. I'm talking about writing here, with the knowledge that a good many of you readers arrived for sports stories. Fear not—there are plenty of sports stories ahead, and they're riveting, compelling, funny, and moving. You'll be taken from the court of Assembly Hall, where the last undefeated team in men's major-college basketball built its 1976 title run, to the Olympic Village in Munich where Mark Spitz made history in the swimming pool and the world got an early lesson in the type of terrorism it would see far too often in years to come.

Bob was there for it all.

You'll get Michael Jordan and Bill Parcells and Ted Williams, and, yes, you'll get Bob Knight. You'll get an unparalleled look at a special era in sports history, and a special era in journalism, when a small-town newspaper could cover the Olympics and the Final Four. But I do want to talk about writing, because you should also be here for Bob Hammel, and Bob Hammel is a truly great writer. He's also a truly great *worker*—I've met few people who pour as much time and energy and relentless effort into the act of improving at their craft, day by day.

Bob doesn't like to hear it, but I think his willingness to teach his craft, to share the lessons of Strunk & White and William Zinsser and, yes, Montaigne, gave me about a 10-year head start on my life's dream of becoming a novelist. I published far, far earlier because of his help than I ever could have without it. I'm but one beneficiary of a man who has a unique and humbling willingness to give of his own time, knowledge, and energy without any need for a return. The causes Bob has championed over the years are legion, and though he claims to be slowing down, I still leave many of our lunch meetings feeling as if I'm lazy in comparison.

I took so much knowledge and joy and laughter away from those basement-office sessions before and during our years together at the *Herald-Times*. The locations of the sessions have changed over subsequent years, but the reward of the time with Bob never has. For a long time, I had the privilege of hearing in private the stories that are now offered to you in these pages, and I'm thrilled that Bob has chosen to share them in this fashion. He has plenty to tell—and he has worked awfully hard to bring them to you with the right words, and omit the needless ones.

MICHAEL KORYTA, still in his mid-30s, already has authored 12 nationally reviewed and admired novels. A product of the Bloomington, Indiana, public schools and Indiana University, he was 20 when his first book, *Tonight I Said Goodbye*, made him the youngest ever to be a finalist for the prestigious Edgar Award for first-time authors, and the youngest ever to win the Los Angeles Book Prize.

(*My quick summation: he has advanced from being America's greatest young writer to America's youngest great writer—BH*)

Prologue

IN LOFTIEST TERMS I WAS A CAREER JOURNALIST, BUT RE-
ally I was a sportswriter. That's not as diminished as it sounds. One
time I went to write about a swimming meet and wound up covering
the start of World War III.

That's why I—an old-school newspaperman left eons behind by today's technology—if given a chance for a commencement lecture to
the bright young people about to leave college and enter today's ever-
evolving media market would title it:

Prepare to be unprepared.

I look back on 60-plus years of writing and realize that as determined
as I was throughout my career to be well-grounded with data and background going into every interview or assignment, the key moments in
my newspaper life—right from its green-as-grass, totally unprepared
beginning—pretty much blindsided me. That most turned out quite
well usually was because of other people's doing.

All those memory-enriching experiences I got paid to write about, all
those giants of sports and even real life that I got to meet and tell about
and some really know, all those events, some historic and some forget-
table, that I tried so hard to give a deserved perspective—all of that the

world, the real world, will little note nor long remember compared to an interruption in my life called Munich.

Munich 1972. The Olympic Games. When I and the rest of a relatively tranquil planet were introduced to the cold cruelty and white-hot passions of terrorism.

We had no idea what we were dealing with then. More than 40 years later, we still don't know how to cope with it. A war on terrorism? Can't occupy it, can't kill it, can't bomb the hell out of it—what kind of war is it when things like that don't work?

Formally, I misspeak with "World War III" references. We haven't christened it as we did the collision of armies and navies and allied countries in the nineteen-teens and nineteen-forties. Warring, though brutal and horrible, seemed simple then, unifying. When we were fighting foreign powers we weren't looking over our shoulders at our own haters, our own gun-happy killers of children and churchgoers. We say terrorism and think internationally, but isn't what happens here almost every other week—when one or two gunmen on suicide missions take a dozen or so innocent victims with them—its own form of terrorism?

Probably, our War(s) on Terrorism(s) will have an ending. Probably, I won't be around to see it.

I didn't expect to be there to see it start.

But I was. And the same "I" was privileged to have a premium coverage spot when much more mundane revolutions happened: when, in a nine-year midpoint stretch of my 42-year sportswriting life, Indiana—*Indiana!*—played in college football's Rose Bowl, Indiana's Mark Spitz conquered the swimming world, and Bob Knight took Indiana and college basketball on an electrifying ride far more historic than histrionic, though both.

Luck, philosopher–football coach Darrell Royal said or stole, is when preparation meets opportunity. So what is it, Darrell, when unpreparation meets unimagined opportunity?

The story of my life.

I was in my 70s when my tolerant wife, Julie—silently enduring my remote-control switchings from between-innings commercial time in a White Sox baseball game to peek in on a Tiger Woods golf tournament, with an occasional sidetrack to an NBA playoff game—asked something brand new in our 50-year marriage:

"If you had been an athlete, what would you have wanted to be?"

I wasn't quick with an answer, because I had none. The question presumed an unfulfilled fantasy. Finally, I said, "Really, honey, I can't say any of them. I *was* what I wanted to be."

I was a sportswriter.

A sportswriter's job, and opportunity, too, it seemed to me, was to tell a story, *the* story. More than that, to watch the story happen, to *see* the story in what happened, and get it.

Every basketball game, every football game, baseball game, track meet, swimming meet—whatever the event covered—deserves to be, demands to be, treated as different because, in some way, it is. My question always, on reading my newspaper account minutes or hours after my work had gone to press, was, Did I get it? Did I pick up what made this game story *news*? Did I spot that difference, and talk about it in casual terms? That part is important, too, maybe most important of all: keeping a perspective on what as well as who is being covered. My writing idol Red Smith's New York *Herald-Tribune* boss, Stanley Woodward, had a splendidly distasteful term for the purple prose that lauded athletes of his and earlier times: "Godding them up." I spent my whole journalistic life with a goal of not necessarily leading the world in scoops but making a good run at the top in perspective: *the capacity to view things in their true relations or relative importance* is the way Mr. Webster defines what I set as an ambition.

I felt my job was not just to report what happened that day but its significance, its perspective with what had been done before, by that athlete, or a player from that team, or a player from any team—and to *know* (so that over time my readers would assume) that what I said was true, fact-backed, verifiable by record books.

I wanted to write. And be right. Goals don't have to be complex.

This act of writing is surely the closest I as a man can come to experiencing the creative, inceptive, painful joy of childbirth.

Sometimes a good phrase, a good story gestates when I'm supposed to be sleeping, my mind at rest. Suddenly I'm aware of this chemistry of thoughts and word combinations in my mind, an entrapped tigercat clawing for life of its own, as words on paper. They flow in a symphony that I know from experience won't be there for me to replay and record in the morning, so I learned to bolt from sleep to life, get up whatever the hour and find a device—a notepad, a pen—for at the least preservation. Notes are not enough. I need to capture the full thought, with all the nuances that seem so clear, so well declared, because they won't be there, they won't flow like that from a cold, daylight restart.

And oh, that flow . . .

A professional lifetime with newspaper realities is probably responsible for my version of what I suspect every writer has: a personal rhythm in transmitting thoughts to fingers on a keyboard. Each time I have one of these midsleep adventures, I realize the pluses and minuses of that rhythm. Once out of bed on one of those, any attempt to record by hand what my mind is spewing out shows me I was not built for the quill-and-ink writing days. My brain races much too fast for my fingers to process with pen or pencil. Later, maybe I can bring it off, but only at a keyboard (fig. 0.2).

Only by typing—a rhythmic wonder of its own. Think just of that act: writing by typing. How does this happen? In a practice older and faster than any computer, the brain considers and rejects and ultimately forms just the right words in just the right sequence—sometimes the punch of a sentence at its opening, sometimes the close, occasionally somewhere in the middle, and none of this by conscious plan. When everything is going right, with maybe a deadline pressuring, it must look to an observer like an uninterrupted flow—no consideration needed for structure in whole thoughts that the fingers, purely by instinct, fast as an electric bolt, convert in fingertip action to perfectly spelled words— a letter at a time . . . with breaks between words, each spelled correctly . . . with just the right punctuation to fit mood and tempo and bring a reader along at the pace intended. And *tell the story*—complete the trickiest part of it all: passing a thought from your mind to your reader's, with clarity and comprehension.

This new work, this child of consummation of creation and dream, can happen in a few minutes, or fifty—but not much longer in newswriting.

0.2. My fingers, my Royal—with round keys that flew (Huntington *Herald-Press* photo by Tom Harrell).

And then it's time to think and dream and visualize some more until there's another tigercat clawing for freedom—till a family of such creatures assembles like young ducks on a single-file walk, so orderly and natural it seems ordained. And that forms an essay, a book, or a paragraph.

Actually, those instances of middle-of-the-night inspiration preservation were rare, probably not even ten in my entire writing lifetime.

Much more common in my 52-year newspaper career was reporting to my desk in early morning, threading paper into a typewriter for most of those years, and ultimately starting to write, something.

As retirement approached—from daily duties as a sportswriter/columnist, just short of 60 years old in 1996—I knew I was going to miss writing... miss being read, but more truthfully miss the daily challenge of a blank page begging, daring, demanding to be filled. Author-professor-thinker Bob Schmuhl, a Notre Dame dean and longtime friend of mine, headed a Red Smith lecture series at Red's alma mater and after a few years put some of his honorees' talks together in a booklet with a marvelous title, *Making Words Dance*. That indeed was each day's goal, and once in a too-rare while, it happened!

But the tryst was daily, a meeting with coitus absolutely in mind: between that virginal white paper and in my beginning a typewriter, with fingertip-round keys and a clang that celebrated the conquest of every line. You don't hear those clangs anymore. The once-cacophonic newsroom now has the stillness of a library, of a morgue (another great newspaper word that technology has antedated).

It really *was* a tryst, that start of a day, start of a column—a love-based tryst hot and passionate, with a short birth process. The offspring from today was there the next morning for me, the proud parent, to maybe beam but also—where it's different from the starry-eyed first look of parenthood—be the first to see the flaws, the imperfections, the maddening shortcomings. And by then it was a new day with a necessity, a chance, to try again.

Lord, that was fun.

Because of my own actions and inactions, mine was a career without a college degree, without classroom exposure to anything close to a college education. I deprived myself of the genuine enlightenment about the dimensions of writing opened to students by skilled professors. That loss was lessened by incessant reading and by hard work and determination, all engendered by recognition of the handicaps I had given myself and the resultant, almost desperate zeal that sparked. Like the difference between arithmetic and mathematics, I wrote as a reporter, not a creator—a photographer, not an artist. There are reporters and there are photographers so very good that their own work is an art form—personal friends Dave Kindred and Rich Clarkson examples. But another personal friend, novelist Michael Koryta, is in mind when I speak of creative writers; I was re-creative, trying to capture and describe what I saw, not what I envisioned—the dull side of the line I associate with Bobby Kennedy: "Some men see things as they are, and ask why. I dream of things that never were, and ask why not." I admire, even envy, the creative. I enjoyed, even treasure, what was available to me as a simple conveyor of snapshots.

I entered my 60s and sports-beat retirement feeling pretty smug. I had beaten The System.

My first full-time job entered me at 17 into a profession I'd hoped some distant day to make. It wasn't a lofty profession: just sportswriting. But I wanted to be in it and lucked my way into it and stayed in it and did all right. My job—particularly in basketball, because of Bob Knight, and in the Olympics, because of many people—gave me experiences and memories that spending a fortune couldn't have bought.

And me? I was on the wrong side of every fitness gauge, but I had good health. I wasn't rich, but I had the lovely, unpressured feeling of being in fiscal debt to no one as I crossed my personal finish line into retirement.

It was then when I met another man newly retired. George Juergens (fig. 0.3) had been an Indiana University history professor, distinguished and even beloved for his lectures that had a singular way of defying boredom and penetrating the brain, and lasting there for a while, stimulating it into some actual thought. We began meeting weekly for lunch: every Monday, same Bloomington place: a back booth at Bobby's Colorado Steak House. Very soon, those Mondays with George ranked among my favorite times of the week, because we were so much alike, and so different.

Journalism has been called the first draft of history. Sportswriting isn't always considered journalism, especially by journalists. But it didn't take many exchanges of two politically liberal minds analyzing

0.3. George Juergens—Sox cap, Dodger fan, premier friend.

the same news for both of us to realize that "first draft" thing had legitimacy. Something would happen, and in conversation I would try to give it an immediate perspective in significance. I would push George for the same from him, but he would be much slower to commit.

Soon we realized our separation: a journalist wants to reach a judgment by tomorrow morning's paper; a historian is disciplined to wait 50 years or so to judge that same event or action by what it caused, or led to, or the way it tumbled into insignificance. The quick newspaper account is a starting point, subject to considerable updating and rewriting on the way to becoming history, or nothing.

George's life was shortened by congestive heart failure. He died at 80 in 2013. And that's about the time I finally grasped the wisdom of the historians' wait. I saw it through a sports event: those Munich Olympics of 1972, as they looked to me 40 years later. As history.

At Munich, I was 35 years old, out of the United States for the first time in my life, covering the Olympic Games for the first time. Rookie or veteran, I wouldn't have been ready for this. The Munich Olympics was much more than a sports event—a major world news event, recognized as that before those Games were even over.

What I didn't grasp in 1972, and what dawned on me when fortieth-anniversary stories and recounts swirled in 2012, was that what happened around me and I wrote about in Munich wasn't just The Biggest News Event of 1972. It was history. Not sports history—*world*.

That unimagined shock—a sports event, interrupted by killers scaling the Olympic Village fence late at night, shooting their way into the building where Israel's Olympians were quartered, holding them hostage while the world watched for long and anxious hours, before a chaotic airport scene that left captors and captives dead—was not just the news of that day but a landmark in time.

It was, I finally could recognize 30 to 40 years later, the world's—not just my, or my country's; the *world's*—introduction to international terrorism.

I've never seen Munich called that. With a sportswriter's propensity for pith and simplicity, *I* call it that. And I have memories of games played when they shouldn't have been, of a hillside full of people blithe when they shouldn't have been, to serve as my evidence. We—Americans, Europeans, citizens of the whole 1970s world—were innocents caught totally off-guard, who just didn't know what life-disdaining, die-for-a-cause, kill-for-a-purpose terrorism really was.

Before and after Munich, I lived in a world of games. But the world around me changed. Things were never the same again, after that terrible 24 hours at Munich, and they never will be. The Middle East that we thought of as deserts and camels and robed sheikhs and annoying fluctuations of gas availability and pricing was a place where our kids would go to die, for uncertain goals. The Holy Land of our Bibles was a hellish puzzle we couldn't comprehend, let alone solve. Was, and is.

And we—or at least I—first *really* began to see it, and feel it, in Munich.

When I had the rather grandiose idea of writing a memoir, of telling the many ways luck steered me through a happy, enjoyable life of sportswriting, I knew I had a lot to tell, some marvelous memories of people and places and events.

I was thinking of sports: my lifetime and pastime.

And then I realized the biggest life experience I had was Munich. When I was 35. That was my midlife crisis. My education.

Horror in the middle of a richly blessed life. Perspective that—my historian friend George Juergens had tried to teach me—came to me only after the passage of time.

But I will say this: it was a really great time.

Bob Knight.

So casually I dropped the name a few paragraphs back.

Truth is, Bob Knight, a basketball coach, is the reason these memoirs weren't written years ago, and that there weren't far, far fewer memories to memoir.

For years I wrestled with how to write my story without making it a borrowed version of his. Without making him such a major figure it violated his own biographical "space." And without cheating him from credit as the primary reason why a small-town regional writer got national and international opportunities.

Certainly not the only personage in my abetting galaxy, but an unquestioned No. 1.

So there, I've done it, with verification to come.

In *Season on the Brink*, the 1986 national best-seller that polarized the Bob Knight–aware into love and hate camps, there were references to long walks the two of us frequently took. And there were car rides, some of them long. Those were times for exchanges of our most private thoughts, family concerns, an occasional dialogue of views on personal feelings about faith, where we're actually pretty much on parallel paths, whatever our language difference—and on politics, where we're not so far apart as most presume: me an unabashed liberal, Bob an unbridled maverick who sees pomposity and preposterosity in pretty much equal portions on both sides.

In 2016, he found a presidential candidate who out-mavericked even him, and he raised some eyebrows by speaking out for Donald Trump. I wasn't surprised. The first time I saw Trump firing back at a news reporter, an image of Bob and a thought flashed in my mind: "There's a marriage coming up here."

When Trump campaigned in the May 2016 Indiana primary, Bob was invited to speak for him at a rally. Hours before the rally I met with him in his Indianapolis hotel room, listened to his planned remarks, then suggested a few ways to sharpen and enliven them. He said with a grin, "You realize you're helping me stick it to that party of yours, don't you?" Of course, I said, "And I hope *you* realize everything you're saying is going against every fiber in my body and I still want to help you. Is that a good-enough definition of friendship for you?"

My overriding rationale was what Voltaire was supposed to have said: "I do not agree with what you say but I'll defend to the death your right to say it."

Truth is I'm not nearly that noble. The "to the death" part overstates. I never was willing to go that far, to find myself trying to explain to

Saint Peter, "I'm up here a little early because I helped a guy speak up for Donald Trump."

And speaking of our forty-fifth president: Past 80, approaching the serenity of senility or the silence of death, I see America, *my* America, in The Trump Age and wonder what have I wrought—I, we, my era? Other eras even in my lifetime have had their passions stirred by iconoclasts voicing the socially unspeakable but *we* have nominated and elected our Joe McCarthy. How will history look at that? How will history—the history of our explodable world, of the children and grandchildren so precious to me—look at the period I have lived through, voted through?

I'm just a sportswriter. Historian George Juergens would have said, "Wait 50 years and find out."

You're on your own for that.

The finality, the fatality of that thought leads me to my only regret at reaching old age.

Getting there has meant going through the burial of so many dear friends.

A life that is so much sadder without them was far better because of them.

Last Press Bus Out of Middletown

In the Beginning . . .

HENRY DAVID, WILLIAM ALLEN, DAD AND MOM

OUT IN THE WOODS, LONG BEFORE CARS OR WORLD WARS OR 50 percent divorce rates, Henry David Thoreau wrote in *Walden*, "The mass of men lead lives of quiet desperation." That observation, so sadly, profoundly true, always has made me think of my dad, and it has hovered in my mind from career peak into retirement as a reminder of how lucky I was.

To me, my father—Dale Theodore Hammel—was a flesh-and-blood representative of Thoreau's mass of men. I saw Dad through a child's eyes in his 30s and early 40s: a smart, hardworking, selfless man who was one of the millions never given a chance to develop or excel or thrive because their emergence into adulthood came during the Great Depression.

No college degree for that mass. No pride of great and visible accomplishment, no inviting stepladder to riches, because for them, as life on their own began, there was no job, period, certainly no job that brought self-esteem and ambitious aspirations. "The Great American Dream," later generations were to call it: hou$e, $port$ car, $ucce$$. From the days his adult life began in his and my hometown of Huntington, Indiana, nothing remotely like that was out there for Dad to dream about, even delude himself about. Just bills to pay, a wife and family to support, a family that included me.

He was a handsome man, wavy dark hair that thinned but never left him, a trim and muscular body that never thickened. A good athlete in a small rural high school, he averaged scoring ten points a game in basketball when teams were averaging twenty. Huntington Township School, its students from the rural areas of the township surrounding the borders of Huntington, had twelve classes under one roof, first grade through senior year, no such thing as kindergarten. Dad, born July 22, 1909, graduated from that school in 1927, and married Mom in 1931, the year she graduated there. Years later I started school in the same building and glowed with an inner pride and a happy blush every time I passed the wall where Dad's 1926–27 basketball team was pictured, alone among all the teams the school ever had—players in separate, individual, simulated-action photos, Dale Hammel right in the middle, the spot for the team star, I always figured.

He attended I think one year at Huntington College—I have to "think," I don't *know* because we never talked about it. Stop for a moment and consider that: inherently curious Bob Hammel, who in a lifetime interviewed thousands of people, probed for details and reasons with questions asking how and when and why—"How exactly did you feel when . . ." and "What was going through your mind when . . ."—can't recall *ever*, even once, sitting down with his own dad and learning as scant a detail as what he did after high school.

That would have been in the Roaring Twenties, when things were good. The Roar was over when in January 1931 he married his 17-year-old sweetheart. Their first home was on a farm, where Dad was a $5-a-week room-and-board laborer, income that jumped to $6 a week for the two of them when Mom married him, moved in, and also worked full time.

I never realized until I first saw pictures half a century later how comely a couple they were on their wedding day. Mom was the one who surprised me. The Mom I grew up idolizing was plain and purposely drab, no makeup, no hairstyling except self-done, always neat and well groomed but never wearing anything more stylish than department stores sold. I never thought of her as beautiful. Just perfect.

I think of her now as the biggest individual influence on what I am today: disciplined not to lose temper or composure, not at all hesitant to show fondness and love, especially toward our children, and theirs. Her birth-certificate name was Beautrice—Beatrice with a *u*, the only spelling like that I've ever seen, pronounced in Hoosier tongue BEW (as in *few*) -truss. Beautrice Mae Davis Hammel was born December 10, 1913, and grew up Betty Davis before the actress made the name familiar. Her home life was shattered when her parents divorced in her early years. Her father—Claude Davis, a Metropolitan Life Insurance salesman whose lifelong name for her was "Babe"—and she shared a deep love, but he saw her rarely after the divorce, moving to Memphis, Tennessee, to live out his last 30 years. She grew up in Huntington with her mother, who—like her ex-husband—remarried.

Today, Mother's exceptional intelligence and absorbent mind might have propelled her to college scholarships and a career of her own, probably as a teacher, perhaps as the doctor her instincts might have pushed her to be. Instead, she married before leaving high school—not for the usual reason: my sister, Joy, wasn't born for three more years. The Great Depression had begun, but her own parents' divorce—not economic hard times—was why Mother's home life without her beloved father around was not great. On January 25, 1931, past the middle of her senior year of high school, Dad drove the two of them about 50 miles to Muncie, found a man with a "Justice of the Peace" shingle on his home, and they were married—they thought (fig. 0.4). Forty years later, Mom was reading the Fort Wayne *Journal-Gazette* and broke out in laughter—nothing loud, just a soft reaction to unexpected discovery of something really, personally funny. In amid the day's minutiae she read of the arrest in Muncie of a man who as a self-declared Justice of the Peace had fraudulently married something like 2,000 couples over a long period of years—the very "Justice of the Peace" who had married her and Dad. Mom was rigidly religious and saw as sacred her marriage and her motherhood. Her laugh showed the news changed nothing; intact and totally undisturbed was her own innate surety of God-approved purity for her unintentional "life in sin." And I never felt the least bit bastardized.

Speaking at her funeral, I said, in humor subtly intended to reflect the humor she'd inherited from her own father, that she actually had very poorly prepared Joy, me, and our younger brothers, Jim and Bill, for marriage, because we never heard the first words of an argument

0.4. Dale and Betty Hammel—the day they thought
they were married.

between our parents. I spoke basic truth. When Julie and I had our first
angry postwedding exchange, the thought bolted through my mind:
*This isn't a good marriage—hostility doesn't happen between couples who
really love each other.* Our kids didn't grow up so deceived.

Mother's quiet, respectful love for Dad came up in a talk I gave long
after both had died. Starting in 1993, I gave the Father's Day message at
my church, United Presbyterian, for 25 straight years (fig. 0.5). In the
seventeenth of those, on Father's Day 2009,[1] I said:

---

1. The last nine, starting with this one (in the year when my late dad would
have been 100), I had email editing and advisory help from Sister Rose Mary
Rexing, a nun at Sisters of Saint Benedict monastery in Ferdinand, Indiana.
I had met her while doing biographical work on Bloomington billionaire Bill
Cook. She and retired Methodist minister John McFarland, another great
friend, gave me consistent, ecumenical, much-appreciated predelivery editorial
help with my prepared "sermons."

0.5. For twenty-five Father's Days, pulpit time.

One year when Mom was about the age I am now, she felt terrible because Christmas came and, physically and financially, she just couldn't get out to buy what she considered suitable presents for us in her family.

For me, she wrapped up something she had picked up years before and waited for the right time to pass it along. She probably got it at what we called a dime store in those days—Woolworth's was our Walmart.

Might have cost her 49 cents—oh, a little more, maybe, because there's a line on there that's personalized and required some engraving. I'd guess a dollar or so, all told.

Its base is cheap wood. Glue binds a thin metal plate to the wood, and over the years the glue dried out and the metal came loose. In a pure financial sense, it wasn't worth salvaging. But this was something worth a whole lot more to me than the sum of its cheap parts.

So, actually a little bit embarrassed, I took it all to a trophy store and said, "Look, I know this is way below the standards you maintain in your work, but could you do anything to make this hold up for me? I really want to keep it." The great, understanding people at that store did the job masterfully, and it's still intact.

I'll read you what it says.

The top line, the one Mom had to have engraved, had just one word: the family name HAMMEL, the key to the message:

You got it from your father, it was all he had to give.
So it's yours to use and cherish, for as long as you may live.
If you lose the watch he gave you, it can always be replaced.
But a black mark on your name, son, can never be erased.
It was clean the day you took it, and a worthy name to bear.
When he got it from his father, there was no dishonor there.
So make sure you guard it wisely, after all is said and done.
You'll be glad the name is spotless when you give it to your son.

My Dad worked days or nights, sometimes days *and* nights, to provide a home, and ample food, for his wife and two, then three, then four kids, not an easy goal at all in those days. He had several brain-numbing factory jobs, one or two that required a 25-mile drive to and from work. In his off time, he was a skilled carpenter, a dairy farmer, a deft butcher, an amateur house renovator and buyer-seller who once bought a house for $6,000, moved us in on a Friday, and moved us out the next Friday because he got a chance to sell it for $7,000.

He was at times a city policeman, a grocery owner, a meat cutter for bigger grocery owners, the last of those the Kroger Company, which separated him from familiar, loyal, trusting customers by firing him just before his fiftieth birthday, lest a retirement commitment take effect. I've boycotted Kroger ever since, because even then, in the 1950s, 50 years old was ancient in the job-seeking market. Unemployed in a thriving economy, Dad fell into a depression of his own, a deep one of the sort medical science still doesn't know how to beat. It knew less then, and was more primitive. At one point Mother's eyes filled and overflowed while she watched her beloved "Bud"—nobody else ever called him that and she never called him anything else—undergo shock treatments as a counter to what was called a "nervous breakdown" in the terminology of the day. "Treatment" is an anemic word for an inhumane electric jolt, usually a series of them. And we thought the Dark Ages were unenlightened.

For a time, he was unable to work. Mom took a job—and excelled— as a doctor's secretary to provide family income. Eventually, through the kindness of a school superintendent named Phil Eskew who later had statewide eminence as commissioner of the Indiana High School Athletic Association, Dad took a job as the maintenance man at the local Carnegie library. The ladies who staffed the library couldn't have treated him better, nor praised him more generously and fondly, veritable saints who fed Dad's depleted self-esteem like resuscitators breathing life into a brink-of-death body. But even back on his wage-earning feet, he surely must have sat at home some nights thinking, *This* is the top of my ladder, after working as hard as I could all my life—in my 50s, a janitor?

The mass of men lead lives of quiet desperation.

But not I. Not Robert Dale Hammel, first of three sons of Dale Hammel, the lucky son who got a part in a family name-passing tradition that linked at least six generations. It might go back farther, but my knowledge of the situation starts midway through the nineteenth century when Ephraim Hammel begat Edward Ephraim Hammel, who begat Theodore Edward Hammel, who begat Dale Theodore Hammel, who begat Robert Dale Hammel, who begat Richard Robert Hammel, who begat two terrific daughters and all that other stuff ended.

Dad had many more skills, could do inestimably more things than I could, but because I lucked into an early job in the one marketable thing I could do—write in a style that worked in a newspaper—I never knew quiet *or* desperation.

But I knew Thoreau was right. And I always wished Dad had known just a little bit of my job happiness, my satisfactions, my essential serenity.

For invaluable contributions to my own sublime life, I say, thank you, Dad. And thank you, William Allen White.

Mr. White and I never met. Couldn't have. He died at 75 in Kansas in 1944 when I was in Huntington, Indiana, and 7 years old. The picture I have of him in my mind was formed much later and might or might not be accurate, but it was my inspiration. From what I have read by and about him, he was a small-town boy who dreamed of a news-writing career, with visions of rising high in the newspaper world, which meant going big-time: ultimately New York, or maybe Chicago or Los Angeles or, an acceptable bare minimum for him, Kansas City.

Instead, he left a job as editorial writer for the Kansas City *Star* to, at 27, buy his hometown Emporia, Kansas, *Gazette*—for three thousand 1895 dollars. He ran all things about that place as editor and publisher, and Emporia was still his base when he died.

He became a Pulitzer Prize winner, an adviser, and confidant to presidents. And his was the real world, in which real news and real presidents abide. Scale that down to the fun and games of sports, and I had the career of William Allen White as my inspiration to make the decision I made in my early 30s: that the Bloomington *Herald-Telephone*, with its 18,000 subscribers and the sports world that it and Indiana University opened to me, made climbing higher in regional and national exposure unnecessary for realization of my own life goals. Writing for thousands, writing for millions: is there really a difference? I never did the latter, so I can't presume to say, but I doubt it. Because first and foremost I always was writing for me: to meet my own standards of professionalism every day and excellence on the best of days. And I'll bet that's true of almost everyone who ever, for a living, put words on paper and enjoyed it.

Before arriving in Bloomington October 24, 1966, I worked at Indiana newspapers in my hometown of Huntington as well as Peru, Fort Wayne, Kokomo, and Indianapolis. My staple was high school sports coverage, but occasionally I sampled what others in the profession considered higher life.

As a credentialed reporter at the four 1964 World Series games in St. Louis, I sat in the press section—not the press *box*, mind you, the press section, which was a few rows of converted upper-deck seats out in the open air. My assigned spot was beside Frank Deford, who then was fresh out of Princeton, amiably conversational in this opening of what became a longtime friendship. Frank was *Sports Illustrated*'s No. 2 guy at that Series; No. 1 Bill Leggett sat on Frank's other side, an affable part of the conversing, too. I name-drop for the fun purpose of showing that in its eleventh year, *Sports Illustrated* commanded no more seating respect from the Cardinals than did the two-month-old, short-lived Kokomo, Indiana, *Times*, which I represented.[2]

Covering sports hadn't gone glitzy yet. So, baseball teams themselves controlled postseason press-coverage rights, and for World Series games at its park, a club took care of its local beat writers first, the other team's beat regulars next, then beat reporters from its own league, then from the other league—and then all outsiders. *Sports Illustrated* to Kokomo.

The night before the Series opener, the Cardinals were host to a press party that filled the main ballroom at the Chase Park Plaza Hotel. I went, hoping to find a few column notes. I *knew* nobody in the room, knew *of* a lot of people who were there, recognized many in an almost star-struck way, but was fully aware that—in a packed room—there wasn't a soul who knew *me*. I got a Coke and some shrimp on a plate and sat down by myself at a large round table. I hadn't been in my chair 30 seconds when a man and an entourage of writers swarmed in to fill the rest of the seats at that table. Because of that man, more note-takers kept coming in numbers that ultimately surrounded the table with quote-hungry, leaning, ear-cocked standing-roomers. The man, covering the Series for *Look* Magazine, was former New York Yankees manager Casey Stengel, who gave me the courtesy of an "OK to sit here?" glance before sitting down next to me on my right.

OK?

Ohhh, yeah!

He sat down talking and continued talking for three enchantingly rambling hours, while crowds of real baseball writers, genuine major league beat writers, in unending replenishment surrounded the table, straining to grasp even one uniquely Casey line or two, plenty to build a sparkling Series-eve column around. Me? I never left that chair, and

---

2. In a 6,000-word autobiographical piece Frank Deford did for *Sports Illustrated* in 2010, he saw a similar picture from a different view: "Before *SI* became a famous girlie magazine, it was new competition for newspapers, and we had a devil of a time even getting admitted to the pews in major league press boxes."

neither did Casey, quite a testimony to our bladders. Especially his, given that I was 28 and he was 75.

I took notes, and kept taking notes, and more than 50 years later wish tape recorders had been more customary then because a night like that with a growingly tipsy Casey Stengel was priceless, and unforgettable, and a sheer, completely unimaginable stroke of luck. The best I could do was a pad of scribbled notes, which I foolishly didn't save. From them came a column that I couldn't write that late, late night, couldn't write until the Series had opened the next day with Game 1 and it could run as a sidebar to my game coverage. The column began:

> ST. LOUIS—His ball club finished as far from the World Series as it's possible to get, but wherever Casey Stengel goes around here, there's a crowd.
>
> The 75-year-old Casey sat down at a table of sportswriters Tuesday night. Early Wednesday morning, he was still there, but by then there were three or four rows of standing listeners, leaning in eagerly to hear everything the manager of the 10th-place Mets had to offer. Meanwhile, manager Yogi Berra of the Yankees sat at a table with four friends . . . and no standers.

Excerpts from the column:

> "I have a lot of fellas on my team who want to go up there and swing the bat a yard instead of like this," he said, demonstrating a punch-type swing with his wrists.
>
> "My men says, 'Who, me? I don't like to swing that way. I can't hit home runs.'
>
> "But my guys strike out and guys like Groat and Richardson[3] swing like that and they are playing in the World Series and my fellas ain't so who's right?"

About the Yankees' pitching ace of the era, Whitey Ford:

> "Well, now, what can Mr. Ford do? You say, 'He can pitch.' Well, sure he can pitch. And you say, 'He can hit and field,' and he sure can do that, but he can do other things, too.

---

3. Dick Groat was the Cardinals' shortstop and Bobby Richardson the Yankees' second baseman, each All-Star caliber who hit for a high average, not power.

"He can keep you on first base, because he's got a great move. And that means you get more double plays because your infielders can play where they want to and let him take care of the runner.

"He can keep the man on second, too, and you better not go to sleep on third because he'll throw it over there, too. What does that mean? Well, that means the fella there maybe only walks a couple steps off third instead of running down the line, and maybe he's out at the plate on a ground ball when he would have scored. That's how this man wins ball games.

"I had him in the 1960 World Series. He shuts out Pittsburgh and we win, 10–0. Then I use him again and he wins, 12–0. But I fouled up, I forgot to use him in the first game, so his arm is stiff the last one and I can't use him three times and I get beat, so I'm a lousy manager."

Ford started and lost the opener to the Cardinals, but my Stengel column ran with that game story and noted:

Before losing he verified Mr. Stengel's judgment by: (1) fooling Dick Groat at first on a pickoff, although Groat got the safe call on a disputed decision; (2) chasing Tim McCarver back to third with a surprise throw that way; and (3) singling home a run.

You're a baseball fan? Tell me the last time you saw a straight pickoff try at third base. By a left-hander.

The Cardinals that year beat the Yankees in the seventh game of what turned out to be the domineering Yankees' last World Series for a dozen years—the last ever for Mickey Mantle, which means that I saw in Game 7 Mantle's last World Series home run. After that seventh game, in pursuit of quotes and grist for a masterpiece that only Kokomo would get to read (and maybe a little bit stupidly), I skipped The Mick. I went to the winning clubhouse, riotous and raucous as it was. Once the champagne sprays were out of the air, I had no problem finding a spot at various lockers to ask some questions and get some notes. One of my last stops was at the stall of game hero and Series MVP Bob Gibson.

Pack after pack had swarmed around Gibson by then and moved on, the big guys of the profession and the local guys familiar to him, asking the same shallow questions and postponing his shower, so a man who had a reputation for being a bit surly anyway had every reason to be dismissive when this lone fellow he didn't know at all arrived to start the silliness all over again. Victory and champagne had done their mellowing. I asked a question—probably something deep and probing like what pitch he had thrown to get some vital out. Gibson looked at me quizzically, his brow furrowed in what seemed to be a genuine effort to come up with an answer, and said with an apologetic grin, "A half hour ago I could have answered that, but right now I'm drunk."

And I had my mine-only-mine quote—not great, nothing to alert Bartlett's to, but *mine*. To Kokomo, Indiana, directly from the Sports Star of the Day.

I offer those few days in October 1964 for, yes, the joy of remembering them, but also for the epochal change they represent. Today, none of those 1964 things could happen to a newspaper guy from Kokomo—or Bloomington, my later and more lasting stop. Choice coverage positions for sports events now go to the highest bidder from network TV, with some allowance for The Major Print Medium, which has its own hoi-polloi-filtering-out system that limits big-event newspaper credentials to those meeting circulation minimums that usually start at 100,000. On its best weekday, the Bloomington *Herald-Times*[4] barely topped 30,000, more commonly in my years hovering near 25,000, which more than doubled the circulation number in the best days of the short-lived Kokomo *Times*.

I mention this modern-day emphasis on bigness with neither rancor nor jealousy but recognition of how lucky I was with my timing. As a very young man, I managed to scramble onto the Last Press Bus Out of Middletown—a town name made generic by a 1920s sociological book/study that made Muncie, Indiana, representative of all small (at the time Muncie's population was around 30,000) American towns. This is not to put down my Huntington, or my Bloomington, but rather to put them alongside hundreds of similar communities way out of the national spotlight and therefore journalism's mainstreams. A combination of

---

4. The Bloomington daily newspaper I joined in 1966 was called the *Herald-Telephone*, its Sunday edition the *Sunday Herald-Times*. In 1989, when the paper switched from afternoon to morning publication, the Monday-through-Saturday edition was renamed the much less colorful *Herald-Times*.

luck and right people got me on that press bus to cover things I would have been denied access to this half-century later.

Let me show you why getting there when I did was not only important in my own professional life but also luckily timed. In the 1980s, my own prime time at Bloomington, the NCAA Final Four and US Olympic organization established minimum-circulation standards way, way above ours at the *Herald-Telephone*. Because I had covered these events before those circulation-based cutoffs began they never did affect me. Both included in their new rules "grandfather clauses" that exempted my newspaper and any others that had been covering their events before. The exemptions remained in effect for the *Herald-Telephone* even after me—until they weren't used, until times changed at the *H-T*'s top, a Final Four came, and the decision to stop spending a few hundred dollars to cover something not directly involving Indiana University lost that special privilege. Bloomington—like all other Middletowns—no longer had NCAA or Olympic exemptions, and never again will.

Me? Protected by that grandfather clause right through my retirement at the end of the 1996 Atlanta Olympic Games, I got to consort with the big-newspaper guys at five summer Olympics in all and twenty-three NCAA Final Fours, with credibility value that got me credentialed for seven other World Series, a dozen or so Indy 500s, a Superdome fight that gave Ali back his championship, and . . .

I was the Bloomington *Herald-Telephone* sportswriter in the press box at

- the Kentucky Derby (just once: for Derby No. 100);
- College All-Star football games (when they still had them);
- baseball All-Star games (when they sometimes had two);
- the biggest football bowl games (a Rose, and the first forerunner of the BCS national-championship games) and some of the smallest (a category that would fit all seven non-Rose bowls in which Indiana University competed during my years).

At US Olympic Trials in track, swimming, and basketball, I was as fully credentialed as colleagues from the *Times* of New York and of Los

Angeles, and the same at NCAA championship events in track, swimming, and soccer.

I was allowed to cover dozens of events that are accessible only by
TV for most people and are unthinkably out of reach today for a fellow representing a small-town daily, even—maybe especially—one
whose newspaper for most of my years had a peculiar and charm-
ing, though indictingly small-town, name: the Bloomington *Herald-
Telephone.*

I was at all those places because a man named Perry Stewart, a blind
man named Perry Stewart, envisioned what a Bloomington *Herald-Telephone* could be and told me about it on an October day in 1966. At the
time, I was tenth man on a good ten-man sports staff at the Indianapolis
News, disinclined to leave there for Bloomington, and Perry—whom I'll
introduce more fully to you later—was desperate, but visionary enough
for both of us.

He is why I live in professional postlude with the blessed and lucky
feeling that I got on—and off—the press bus at just the right time.

I speak of a span that exceeded 50 years. Within that was up-close-
and-personal coverage of

- some of the best college basketball ever played, composed and
  conducted by a maestro named Bob Knight;
- *the* best collegiate swimming era ever, with a genius named Doc
  Counsilman and an artist named Mark Spitz as headliners;
- a parade of American track Olympians recruited and trained by
  another coach of exceptional gifts, Sam Bell;
- Indiana University's only Rose Bowl season under national
  Coach of the Year John Pont—*and* football All-Americans playing for a coach denied by the big-time college game's harsh caste
  system the Hall of Fame recognition he deserves, Bill Mallory;
- and, oh, so much more.

I had personal exposure to a more varied cornucopia of sports
achievements and achievers than surely anyone whose career topped
out at a newspaper circulation level close to mine *ever* had.

But most of that career, most of my job, was done far from the national spotlight. For every Big-Time Event where I was one person in a reporting battalion, there were hundreds of other events where I was the only writer there, soloing at games some no doubt would consider boring . . . bush. Counting everything, I saw and wrote about more than 2,000 college and high school basketball games, and maybe 1,000 college and high school football games, not to mention track meets and swimming meets and golf tournaments and baseball games, even a few top-level soccer games including a national-championship game . . .

And I covered a *lot* of practices.

I loved it all, right up to my day of retirement, suppressing a smirk because the scam of it was that every one of those games and practices and attendant events came under the generous heading of work.

Big-league baseball was the sport where, except for those postseason and All-Star games or times in a press box, I usually stepped out of my "working" role, sat in the stands, and just watched or listened as a fan. I've seen or heard broadcasts of I suppose twice as many baseball games as all those events I've covered added together. I'm 82 now—older than Casey Stengel that night in St. Louis, than William Allen White when he died. When I was eight and nine and ten, I was pressing an ear against the rounded, vertical wooden bars protecting the cloth front of a tall brown Philco console radio, on stormy days trying my hardest to separate from static the key words I needed to keep up with a White Sox game, even keep score.

Broadcasting was my dream then. Play-by-play. What a glamorous job—watching a major league game, every day, and telling people about it, and knowing the players and managers, and traveling with them. For a whole summer!

Alas.

I left puberty with a distinctive but decidedly not-beautiful voice. Broadcasting therefore was never a career option. I grasped the next-best possibility. I got a job typing my observations onto paper rather than speaking them into a microphone. My surprise discovery: that role had its own unimaginable rewards.

I grew to revere Red Smith, the best I've ever read in telling about sports and sports people and a few peripheral things such as history, literature, and sociology.[5] I never met the man, but a few times I was in the same press box, covering the same event that he was, excited by realization that each of us this day was armed with the same equipment—two eyes and the English language—as we set out to do our identical job. Another alas is called for here: in all those times of equal opportunity, the quality of my finished product never approached his.

But I've always felt my career had an advantage over Red's in one proximitous category: I covered Indiana high school basketball and he didn't even like the sport, at any level. He would have, I know, if—poor, unenlightened fellow—he had grown up in Indiana. My spawning was in Huntington, in northeastern Indiana—Dan Quayle–ville to some, population 13,902 in my day, a satellite to much bigger Fort Wayne. I grew up to a good life that, unlike poor Red's, let me cover twenty-nine Indiana high school basketball championship games. At 18, I covered Oscar Robertson's team's victory in the nation's first integrated state-tournament final between two all-black teams.[6] And I saw Oscar and his Indianapolis Crispus Attucks team repeat as champions the next year, and twenty-seven other outstanding teams come along after him to win the greatest high school basketball tournament of them all—all schools in the state, as many as 700-plus, competing for one grand prize: *the* Indiana state championship.

---

5. Dave Kindred and Frank Deford are my nominees as the Red Smiths of my generation. Just as Red had challengers (e.g., Bill Heinz, later Jim Murray), so do Dave and Frank (a personal favorite: Indiana-born Mike Lopresti of *USA Today*). It's a profession with lots of superb craftsmen, not all of them blessed with the Smith-Kindred-Deford-Lopresti blend of integrity and judgment. Today's trend toward bloggery, sans editing, seems a terrible one to me, but don't all generations go out carping?

6. In 2016, Indianapolis filmmaker Ted Green produced *Attucks: The School That Opened a City*, a wonderful work. In the process, he called me and said, "I heard you covered that 1955 tournament? How old *were* you?" I said eighteen and heard back: "*Eighteen?* And you're *eighty now?* There can't be another man alive who covered that tournament!" Never thought of it that way.

My timing was impeccable and lucky there, too; every one of the twenty-nine I covered was in the delicious era before people in principal positions "protected" Indiana's unique crown jewel right into obscene class-divided obscurity.

You've seen the 1986 movie *Hoosiers*, always up there No. 1, 2, or 3 whenever the greatest Hollywood sports films of all time are ranked. If you've seen it, and joined the millions who let themselves get caught up in its theme, you know why I thank God I had retired before having to cover something less than what writer Angelo Pizzo and director David Anspaugh—born-and-raised Hoosiers reberthed in Bloomington now and friends of mine—so lovingly captured.

Now, instead of one basketball state champion, Indiana crowns four, the fields differentiated by enrollment count, just like all those other states who never knew high school basketball grandeur.[7]

It's just another dimension of how I, star-blessed Bob Hammel, not only got on that Last Press Bus just in time to enjoy a long and treasured ride but also got off it at the perfect time to avoid the heartbreak of the newspaper world today.

When Bob Knight basketball came to Bloomington, my world expanded unimaginably. It was an educational experience in adaptation to sudden and privileged coverage of rarefied levels of excellence.

Covering teams that are *really* good, national-championship good, brings another test: fidelity to the neutrality/objectivity conveyed by sportswriting's inviolable vow of journalistic chastity, "No cheering in the press box."

I have as phlegmatic a face as anyone could imagine when competition is on, a mask of unemotion mastered in my teens covering high school basketball games when almost always both teams involved were

---

7. Indiana actually now crowns eight state high school basketball champions: four boys and four girls. The boys' tournament got a 65-year head start on the girls, until Title IX–based expansion brought the first state girls tournament in 1976. That change was as beneficial as it was overdue for women's education of all types. And it had Hoosier parentage: Indiana Senator Birch Bayh Jr., whose dad officiated seven boys' state-championship games, was Title IX's author.

from my coverage area. Not a crack of a smile, not a crease of a questioning brow when anything happened benefiting one team and hurting the other.

But did I care when Keith Smart's shot went in to change Indiana from an NCAA runner-up to national champion in 1987? Of course I was elated that kids I had watched struggle in down times had a champion's spot in history, forever . . . that a coach I had watched polish and burnish, add and subtract, nosed his team across the finish line with just the right combination . . . that my newspaper would sell a lot more papers tomorrow. Of course I enjoyed victory by the university that, when I was 8 and could root, I *had* rooted for, and followed with personal identification ever since. I don't deny, don't regret, never made any attempt to repulse tears that welled when the flag went up and the anthem played at the Olympics for kids I had covered and grown to know and like, or when ultimate championships came to teams and athletes and coaches I had watched sweat and practice and fall short at times and press on. My always-governing concern about dealing with things in the proper perspective was absolute where the printed word was concerned, but certainly I—internally—felt gloom, felt joy, felt sick, felt euphoric hundreds of times behind that face that never creased, those fingers that were never released from professional inhibitions to exult or groan, rather than report. I'm pretty sure I had company in that. I saw too many expressions of warmth and fondness in reports by professionals who covered the New York Yankees when Derek Jeter's days ended to think that others didn't feel an emotional stirring now and then while—and I won't put quotes around the word because I employ it sincerely—objectively reporting about sports people and teams they knew well.

That Keith Smart basket . . .

Two days before, that 1987 Indiana team had reached deep into its well to beat a more athletic, probably better team—No. 1–ranked UNLV—in the Final Four semifinals at New Orleans. Maybe those Rebels were a tad overrated—probably not but maybe. For sure, the Syracuse team Indiana had to come back and face in the finals was greatly underrated. Three of its starters went on to outstanding 10-year careers in the NBA. Indiana, with nothing close to an NBA lottery pick, was favored because of its UNLV victory and its storied past—but physically worn out. Syracuse, which had cruised in the semifinals, maybe was downgraded because previous Orange teams had flamed out in Final Fours—totally irrelevant for this team, this game, and this team's unquestionably top-rank coach, Jim Boeheim. Indiana led at halftime but trailed almost the entire second half, more likely it seemed to fade out of contention than surge ahead. But at the end, there was a chance: a free throw was missed, Indiana claimed the rebound and—one point behind, 30 seconds left in the national championship game—had the ball. As taught, the Hoosiers called no time out; the ball came downcourt, the teams set up to attack and defend, the ball moved from one Hoosier to another with cuts and screens and defensive pickups all over the court, eyes of both teams trying to keep in vision the ball and its likely ultimate destination, Indiana shooter Steve Alford. The clock ticked down, and suddenly—from a spot near the baseline on the side of the court opposite where Alford and Syracuse's defensive focus had gone—Smart went up for a shot. I don't remember feeling a particular personal tension, just watching the arc of the ball up from his fingertips and down through the basket. The thought in my mind was not wild at all, just *Well, I'll be darned . . . they're actually going to win.* And probably the crease of a smile, more in genuine wonder than crazy joy. And, I'll be darned, they actually did win. Thirty years later it's still the latest point in a championship game when on one play a March Madness team went from loser to national champion.

I covered two other IU national basketball championships, both times the winning margin in double figures at the end so the "I'll be darned" realization those times was more diffused. But even then— say, in 1976 at Philadelphia when always-cool, determinedly unruffled Quinn Buckner was jumping in glee on the sidelines and hugging his take-nothing-for-granted, first-time-champion coach as time ran out— there probably was some welling in the eyes.

A different memory from that night: Dave Cawood, head of NCAA press operations, in the closing minutes of that 86–68 game asked me if at game's end I could go on the court straight to Bob Knight and try to get just a comment or two for distribution to press-row writers on tight deadlines. I said sure, the game ended, I left my seat to go onto the court and carry out my accepted duty, and about two steps onto the floor I was enveloped in a tight grasp from behind by a Philadelphia policeman who was saying something—as I recall—about throwing my ass out of the building. I had a brief thought about how to explain to my editor that I might be a bit late with my story because I was in jail, when Cawood happened to see what happened, intervened, and I was back on my way to get a few words from Bob Knight.

A long time later that night, after I had gone to the Indiana locker room and talked to several players and joined in the general interview of Knight and picked up a few things from locker room drop-ins such as John Havlicek and Pete Newell, time had come to leave the arena— Knight with Havlicek to go straight to the hospital where Indiana starter Bobby Wilkerson had been taken after an early-game blow to the head and severe concussion, me to my hotel to start a rush to deadline for my newspaper. I was a step ahead of Bob as we started down The Spectrum's outside steps, and a thought crossed my mind: this *was* his first national championship. I turned, put out a hand, and over a shoulder said, "Oh, by the way, congratulations." I'll never forget his eyes. They looked a bit over me, less twinkly than wistful, and he said, "Thanks . . . but it should have been two."

A year before, he had another unbeaten, No. 1–ranked team that lost star Scott May to a broken arm in February and was eliminated 92–90 by Kentucky in the regional finals. Bob knew that team deserved to win the championship and felt it might have been even a little better team than this one that had just completed a historic title run. The 1975 seniors who didn't know that ultimate feeling in Philly, the first recruits he talked into coming to Bloomington and starting a brand new program, were in those eyes, in those words.

And we split.

Back in my hotel room, I went to work. Because we were a "p.m. paper," delivered in the afternoon, my deadline wasn't immediate. First for me that night was the mandatory stuff: typing the box score, then the story of the game. Then, an accompanying story or two, with comments from players, from the losing Michigan side. Then, the perspective: a column. Of all nights, this was one that called for, screamed for, perspective.[8]

All the supporting books and data I normally would have around me doing this in my office weren't in that Philadelphia hotel room. It was just me, my notes, and my memory—which I had learned to, *always*, treat in Reagan terms: trust but verify. Indiana was the seventh unbeaten national champion, not the first, but I felt strongly that this team had made it through a harder route than any of the others. I thought of an angle I wanted to pursue, wanted desperately to verify in specifics but couldn't, and trusted anyway.

I love baseball. The ultimate achievement in baseball is a perfect game: twenty-seven straight outs. Twenty-seven: exactly the number of games this Indiana team won to go into the tournament unbeaten. And then for this basketball team there were five hard outs to go when tournament play began. I thought of the most impressive five-out stretch I'd ever heard of in baseball: when Carl Hubbell in the 1934 All-Star game struck out in order five straight future Hall of Famers, starting with Babe Ruth. I thought I knew the names, and the order; back home I'd have checked. In Philly, I decided to gamble. I wrote:

> PHILADELPHIA—Calling it a perfect season understates the basketball achievement Indiana's 1975-76 team completed Monday night.
> It was better than perfect, these Hoosiers' 32-0 season. It was unique.
> It came in two parts. It was a nine-inning no-hitter, each out a day or two—sometimes five or seven—apart, in 14 different cities. Time to

8. In 2013, for its seventy-fifth men's tournament, the NCAA ran a national poll to pick the tourney's all-time No. 1 coach, player, and team. The coach was ten-time champion John Wooden of UCLA, the player three-time champion and Outstanding Player Award winner Lew Alcindor/Kareem Abdul-Jabbar, and the team was Indiana 1976. That team's seniors (Scott May, Quinn Buckner, Bobby Wilkerson, Tom Abernethy, and Jim Crews), junior center Kent Benson, and coach Bob Knight were brought to Atlanta for Final Four recognition. A commemorative sign hangs in Assembly Hall.

think before each try, a dozen days killed in hotel rooms waiting for one more inspired opponent to take a cut, one more revved-up crowd to do its imploring for the interruptions that never came.

And, after the 27th out, there stood Ruth, Gehrig, Foxx, Simmons and Cronin. No slips allowed.

And none came. A perfect year, a national championship like none before.

No?

Find another team that stamped itself No. 1 with as bold and thorough an opening victory as Indiana's over the reigning national champion, UCLA, way last November . . . and stayed at the top, the No. 1 target the whole year?

Find another that threw back so many credentialed challengers—11 of the Hoosiers' 27 regular-season opponents were ranked in the nation's Top 20 when they got their shot.

And forget about finding a tournament path to match the one that this Indiana team paved into an avenue to immortality—no challenger left standing with a chesty claim because all had been personally dealt with.

There was an obvious nasty side to a tournament path that laid St. John's, Alabama, Marquette, UCLA and Michigan in front of the top-ranked team.

But there was a poetic side, too. Marquette, No. 2 virtually all year long, was convinced, 65-56. Alabama, fresh from thumping a year-long Top 10 club, North Carolina, to solidify its own membership, was hurdled.

And there were St. John's, UCLA and Michigan—by coincidence regular-season opponents that for special reasons weren't convinced No. 1-ranked Indiana was all that superior. Under tournament pressure, St. John's lost by 20, UCLA by 14.

Which left Michigan, in the odd position of being able to take a national championship by "winning" a three-game series one to two. When the Wolverines fell, 86-68, there were no straw men to prop up. Indiana was No. 1. N-C-Double-A, the Hoosiers had gone all the way.

All things considered, including by now it was past 4 in the morning and I was dead tired, and my Ruth-Gehrig-Foxx-Simmons-Cronin memory did prove right, it may be my favorite column.

And, as the years go by, and the fortieth anniversary of that championship season has passed and the 1976 Hoosiers are still men's major college basketball's last unbeaten champion, that game, that season, that championship, those memories are right up there competing for No. 1 with me, too.[9]

That perspective thing wasn't tested only in basketball.

In 1992, America's premier distance runner, Bob Kennedy, came back from the Barcelona Olympics to use his last semester of college eligibility running on the Indiana University cross country team. Especially pulling him back then was timing: the NCAA cross country championships that year were being run on the IU course in Bloomington.

Kennedy had won the NCAA cross-country race four years earlier as a freshman. In his college years, he won an astonishing 20 Big Ten championships in track and cross country. Foreign athletes, particularly Kenyans but stars from other African nations as well, had taken over international and even American collegiate distance running in those days, and Kennedy recognized that. Eventually, rather than duck the Kenyans or concede any sort of inherent superiority, he arranged an agreement that let him work with them in their training program, on their grounds, and he came back from that experience to take the American 3,000- and 5,000-meter records down drastically.

But this was still the young and collegiate, on-the-way-up Bob Kennedy, running in crisp November Indiana air, on his own turf, for the last time as a collegian, taking on the best collegiate cross-country com-

---

9. I've kept a chart since 1976 of each season's last major college unbeaten to fall. The average date has been February 8, but it has happened as early December 30 (2017, 12–0 Arizona State losing to rival Arizona, 84–78). Only a few teams on that reached the tournament unbeaten. In 2014, Kentucky got to the Final Four undefeated. That gave the '76 Hoosiers a week of new media life— comparisons, interviews, anticipation of the end of an era. But the Big Ten's Wisconsin extended IU's reign, 74–67, before losing the championship game to Duke. UNLV also got to the Final Four unbeaten in 1990 (Duke ending that in the semifinals en route to its first championship). The undefeated team that got the farthest since Indiana? Indiana State, 33–0 with Larry Bird in 1979, beaten by Magic Johnson and Michigan State in a classic final game. Less known: in those years there hasn't been a once-beaten champion, either. Every titlist since '76 has lost at least *two* games.

petition, Kenyans and all. And he ran away from them. The runner-up, a Kenyan, wasn't in camera pickup range when Kennedy crossed the finish line—26 seconds behind, a football field and a half. Kennedy's wife, Melina—the Melina Kennedy who was to have an outstanding legal career and run as the 2011 Democratic candidate for mayor in Indianapolis—told me in a 1992 note that Bob that evening, soothing out muscles sore from the six-mile-plus late-afternoon race, idly said, "I wonder how that margin compared with the meet record?" Melina said, "How can you find out?" She said his answer was, "I'll pick up the paper in the morning. Bob Hammel will have it."

Though of course unaware of it, I came as close as I could to living up to that high faith. I went back to the office from the race and for more than an hour poured through old NCAA guides and record books, typical of stores I kept in all sports for just this kind of researching emergency. I traced back, year by year, to a time when the race was less than half as long, therefore extremely unlikely to have so wide a margin, and declared it apparently a record—almost double (in seconds) anything else ever done at a similar distance. Since then the NCAA has certified that margin as a championship record, and it still stands.

The point Bob Kennedy's comment illustrated was that the sportswriter inherits an obligation—a public expectation—to know, or at least diligently seek the perspective on a special achievement, however out of the blue it might be. Hearing of Bob's confidence in me made that day's search, and all that had come before in establishing his faith, wholly and satisfyingly worthwhile. But doing it would have been anyway.

That was essentially my approach in every ball game I covered. I sought out comments from people involved, yes, but personal observation and analysis emboldened me on my way to postevent interviews to settle on what play or plays I thought decided this particular game, then point my questions toward establishing what went into those plays, what those playmakers had to say about what happened, and why— how they felt about it at the time, and afterward. And, what did it all mean, all these one-game happenings, in deciding a championship, in the perspective of history: for this day, or this week, or this season, or for all time? If anything . . .

Yes, really. Every time. Every game. It seemed to me a delightfully simple job, and a simply delightful job. I loved it, for 42 years. Then I stepped aside.

Yet I confess to always having a deeply recessed curiosity about how my life would have turned out if—instead of starting at 17, never having taken a journalism class—I had followed an orthodox path at Indiana University and come out with a degree in journalism at 20 in the spring of 1957. I could write. Maybe I would have been polished and formalized and steered toward editorial writing, toward a career more like William Allen White's. Maybe, unlike Mr. White, I couldn't have resisted taking my remarkably developing and broadening skills (remember, this is the World of Maybe: i.e., fantasy) up and up in the newspaper world to Chicago, Los Angeles, New York; to Pulitzers, wealth, renown.

Or maybe I would have failed colossally. At writing. At being an editor. At marriage.

The last is the jolting one. A different life, even a wildly successful one, probably would have meant a different assortment of acquaintances and friends, likely a different wife, a different family. No, thanks. Even in dreaming, I back off that gamble. I won big with the hand I was dealt, above all with Julie and our kids, and subsequently our grandkids and in-laws. I'm happy with being happy. And grateful for so very much good luck.

Book One

JOURNALISM AND I

Of course you need a college degree,
And an internship or two for experience—

Unless you're blessed with a lot of luck
And survive the scariest of possible words:
                                        "Should we keep him?"

MY FUTURE AT AGE 17½ WAS NOT WHAT WOULD HAVE BEEN considered a growth stock. That young I had reshaped natural promise into a likelihood of failure. I was about to be kicked out of Indiana University, without one class hour of credit or one minute of experience in the field I hoped to enter. I had every reason to be in the psychological pits, but suicide was never a thought. Neither did an alcohol binge ever occur to puritanical me. Drugs as an escape might have been a possibility in another generation, but not then, not in the early 1950s, when the movie equivalent of the dime novel *Reefer Madness* was the only remote connection I and my immediate peers had with times that already were a-changin' in places more sophisticated than the naive, insular world in which young Bob Hammel lived and flopped in spring 1954.

Mine right then, as a second-semester college freshman, was a sudden, unexpected, and absolutely unimagined world of failure, of blown opportunity, of incompetence of the worst sort—defeat undignified by even token effort, even minimal competing.

Classroom failure—F's across the board—loomed, which might have scared or at least worried me except I was academically shell-shocked. I had failed and accepted it. Robotic might best describe my mental state right then, in April 1954. Catatonic would work, too. I was a zombie, reduced to walking straight ahead, in an irrational "somehow it will all work out" stupor, day after day, every day, putting off any thoughts about the future I was jeopardizing with unexplainable sloth. I slept in my dorm room on campus; I got up every morning and did my post-office job; I just stopped going to class, at all, my brain numbed by realization that the academic weight of a French class I was failing was going to cost me the scholarship that was my only way to stay in school. I don't ever remember thinking, "Oh, my God! I'm going to flunk out! Where do I go from here?" But that's exactly where I was. Maybe suicide *would* have been an option, if I had realized the extent of my vocational disarray and its likely effect on the long, long life ahead of me, consigning me to 40, 50, 60 years of mediocrity and frustrated unhappiness. I wasn't thinking clearly enough to see that and panic.

Seven months before, I was still 16 when I enrolled in my first Indiana University courses, checked into my first dorm room, met freshman Charlie Winslow from Indianapolis Howe High School, my first roommate,[1] went to my first classes. Fifteen academic hours was considered a full load; I was assigned and confidently accepted a seventeen-hour class load because test scores and my ego said I could handle it, no problem. I was a journalism major who, under university rules, couldn't take any journalism classes the first year. Instead, my curriculum was all liberal arts, designed to fulfill mandatory Arts and Sciences degree requirements: psychology (hour-long lecture Monday, Wednesday, Friday, 7 a.m.), French (Monday–Friday, 8 a.m.), a few other things wrapped around the one Tuesday-Thursday delicacy for me: English Composition W-102, where I got to write. Through pre-enrollment testing, I had been waived through the introductory W-101. I loved that "comp" class, respected and almost revered Professor Merritt Lawlis, who I learned later was then only a few years out of a World War II Japanese prison camp that had left him, a quiet, mild, and scholarly man, permanently embittered against his captors. None of that showed in his soft lecturing style, his handling of papers I submitted as class assignments. He taught well. I learned.

---

1. Charlie Winslow, my only college roommate, was on the same Residence Scholar program as I was. Our room was in Rogers H, one of a row of wood-frame World War II barracks ticketed for demolition when funds could be found to build real student dormitories there. He went on to become a distinguished scholar and political science professor at the IU–Purdue campus in Indianapolis. His book *Lebanon: War and Politics in a Fragmented Society* gave him such standing about Middle East politics that he frequently was interviewed on Indianapolis TV when first Iran, then Iraq became major US trouble spots. Once, Charlie attended a Bob Knight talk in Indianapolis, and afterward mentioned his connection with me. It led to a reconnection that included an exchange of books and a dinner together. I still have a handwritten note he sent, to which I hope I responded, because I greatly enjoyed reestablishing a relationship.

And that's about the only place that sequence happened for me—
that one two-hour, one-semester class—in my year as a college student.
The shortcomings were mine, not Indiana University's. I had never
learned to study. So, on my first day in a college classroom, I realized
that dodging every attempt high schools had made to get me into a
foreign-language class was about to exact its price.[2] The first or second
day of attendance I saw I was the only student in that French class who
had *never* taken a foreign-language class, and from Day One, I was behind and sliding. Midterms came and I had an F in French—a B or A
in everything else, but a totally inconceivable, made-for-other-people F
in my five-hour class. The grades most terrified me not on their own but
in what they meant: that my GPA, grade average, was going to be too
low—far too low—to maintain my vital scholarships. Without them, no
college for me. The first sense of hopeless resignation seeped in.

The rest of the semester, I flailed away in my frantic, undeveloped
form of studying, devoting every hour I could to French. I progressed,
but not enough. Semester grades came and I had moved French up, but
only to D, and every other class, except W-102, had dropped a letter.
My overall grade average was worse than before, my scholarships all
but death-assured. I came back to school in late January inwardly hu-
miliated, whipped. I behaved unaccountably: I enrolled in my full load
but very quickly stopped going to class—including W-103 (a step up
in English Comp, which was not under Professor Lawlis). Every day, I

---

2. My freshman and sophomore high school years were at Clear Creek, a
small rural school with limited curriculum choices. My last were at much larger
Huntington High, but by then I was out of step from where guidance/counsel-
ing normally would have taken me, particularly in foreign languages and math.
That was no one's fault but mine—I had options and took the easiest path: no
foreign language at all, no geometry, trigonometry, or calculus, nothing that
required or developed study habits. I paid for my academic laziness at IU. I did
enjoy the years and the friendships. Clear Creek had its own pluses, and Huntington, though without a school paper or a journalism class, had (and still has)
its own radio station. My introduction to media life came as a senior, as the station's football and basketball play-by-play announcer. Easily the youngest one
in that HHS Class of 1953, I didn't look it. Witness: in casting for our senior play,
Old Doc, I got the title role, and died in the second act.

slept in as late as I wanted, bed a form of escape. Evenings I played ping-pong a lot, bridge, got pretty good at both. I worked every hour I could at my 50-cents-an-hour campus post-office job (where my carrier route included the office of professor-author Alfred Kinsey, his second sexual behavior book just out, research at his renowned sex institute already underway on pornography, which meant every day two or three large, plain-brown envelopes came in, usually from West Germany, always marked "May Be Opened for Postal Inspection," and by the time they came to me for delivery, always had been. I was a good and diligent post-man, a fast-improving ping-pong and bridge player, a marrowless and moraleless nonstudent resigned to losing not just my scholarship but also my status as a student. That was my state of mental being: hollow resignation, an academic Dead Man Walking.

One April day, two miasmic months of "school" still ahead of me, a letter arrived. I had worked my high school senior year (fig. 1.1) in a circulation job in the mailroom of the Huntington *Herald-Press*, my hometown newspaper, and formed at most a nodding acquaintance with the man who wrote that April letter to me in Bloomington: editor Howard Houghton. He knew how to get in touch with me at IU because my sister, Joy, worked in the newspaper's business office. I had never written a newsish word for him or for anybody else (Huntington High School had neither a journalism class nor a school newspaper), but he knew somehow of my intended major. Frivolous warm-up wasn't the style of the white-haired, austere gentleman known in his building and his town as Judge. He started the letter by saying his sports editor was leaving and he wondered if I would be (1) capable of and (2) interested in filling the role during the summer while he looked for a permanent replacement.

Interested?

!!!

Capable?

I never really felt a doubt.

But should have.

I was too dumb to know how very, very much I had to learn, just to be mediocre in a small-town newspaper that had a news staff of five: (1) managing editor (and page-layout man), (2) City Hall and police

1.1. Bob Hammel, high school senior—16 going on 30.

reporter, (3)Court House and sheriff's department reporter, (4) "society" (or women's page) editor, and (5) sports editor. Each was a title with tentacles. Each person did what the title said and took on anything else that was needed that day, then maybe something or some things altogether different the next.

Starry-eyed over that out-of-the-blue job offer, I thought nothing of any of my shortcomings, nothing of fear. What I knew was Deliverance. After that "somehow-it-all-will-work-out" daze that had kept me going for months, the "it" that "will work out" was in my hands. Only for the summer, only if I passed the small test assignment Mr. Houghton gave me ("Find some sports event happening on campus in the next few days and write it up")—but "only" wasn't in my suddenly euphoric state of mind. Instead:

Wow!

I came to college to be a newspaperman and I am one!

Wow!

A job, a dreamed-of opportunity that I had done nothing at all to earn had dropped in my lap.

The story of my life . . .

I have two memories of my first newspaper days. One was thrilling, giddy. The other was chilling, terrifying.

My last IU exam was Monday, June 7, 1954—which I actually took, for reasons I can't explain even to myself now, maybe to carry out something of a charade for my parents, who drove to Bloomington from Huntington that day to pick up me and my belongings. All I remember of the trip home that day is, as we left town—and this I remember distinctly—looking back over my shoulder, out the rear window from the back seat, thinking, "Goodbye, Bloomington. . . . I'm sure this is the last time you're going to see me."

About 36 hours later, at 7 a.m. on Wednesday, June 9,[3] I came through the door to the Huntington *Herald-Press* newsroom and was pointed to

---

3. Historical note: June 9, 1954, the day my newspaper career began, was the day of the Army-McCarthy hearings when counsel Joseph Welch asked Senator Joseph McCarthy: "Have you no shame?"

1.2. Reunion time for Bob Hammel with first "journalism professors"—
Huntington *Herald-Press* editor Howard Houghton and managing editor
George Frye (Huntington *Herald-Press* photo).

the first chair and typewriter, no more than five steps inside the door.
My assigned desk butted up against the desk of the managing editor,
George W. Frye, a prematurely white-haired ex-marine whose sportswriting before he advanced to his management role was among the first
things I ever read. I inherited a black 1948 Royal upright typewriter
with round keys that wanted to race. My first-day assignment was to
type one-paragraph stories and box scores from scorebooks submitted
on two games that had been played the previous night: a semipro men's
baseball game and a women's softball game. Words came hard for rookie
Bob Hammel that day. But nowhere near so hard as the tabulated box
scores. Stone carvings have been completed quicker.

"Coach" Frye (fig. 1.2) got me through the day. After lunch, the newspaper out, he told me of the news beat I would cover each day once my
day's work in sports was done. Included was a stop at the local army
recruiter's office to check for new sign-ups. Frye also told me he wanted

me to start a sports opinion column as soon as I could, especially for the showpiece of each week: the Sunday morning edition. I did some thinking, some reading. By Friday, my third day as a professional, I had my first column ready, cribbed from a magazine feature I had come across on a young Huntington County man who in his 20s was gaining attention as a TV sportscaster in exotic New York! That first Bob Hammel column ran on Sunday, June 13, my fifth day as a Journalist.

As his star in the TV firmament continues to shoot upward, Chris Schenkel, Huntington County's gift to the sports archives, gathers more and more prestige and favorable comment from his very numerous critics, ranging from boxing's elite to John Q. Phan.

Chris was born in Wabash Aug. 21, 1923, to Phillip and Theresa Schenkel, but at the age of six moved to Bippus, where his family still resides. At Bippus High School, he participated in three sports, naturally favoring basketball. At the conclusion of his high school career, he moved on to Purdue University, where he received his diploma in 1943. While at Purdue, he began his radio career, describing Boilermaker football and basketball contests over the school station, WBAA, and working summers at station WLBC, Muncie.

Uncle Sam beckoned upon his graduation from college, and he wore khaki until September, 1946. He returned to radio that fall, working in Richmond's WKBC. He moved on to Providence, R.I., where he covered, among other things, Brown, Holy Cross and Boston College football games.

His big break came in the summer of 1952 when an ad agency asked him to help Marty Glickman cover New York Giants pro football games. That fall, he was selected to work the pro football championship game between the Detroit Lions and the Cleveland Browns.

He achieved his present position, that of the DuMont television network's Monday evening boxing announcer, quite unexpectedly, temporarily replacing Ted Husing, his boyhood idol, when Husing became ill one Monday afternoon before his scheduled broadcast from Eastern Parkway Arena. When the new announcer became extremely popular, he was retained, much to his surprise and delight.

Unmarried, Chris now resides in New York. Proof of his rising popularity lies in the January issue of *TV Boxing*, in which Steve Snider features Chris in an article entitled, "Chris Calls the Upsets," an honor seldom accorded an announcer. One can only wonder now how far that Schenkel star will rise.

OK, a little gaga. More than a little . . . kind of awful, and amateurish, and—at 325 words—short for what became par for me. Borderline
plagiarism, too, though I'm not sure I knew of the word let alone the
laws then. Essentially, I just paraphrased huge chunks from one *TV
Boxing* magazine article, though I was honest enough to give the article
some attribution. With all that, the subject and the timing weren't bad,
and with the column I did hitch myself to a real star on the rise. Chris
Schenkel said, or at least pretended in a friendship that subsequently
developed, that he read, loved, and always remembered that column.
All I remember is, that night when the presses started rolling and I held
a fresh newspaper in my hand, that column felt golden. The Sunday
morning edition came out at about 1:30 a.m. In the newsroom, our job
when the first papers came off the press was to scan for egregious errors,
the embarrassing kind that landed us and others at times in the *New
Yorker* and other snooty scoff-at-the-rubes publications. All I saw that
night was my column, which I read in awed wonder.

I was still living at home. At 2 a.m., I walked cloud high the four
blocks from the newspaper to our house, flipped on my parents' bedroom light, and handed the prized paper to my mom. She read it, and
exceeded my awe and my wonder—"rave" a word too tepid to describe
her review. *"Oh-hhh, Bob!"* She handed it to Dad, who glanced at it and
went back to sleep. One happy reader, one bored: not a bad ratio for a
columnist, I was to learn.

That was my "thrilling, giddy" beginning. The "chilling, terrifying"
part came about two weeks later.

I was assigned to fly to Camp Grayling, Michigan, on a spartan DC-3
airplane with the Huntington unit of the National Guard, to do a feature on the guardsmen on summer maneuvers. Fine. Story went well.
It was a photo feature. I had been quickly broken in on how to use a
4×5 Speed Graphic camera, the basic press camera of the day. The 4×5
numbers were inches, for the size of the sheet of film inside each of the
two sides of a slide that fit into the back of the camera. Before shooting, a light-proof guard had to be pulled out, exposing the film when

the shutter was tripped. I did all that great, for a fellow who had never clicked anything more sophisticated than my mother's home camera, a "Brownie" by popular name.

One problem: the Brownie had one lens setting, prefocused. The Speed Graphic lens had to be wheeled into sharp focus, *then* the slide pulled and shutter triggered. I had no idea about that focusing part. I brought back my slides, they were processed—and every piece of film was exposed very nicely but hopelessly out of focus, unusable. I was disappointed. My editor, the benefactor who had hired me, was more than that: lip-biting angry. Not right away, of course. He read my story in his upstairs office, then came down to the desks that George Frye and I shared, and the conversation went:

Houghton, beaming: "So how do the pictures look?"

Frye, mumbling in a near whisper: "Uh, they didn't come out."

"Whaddya mean, *'They didn't come out'*?"

"The pictures are no good. He didn't focus the camera."

Eight feet away, head down, I kept frantically typing. I listened for a response, but none came. Just a pregnant silence.

Then, I heard—and I will always tremble when my memory replays it—the austere "Judge" Houghton whispering a cold verdict request to Frye:

"Should we keep him?"

That thread-thin was my newspaper career in that moment's electric atmosphere. Still typing, I remember a desperate man's demand for mercy exploding in my mind: "How unfair would that be! I wasn't hired to be a photographer!" I never heard Mr. Houghton's question answered. I kept typing.

That was my newspaper start. My own start, in life, is less documented and much less remembered, even by me.

I can't tell you much about my birth except it wasn't in a manger. Nor a hospital. October 6, 1936, was so much a depth-of-the-Depression day that, of my parents' four children, I was the one who was born at home, to save the price of a hospital. Home then was a neat little red-brick bungalow that was still standing, and still neat, into the 1970s. It

1.3. Birthplace—as captured (and autographed) by Olympic gold medalist and Bloomington *Herald-Telephone* photographer Kevin Berry.

was at 1901 College Avenue, near the Huntington College campus on Huntington's north side. Once I had attained driving age and still was living in Huntington, I enjoyed cruising by the house occasionally to check on its upkeep, the silly thought deep in the back of my mind that it would make such a nice Bob Hammel Memorial Museum someday.

Many years after those musings, the place had a visitor. Kevin Berry, who won a gold medal as a teenager swimming for Australia in the 1964 Olympics at Tokyo, later swam for Doc Counsilman at Indiana University and stayed on after graduation to work alongside me at the *Herald-Telephone* as a news and sports photographer. Kevin became a friend of mine. When the time came for Kevin and wife Julie to return to his native Sydney, he did something remarkably fortuitous for me: he set aside one pretakeoff day to take his camera on a 150-mile trip from Bloomington to Huntington, this town he had heard so much about from me and another Huntington-Bloomington friend of Kevin's, professional photographer David Repp (a year behind me at Huntington

High). I gave Kevin the address of the little brick house, he found it, shot a picture (fig. 1.3) that he printed up eight-by-ten, black-and-white of course—and signed it, even. It hangs on my wall at home, my reminder of the museum that never was, except in my prone-to-dreams mind, and of Kevin, who after returning to Australia and playing a lead role in landing the 2000 Olympics for his native Sydney, died quite young.

Kevin's timing with the farewell photograph was providential. Just months after it was taken, the house was gone, victim of creeping Christianity. The little house, a hair stylist's operating base in its final days, was on the southeast corner of a block that had on its northeast corner a United Brethren in Christ church, the headquarters church for the denomination that has as its educational landmark Huntington University—one of its key founders Bishop Milton Wright, father of aircraft history's Wright Brothers. In the 1970s, the church's membership outgrew its original quarters, and building expansion gobbled up the whole block, including my museum—flattened ignominiously for a parking lot. But I have the picture and warm memories that keep it alive in my mind.

The one drawback of my low-budget entry into life: I don't have the niceties that go with a hospital birth—no official length and weight, for example. I'm told Dad pulled out his butcher's scale that day, put me on the silver holding tray, and declared me ten pounds, which he told me once with a caveat: "Your head was hanging over the side of the tray— that was ten pounds without your head."

Time has taught me some other things about my birth. I heard in one of those weather facts, thrown out on TV every day with the highs and lows, that the coldest day in Indiana history was January 6, 1936. My mind hummed into calculation: hmmm, that coldest-ever day was exactly nine months before October 6, 1936 . . . so maybe that's why a young couple that already had one child and probably didn't need any more mouths to feed in those Depression days wound up having another. I was probably the accidental product of a cold night's cuddle. Then I heard another weather fact: the hottest summer in Indiana history was July and August 1936. Day after day, weeks on end, of upper 90s, even well into the 100s, including the all-time state high of 114. Poor

Mom. Carried me at six and seven months ballooning through those miserable summer days. And still she loved me.

I have no memory of life in my College Avenue birthplace. "Memory" is a somewhat sensitive word for me, because—though what's up there is OK—I have really an embarrassingly stark void of memories at all till I was 8, an unexplainably late start in ready recall. I've never met another person—I truly mean not *one*—who remembers almost nothing about his or her life before reaching age 8, but now you have met one. It's humiliating. I've read the memoir of Colombian writer Javier Gonzalez Marquez, who frequents his growing-up-years account with vivid descriptions of things he remembers from age 4, or 3, even 2, maybe 1—and I can't go beyond 8. And by then I was in fourth grade.

Which is another story.

Those early years were eventful and formative for me, even if not personally recallable. Sister Joy—born Carol Joy but always known by her melodic middle name—was three years older, born August 16, 1933. I was told she came home from our no-kindergarten school every day her first-, second-, and third-grade years, made me a sitting prisoner, and forced me to learn everything she had been taught that day. She says she did it out of the shock of seeing kids in her class who didn't learn quickly, and she proclaimed to our mother in unpolished vernacular: "I *can't* let him be a dumbbell!" Clearly, she thought me capable of being one so she went to work, hard. She became a career teacher, an outstanding one, but I had her at her most effective, unrestrained by state laws and niceties. When my mind strayed, she regained my attention with a backhanded *whack!* across the cheek. Intelligence had relatively little to do with my being able to read fluently and to handle long and fairly complicated arithmetic problems by the time Mom talked school authorities into letting me enter first grade a little early, at 5-about-to-turn-6, in September 1942. I certainly don't remember, but I've heard that on my thirteenth day of school, the teacher was out of her classroom for a moment and came back to find me reading a book to the other kids, grouped closely around. She left quietly, brought the school principal in to observe, and I was moved to second grade. Mom said a few days later they recommended third grade, but she rebelled: "He's already going to be 15 starting his senior year. No! No more!"

Now, I figure if Joy had been a *really* good teacher/relayer, I should have gone straight up to fourth grade with her. But I mean her no criticism . . .

Fourth grade. I don't remember a single day in the classroom, but fourth grade—when 1944 turned into 1945, when in October I turned from 7 to 8—is when the lights seemed to come on for me, when my world expanded and my memory began to record.

I wasn't much into radio news then, couldn't begin to understand why Dad subjected himself night after night to the dreary reportings of Lowell Thomas, H. V. Kaltenborn and the like. I don't remember the momentous happenings of Pearl Harbor or June 6, 1944, D-Day at Normandy, but—why, I have no idea—I do remember about that time listening on radio to the Republican convention when they nominated Ohio governor John Bricker as vice president on a ticket with New York governor Thomas Dewey. Yes, I remember the Bricker part, not the Dewey.

And I remember coming home from school around my birthday and finding Dad—a city policeman at the time, on duty from 7 a.m. to 3 p.m.—at the kitchen table listening to the Cardinals and Browns play in the World Series. Dad was actually keeping score of the game, in a primitive, unofficial way, but recording it, pencil on paper, batter by batter. That was my introduction to what became a lifetime fixation for me.

In March 1945, the hometown Huntington High School Vikings beat No. 1-ranked Kokomo and reached the four-team State Finals. I had discovered basketball, and the Indiana high school tournament.

And then there was April.

Coming home on the school bus on the afternoon of the 12th, I saw people out of their homes onto the sidewalks, talking and crying and hugging each other in universal grief, because President Franklin D. Roosevelt had died of a brain hemorrhage. History was in a rush then. Before the month was over, I remember older kids on the bus joking about the way Italian dictator Benito Mussolini had died by mob, their bodies hung upside down... and days later, still in April, his hated German partner, Adolf Hitler, was dead, too. And, a few days later the war over there was over—VE Day they called it, Victory in Europe. Then we heard of this superbomb dropped on two Japanese cities we'd never heard of: Hiroshima on August 6th, another on Nagasaki on the 9th, leading to Japan's surrender on the 14th—that nightmare called war suddenly over.

By then I had discovered baseball. When the 1945 season opened, the Chicago White Sox won their first five games—only team in the majors to do that—and at 8 it was a come-on I couldn't resist. They hooked me for life. No complaints; 2019 is my 75th year as a devout Sox fan, with one World Series championship, and millions of memories (fig. 1.4).

Then in September 1945, I listened in on radio as Indiana University opened its football season by winning at Michigan. Even by radio it was a spectacular game, its star an 18-year-old IU freshman whose name was new to everyone then but soon became legendary: running back George Taliaferro. He's in the Pro Football Hall of Fame at Canton, Ohio, for being the first African American drafted by an NFL team, and in mine for several reasons. His debut at Michigan was a good start, but two years later, as a seventh grader, I talked my way into a High School Day ticket and a school bus ride that took me to Bloomington for my first college game. IU routed Pittsburgh that day, and the highlight was a zigging, zagging touchdown punt return by Taliaferro—who a good 50 years later, by now he and wife Vi good friends of mine, signed the game program that I had treasured all those years.

He wasn't the only reason I adopted IU. I liked lining up behind my state's name, and those '45 Hoosiers of Hall of Famer Bo McMillin did finish unbeaten and win the Big Ten championship outright—IU's only time in now 74 years. Again, no complaints. Even with recent downers, my lifetime record with the White Sox is about a hundred games over .500. I more than gave that back with IU football. Win some, lose some, but I'll always remember '45.

I have another great reason to remember 1945 fondly. By then we had moved to the south side of Huntington, close enough to Huntington

1.4. Didn't everyone wear a jersey like this to work the morning of October 27, 2005—after the White Sox' first World Series championship in eighty-eight years? (Bloomington *Herald-Times* photo by Janice Rickert).

County Hospital that Joy and I walked there and waved up to a third-floor window to Mother, who on March 20, 1945, gave birth to the brother, Jim, who made us a family of five.

I was 8, Joy was 11, which gave us an early taste of diaper changing and the like. I loved to read to Jim. One winter morning when he was 3—we had moved again, to a country house about six miles north of Huntington—I sat at one end of a sofa, reading to him as he lay on his back on a sofa pillow beside me. Suddenly he grabbed the sides of his head and began screaming, in obvious agony. Mom rushed in, picked him up, laid him out on the kitchen table, and, as the screaming continued, began frantically trying to learn the cause and ease the problem. Jim contorted in pain as he cried, still clutching at his head. Mom ran to our wall-mounted telephone, cranked to get the operator, and shouted her Huntington doctor's name and number, then held on . . .

We were on the Bippus Telephone Company exchange, which had one central switchboard operator, Blanche. Every call passed through her headset. A community joke was that no one had any secrets that Blanche didn't know—teasing, nonmalicious neighborly humor that branded her the font of all gossip. That night, our family doctor didn't answer. Mom knew one other doctor, tried that through Blanche, and again got no answer. By then, she was frantic, Jim's plight getting steadily worse. Blanche cut in, "Betty, you take care of your baby. *I'll* get you a doctor." Within minutes, a doctor we had never met came through our door—Jim's body blue by then—and after just seconds of observation shot a needle directly into his heart. And Jim lived. Forever after, Blanche was anything but a joke in our eyes—much more a watching angel. And Jim, as much as my Bible-quoting mother didn't want to have anything approaching a favorite among her kids, took on a gift-from-heaven status that did make him special.

Another eight years passed, and we added a fourth sibling—brother Bill. Now, that was different (fig. 1.5).

I was excited, welcomed the addition because of the fond brotherly relationship I had built with Jim—Dad was working two shifts much of the time then, so I was the one teaching Jim to shoot baskets, to field ground balls, to hit, to pitch, to throw a football spiral, to be a boy, to

1.5. Golden Anniversary gathering—siblings Bill and Joy (left), Bob and Jim flank their raison d'être.

be the athlete I always worked to be but wasn't. And Jim was good, the athlete of the family, which led to a college football scholarship and an ultimate Hall of Fame career in high school basketball coaching. But . . .

When Bill was born, I was a senior in high school. The whole idea was embarrassing. A senior just doesn't feel like telling his peers what his dad and mother obviously had been doing, at *their* age! Still, Billy arrived just as welcomed, just as loved, just as much the signal of a new alignment at home—which, by then, didn't include Joy. Two years earlier, with me as the 14-year-old "best man," she had married her Clear Creek High School classmate and longtime sweetheart, John Kennedy (John W., not F.), and in 1953 she was eight months behind Mom in producing her own first child. Uncle Bill and niece Cheri marched together as graduates in Huntington North High School's Class of 1971.

Joy and I grew up outside the Depression, our childhood years in the 1940s. But we were Depression Kids, and I've always felt helped by that.

As children of parents who during the Depression did the real suffering, who endured family-provision, meal-to-meal worries, maybe Joy and I soaked in enough to be a little more inclined toward paying our way as we grew up and wanting to improve our *own* habitat and lifestyle as we could pay for it . . . a bit more prone to consider the risk part of risk-reward business ventures. Paul Samuelson, the great, longtime *Newsweek* financial columnist, was in his 90s when he said something that spelled it out. In March 2009, when the nation's major financial institutions and the government seemed helpless as all about them was melting down, Samuelson in an interview with the *Wall Street Journal*, said:

> I have great admiration for Ben Bernanke [chairman of the Federal
> Reserve System under both presidents George W. Bush and Barack
> Obama]. But having been born in 1956 he did not have a feel for what it
> was like. If you were born after 1950, you really don't have the feel of that
> Great Depression in your bones. Being a bright boy at MIT, it's not really
> a substitute for that.

"The feel of that Great Depression in your bones."

Is that what it was, when the credit card era came, after a brief taste of debt accumulation and desperation and usury, that made me keep my account *always* up to date, balance paid in full, and thus uninvolved when so much of early twenty-first century America found itself engulfed by soaring balances and rapacious interest rates? Or why in 2000 when we bought a new home, with a six-figure loan, my happy banker had no reservations about giving 64-year-old me a 30-year loan, but *I* did. I wondered how those loan payments that seemed attractive then would feel when I was 80 . . . 90? I kept remembering a decade before when I made the last payment on my previous home, and it was mine, all mine—no Depression-imbedded confiscatory worries, no obligations except for meeting yearly property taxes. With that last payment, a palpable load left my shoulders—I consciously *felt* the muscles relax. Even at that time I was hearing the prevailing wisdom, "You're dumb to have your house paid for—you should take out a mortgage and put that money to work, and . . ."

So in 2004 when we came into some money and I was hearing "invest, put that money to work," instead I used the money to eliminate the mortgage. Because I did, I entered my 70s in a paid-for home. Had

I been "smart" and "put that money to work," I'd have lost nearly half of it—*poof!*—only a few months later in the stock market crash . . . and still had a mortgage to pay off.

Thank God (and Dad, and Mom, and FDR) for "the feel of the Great Depression" in my bones.

MY "SUNDOWN TOWN"

We moved a lot in my childhood. In 1956, when Dad and Mother celebrated their Silver Anniversary, I got Mom to list on paper, one by one, the houses they had lived in during their marriage. Her astonishing memory came up with 26 in 25 years.

The first one I remember was a few blocks north of my birthplace, across a wooded ravine from the Huntington College campus (one building then, plus a gymnasium).

Living in that house on Wildwood Drive is one of my few, vague pre-8-years-old memories. Primarily I remember it because Dad and Mom paid a few bills by taking in a college student as an upstairs roomer. His name was Gilbert Carter, and he was black.

That would be one thing in most 1940s towns. Huntington, my hometown that I love and always will, was not "most towns." It gets prominent mention in the nationally recognized 2005 book *Sundown Towns* (by James W. Loewen, published by The New Press). Mr. Loewen explained on page 3: "Towns are often called 'sundown towns,' owing to the signs that many of them formerly sported at their corporate limits—signs that usually said 'Nigger, Don't Let the Sun Go Down on You in . . .'"

I lived in Huntington through age 26 and never saw a sign anything like that, but Mr. Loewen's ground rules don't consider signs essential to my town's labeling.

> A sundown town is any organized jurisdiction that for decades kept African Americans or other groups from living in it and was thus "all white" on purpose.
>
> I identified a total of 231 Indiana towns as all-white. I was able to get information as to the racial policies of 95, and of those, I confirmed all

95 as sundown towns. . . . Some places have built national reputations as
sundown towns. . . . These would include . . . Elwood, Huntington and
Martinsville, Indiana.

Of course I'm not proud that my town is on that list. I would prefer
in retrospect to have grown up in a polycultured world. I think the genius of making public schools a primary tool in attacking segregation
nationally is that daily exposure to different races and cultures educates
us to our sameness. Like the Bible, Shakespeare has many passages
that jar against today's mores, but one in particular—from Shylock,
the persecuted Jew in *Merchant of Venice*: "If you prick us, do we not
bleed?"—communicates that essential sameness.

But bigots grow up in integrated towns, too. Towns don't make individual decisions; individuals do.

Loewen quotes an email exchange he had with one-time Huntington
resident Roger Karns, who thinks "growing up in an all-white community is detrimental for the white kids" because it "allows you to sus-
pend your normal respect for people. Some of these kids don't see a
person walking down the street, they see what amounts to a character."
Loewen goes farther: "These Indiana young people would doubtless
deny that they meant anything by their comments and antics. Denial
is a peculiar characteristic of the talk in sundown towns."

Makes it kind of hard to feel untainted. But I don't feel tainted or
generalized, or in denial. My weaknesses and failures are mine, not
Huntington's, and they don't include racial bias.

Loewen also says:

> Many towns that would never let them stay in houses permitted African-
> American and African college and prep-school students to live on
> campus. . . . In the 1960s, missionaries of the United Brethren Church
> in Christ recruited students from Sierra Leone to attend Huntington
> College in Huntington, Indiana. . . . The town let the Africans live on
> campus. . . . Again, it helped that townspeople knew the students were
> only temporary.

Again I mention Gilbert Carter, who—in the 1940s, when the US
Army and baseball and Big Ten basketball were still segregated, a
decade before *Brown vs. Board of Education* and two decades before

Selma—lived in my Huntington house, off-campus, and, indeed, on the rare times when my stay-at-home parents needed one, was the babysitter for Joy and me.

This is not to contend that my town was terribly mischaracterized. An all-white town with its all-white schools does carry some obvious self-incrimination, though in my teens I did sometimes raise the possibility to friends that maybe Huntington stayed white by African Americans' choice—apparently nothing about Huntington attracted them.

Also, Loewen doesn't mention—which means he obviously didn't discover—that the town deserves an eternal scar for an incident there around 1940. The story I and my generation grew up hearing: At a downtown intersection of two heavily traveled highways, a car from Detroit carrying four African American men collided with a speeding Huntington fire truck, with horrible results: four dead, two firemen and two from the car. There also were grave injuries, and—according to the oral history we grew up hearing—the injured African Americans were denied admission or treatment at the Huntington hospital. Justifiably, this outrage made national news—"Cruelest town in America," a magazine of the day is said to have headlined its account. The town took on a notoriety that its continuing all-white makeup hasn't diminished. We of my generation grew up with that story, and heard it told sometimes with a smile of repugnant pride. So, guiltless, undeserving of a terrible racial image my town certainly was not. But neither was my country at that time. Neither Huntington nor America has an excuse for that, 75 years after Appomattox.

When my time came to move from Huntington, I wasn't sure if anyone outside, especially African Americans, had ever even heard of Huntington, Indiana, let alone knew of its dirty secret. In spring 1964, my job at the Fort Wayne *News-Sentinel* was mostly as a copy editor with an occasional reporting/writing chance. One of those came when Indianapolis lawyer Frank Beckwith, reputedly the first black person ever to run in an Indiana presidential primary, spoke in Fort Wayne a few weeks before the May election. At the south-side African American church where he was to speak, I arrived early, the only white person among about twenty church members. Beckwith was late, and as we waited a man beside me asked casually, "Where are you from?" My Huntington apprehension kicked in; I said, "The *News-Sentinel*."

"No," he said, "where are you *from*?" Before I could answer, another conversation in the room caught everyone's attention. A woman, probably in her 40s, was discussing *the* issue of the moment, her voice strained but under control. "I *believe* in Dr. King—I *believe* in nonviolence, all those things," she said. Then her eyes flashed and, biting off every word, she said: "But if *I* had been the mother of one of those *little girls in Birmingham*, I'd have *got* me a *gun* and *shot every white man* I saw!"

I couldn't change my skin color, and to the extent I could I shared her outrage and passion, but I *was* very glad we weren't in bomb-shamed Birmingham, and I hadn't let my Huntington roots slip.

About then Frank Beckwith arrived. I introduced myself, and he said amiably, "Why don't you sit up here with me and be my son for tonight?" I came out of it all with a story to write, and my background unbared.

But getting back to Gilbert Carter, which I tried to do more than a half century after he stayed in our home . . .

I was out of sports and writing a Sunday op-ed column for the Bloomington *Herald-Times* in 2002 when a column idea came to me: *I wonder if I could find and talk to Gilbert Carter now? I wonder if he remembers those days with the Hammels in Huntington? I wonder if he* (whom I remembered as soft-spoken, friendly, obviously intelligent) *had or has any idea of how much he influenced my own feelings about blacks, he and that song I sang with full belief: "Red and yellow, black and white, they are precious in His sight. Jesus loves the little children of the world."* From childhood up, never did I have the slightest doubt about Negro (the term we used then, though not all in Huntington or other 1940s places did) equality, because that Sunday School song said Jesus treated them equally, and Gilbert Carter in manner and intelligence was obviously at the very least equal to us.

As far as I knew, there never were any Christmas cards or other communications between Gilbert and my parents after we moved to the opposite side of Huntington, removing any reason for a Huntington College student to stay with us. In 2002 I called the alumni affairs office at now Huntington University and asked if they had any postgraduate record of Gilbert. I got information that substantiated his student years, his degree, and traced him to 1960s residency in Michigan. My young novelist friend, Michael Koryta, doubled then as a private investigator. From those 40-year-old alumni records, Michael found Gilbert Carter and a recent Michigan address and phone number. I called, got no answer, and left a voice mail. I wrote him a letter at the address, telling him that my wife and I—this was happenstance but true—were coming through his area on a vacation trip later that month. I gave him my email address, home and office phone numbers, and mailing address, and asked if there was a chance we could get together.

I never heard back.

I've wondered since if what he remembered of Huntington, what he remembered of us, my parents and their two kids, was strikingly different from my idyllic picture. Maybe my call was to the wrong Gilbert Carter. Maybe the address was wrong and that's why he never called back. I hope so.

RELIGION, POLITICS, AND ME

Were they still alive, my dad and mother—like most of the rest of my family, though decidedly not me or brother Bill—would probably be conservatives, Republicans, and in the "Christian Right." And that is testimony to how things have changed over the years.

Having married in the harshest ravages of the Great Depression, Dad and Mom felt blessed at the time to have even a menial job and a roof over their head. They became grateful, devoted FDR Democrats, though Dad's even then was a mostly Republican family, in a mostly Republican city and state.

In my childhood, because of their voting affiliation, I identified with the Democratic Party. Consequently, from childhood up, in my own reading and radio-then-TV absorption, I heard and viewed Democrat candidates sympathetically and Republican negatively; I tended to read liberal writers approvingly and reject conservative. And I've wondered ever since: What part does inculcation play in our deepest root feelings? How much political truth is there in Alexander Pope's "As the twig is bent, so is the tree inclined?" As ardent a liberal as I am now, could different early inclination have exposed me to different reading, inclined me toward different political heroes, made me right-wing? Or, my bitterest enemies left? Is this national fissure that divides us so sharply really that shallow?

Growing up with Dad and Mom also meant I passed through stages as a young member of the Church of God. Already I have misspoken, if what I remember is true: our Church of God didn't have "members." The denominational belief as I understood it was that your relationship is not with a building or a pastor or a congregation but directly with God: He and only He knows if you're in or out.

I still like that.

You hear the term "straight and narrow" sometimes, regarding the path devout Christians are to follow. The path I walked as a child, behind Dad and Mom and sister Joy, was indeed straight and very, very narrow.

Let me give you an idea how narrow. Definitely not welcome on that path—though undeniably Christians—were Catholics, of which Huntington had many. I first was smitten with a version of puppy love as an eighth grader, when we moved to a new home and I entered a new school and found the most gorgeous girl I had ever seen. I'm not sure if I was comparing her beauty with anyone before, because I don't remember thinking of girls as . . . girls, before that.

I certainly did not want her to know I felt like that, not at least till I knew whether maybe she "liked"—that was the word—me, too. I couldn't really ask her, couldn't say anything to her at all; tipping my hand would have been mortifying. So I kind of moved around her in the classroom or school hall or playground in what amounted to slowly shrinking circles. I'm sure I could find animal species where mating works something like that—NOT THAT I WAS THINKING *MATING*, FOR CRYING OUT LOUD.

Or maybe I was. Of course I was. Otherwise why, the time I heard one of her friends talking to her about a church class she was taking called catechism, did I feel like my world collapsed?

I couldn't sleep that night. I thought of catechism as a Catholic term and at that stage of my life it was an absolute given that I could never think of "liking," let alone dating or—oh God, forgive me for even letting the idea cross my mind—marrying a Catholic girl. And when I learned a day or two later that her catechism class was not in a Catholic church at all but a Protestant church that used the term, I felt elation and liberation—circling permissible again, because she wasn't a Catholic!

That's how narrow I thought our path to heaven from that little brick church was.

And here, too, as in school integration, increased exposure to practicing Catholics as I moved up through school and into adulthood showed me the folly of my prejudiced blindness. I was 21 when Julie and I married, and my best man was Catholic (Dick Morris, my senior class's president). My barber, a Catholic, was as close a friend as I had in the follow-up years. By then, and for the rest of my life, I never even thought about it, never cared. Mixing, observing, removing the blinders of bias worked wonders.

But there *was* the first Monday night in November 1960—I'm 24 and, finally, beyond the 21-year-old voting requisite and able to cast my first vote for president. And I'm young and liberal and excited, because young and liberal and exciting John F. Kennedy has a chance at the presidency. I'm married and a father and that night before the election I am at my parents' home earnestly pleading with them, reasoning with them, on how it made no sense for them to break away from the convictions and life experiences behind all their years of Democratic votes, that they were just too level-headed to let the Catholicism of Kennedy scare them into switching to . . . Richard *Nixon?* By now I was outright begging: Nixon is just *not* what you two *believe* in, what you *stand* for, what you've spent all your voting lives *rejecting*—he's from the party of *Hoover*, for heaven's sake.

Dad didn't say much. A few times Mother said, "Yes, but . . ." but she listened. When I left, Mom gave me a loving look that came across to me as *Yes, son, you're right, we'll vote Democrat.*

That night, I slept well.

The next night, I sweated out the news as the vote totals began to trickle in. Driving home to do my sweating-out and watching there, I stopped by my parents' house. Mom greeted me with a guilty look and with teary eyes said, "I've got to tell you. We voted for Nixon."

Dad didn't surprise me. He hadn't argued the night before, but he hadn't openly agreed, either. But Mom? I was stunned. What she said she'd do she hadn't, and that wasn't Mom. My reaction came in a lame, choked-out "Why?"

"Honey," she said, her eyes flooding, "I'm sorry . . . but I got in that voting booth, and all I could see was the Pope."

Dating was never a part of my high school life. My age probably didn't help; I was 15 through the first several weeks of my senior year, and never did get around to getting the driver's license that all my friends had.

That didn't leave me wheel-less. One friend's parents gave him unlimited use of the family's big Buick, unlimited until his report card included an F in English Comp and he was told to get that grade up, immediately and considerably, or he would drive no more. I happened to be taking the same English Comp class, and my friend's car had been providing both of us with rides. I didn't think of it as cheating, just as right—helping a friend a little. But . . . the spelling and grammar in his assigned papers did improve remarkably, almost immediately after the parental threat. So did his English Comp grade, and even more than before I had a free ride any time I wanted.

Of course, that meant my friend came with the car privileges: he was driving, not I, so dating on my own wasn't feasible. That's a cop-out. I wasn't in what I would term a dating way with any girls anyway, although by now I was no longer circling. I actually had amicable conversations regularly with several, but the only real date was when I took Sheila, a really neat, attractive, exceptionally bright girl, to our senior prom. I liked and genuinely admired her a lot, but we didn't date again afterward, which tells you all you need to know about me as a teenaged charmer.

≈

It wasn't until my newspaper life had started that I actually began to date: one girl, whom I ultimately married . . . and I probably would never have met if she hadn't been the kid sister of my best friend at the time, so she and I didn't have to go through any kind of introduction.

By the time I left that job at the Huntington *Herald-Press*, sweet Julie Sowerwine Hammel and I were four—son Rick and daughter Jane joining us. In later years, Jane, a career primary-grades schoolteacher, has found great fun in pointing out to people the boundless imaginations of her parents as name givers. "My dad is a *writer*," Jane will say, "very creative, imaginative, reads a lot! And he named his two kids Dick and Jane."

Those two kids were such blessings in our lives—for all *their* lives, from birth to today, when grandchildren and great-grandchildren have followed—that career bumps became small. I traveled a lot, missed whole days often and got home late, late at night many, many times. Those nights when I got home after the kids were in bed, I *always* made it a point to stop by each's bedroom, lean over, and give them a kiss. Yes, there was a risk that I would disturb their sleep and wake them, maybe even frighten them, but I felt it a bigger risk that just once they might hear me come in, expect that stop for a kiss, and not get it. That never happened, and they rewarded both of us by growing to be great teens, then great adults, great contributors to life . . . and always great, loving kids. We can take all the credit in the world for being terrific parents, but we both know many friends who worked every bit as hard at being terrific parents, too, but for various reasons beyond their real control knew heartbreak. We were lucky, and blessed.

Those kids became:

> Dr. Richard Hammel (fig. 1.6), MD, MPH, not a patient-treating physician but ultimately a career executive with Procter & Gamble in Cincinnati, husband of Marcie—exceedingly bright herself, a Purdue graduate who was on her way to a business career when she and the man she calls Richard and we call Rick met, married, and had the two girls who brightened our lives in brand new ways: Mackenzie and her 13-months-younger sister Cameron, each exceptionally accomplished

1.6. While earning a master's degree from North Carolina and completing residency at Duke, son Rick rankled at ACC basketball haughtiness and celebrated Indiana's fifth NCAA championship in 1987 by getting and using this license plate: accurate accounting at the time.

as students and (all thanks to Marcie) musicians. Mackenzie, a harpist, appeared on the PBS program "From the Top"; Cameron, a flutist, was All-Ohio first chair through high school. Mozart and others wrote many exquisite compositions for harp and flute that let them perform together in ways even their unmusical paternal grandparents could savor and treasure (e.g., playing for weddings when both were preteens). Both chose to attend Indiana University, so for five years, and especially the core three when both were in school at the same time, Grandma and Grandpa were spoiled. Mackenzie graduated in business in 2013, Cameron in prelaw in 2014. Both went on to graduate degrees—Mackenzie an MBA with honors from Carnegie-Mellon, a degree achieved largely online while

1.7. Mackenzie (top) and Cameron Hammel—climbing professional ladders now, way above Grandpa.

working uninterrupted at Procter & Gamble in Cincinnati; Cameron completing law school at Duke, graduating first in her class in international and comparative law, and taking a position with Gibson, Dunn, Crutcher in New York (fig. 1.7).

Jane Hammel Priest, a career elementary teacher with—like her brother—two Indiana University degrees. Jane perplexed her parents by—though attractive, bright, cheerfully conversational, happily successful in her field, active and beloved in her church—staying single into her 40s, waiting for the right man. Better no marriage than a bad marriage, I kept reminding/consoling myself, her growingly anxious mother, and even Jane herself at times. At 44, she married Fred Priest, who was in his 50s and had lost his first wife to cancer. Jane felt it was too late to become the mother she had dreamed of being, but she got her family anyway. Fred brought along two daughters and six grandchildren, which later became seven. So, when Jane told me she was going to wed, I was elated of course and said with a teasing grin, "Congratulations, honey! And how does it feel to be an instant grandmother?" The kid was around me too long. She smiled even more teasingly and retorted, "Great! And how does it feel to be an instant *great*-grandfather?" That thought hadn't occurred to me, but on consideration it felt and still feels great, almost as great as that awaited moment on December 27, 2007, when I walked her down a church aisle.

Julie and I (fig. 1.8) were blessed, bountifully, and Julie was the one who did the heavy work. She was the omnipresent mother, helping it all happen. Julie endured without complaint a secondary life as "Mrs. Bob Hammel" in a college town and world where women were increasingly and deservedly intent on shedding such subordinated identification. At home, she certainly never acted subordinated, while working the magic of motherhood and enjoying its payback: the kind of people those kids she raised turned out to be. She was the one who—by far—did the most to help *that* payback happen.

Julie is why the Church of God and I parted. She was a Presbyterian. In our time the unofficial book of rules on How to Do Things said that when marriage time came, it should be in the church of the bride. The pastor of that church let Julie know that she would be a lot more welcome to use its building for her wedding if the groom were also a member. So I joined.

1.8. Bob and Julie Hammel—after 50 years, now 60.

We got married at Huntington's First Presbyterian Church,[4] June 22, 1958. Originally, Julie and her mother had picked August 10, and when her engagement picture ran in the newspaper one Sunday in January, the last line in the picture caption said, "The couple plan an August wedding." It happened in June. Usually in the Huntington of the 1950s when a wedding date suddenly got moved up two months like that, it was for a reason. This was suddenly moved up, but not for *that* reason.

The 1958 American League baseball schedule came out in February, and the line that jumped out to me was "New York at Chicago, June 23–26." The Yankees were coming to Chicago to play my White Sox in late June!

I wasn't dumb enough to tell Julie or her mother I'd like to move things up a little because of the baseball schedule. Instead, I reasoned with almost romantic overtones, June is just . . . the *traditional* month, the perfect month for weddings.

Darned if I didn't get that through. And they agreed that Sunday, June 22, seemed just a great time. The first day of summer.

There was still the matter of getting us honeymooning in the right city.

Sometime in there, I interjected, "Honey . . . what would you think of going to Chicago? The *Herald-Press* has this due-bill thing that would let us stay almost free at the Congress Hotel right in the heart of Chicago. And right there close would be the Schubert Theater where the stage production of *My Fair Lady* will be playing, and the Chicago Theater, where they have great acts like the Four Aces along with movies like *South Pacific*, and they've got the art museum, where your grandmother used to go to sketch . . . and, maybe we could catch a Sox game or two."

---

4. The wedding wasn't the absolute end of my Church of God connection. In 2000, Julie and I moved from our 25-year home on Bloomington's east side to a newly built west-side home, the first to go up in Stoneybrook subdivision. Construction soon started on its second building, across the street from us. It was a church, unidentified at first, till a sign announced it as the Stoneybrook Church of God. Both my parents had passed by then, but I told Julie, "Honey, Mom hasn't given up yet."

Julie and I did get to two White Sox-Yankees games on that honeymoon—on Tuesday and Thursday after our Sunday wedding. Would have been three, but—terrible luck—the Wednesday game was rained out. Julie took full advantage: we went to the Art Institute of Chicago, where her maternal grandmother had spent many young hours on pencil drawings that are admirable parts of our wall adornments today. I'm not proud that I was as little into art as Julie was baseball. I slogged through the whole visit—masterwork by masterwork—around the museum, finally got back to the entrance and, just as I saw the exit door and triumph was lighting up my weary face, she said, "There's a second floor."

Oh, what a day. And the Sox lost the two games we did see. God denied me *real* pleasure from my slick subterfuge.

MY COLLEGE YEARS, IN A NEWSROOM

My professional launch out of my nest into my true world was with—shall we be crude here?—the most velvet-gloved goose imaginable.

Before that, I was happily on career cruise control.

As my first couple of newspaper years went by and my return-to-college ship disappeared over the horizon, I found more and more to like about the unusual opportunities offered an untrained kid. What I had as a developing writer at the Huntington *Herald-Press* was certainly not autonomy but precious little supervisory pressure. Most of the things I did went unedited straight to the Linotype machine. From the beginning, I typed "clean" copy, minimally uglied by mark-outs and penciled editings—until they got to "Judge" Houghton. The ones he saw were rare: an opinion column or a major Page 1 piece that had to be cleared by him before going to print. And with those, the same thing happened every time. *Always,* my clean copy came back with alterations aplenty, and strike-throughs—words or whole passages he obviously considered too bad to alter, better dead than read. In my juvenility, I usually thought, *Those things he changed weren't really wrong, the stubborn old coot just changed them to be changing—to keep me in my place.*

Editings were one thing; butchery was another. I came into the business with a gift for the concluding paragraph, an insightful, almost poetic summary of all that had been said before. A digest. A summary. Always, those came back from "Judge" Houghton missing. Not altered—killed. Snipped right off the bottom of the page. The first few times it happened, I was a little piqued. It kept happening. I got piqueder and piqueder. I'm not sure how many repetitions later I actually read the shorter version and it sank in to me that it read better—more virile, stronger—without the summary 'graph. Just fact, fact, fact, fact, boom. Draw your own conclusions, reader. You're smart enough to do it without me.

It may have been my best long-term journalism lesson: trust your reader. Do your job, present your facts clearly and concisely, then get out of the way. Let the reader take it from there. It's the only way to write a news story, obviously, but it works effectively on opinion pieces, too. Stimulate thinking, don't assault it.

In my fourth year, now 21, the age of a college junior, I was feeling veteran and frisky. The Fort Wayne South team that won the 1958 state high school basketball championship had a seven-foot center, Mike Mc-Coy, who was named Indiana's "Mr. Basketball," best player in the state. South regularly played Huntington and that year murdered the Vikings, 81–41. In print I cleverly referred to South's big center as a "glandular error." Sixty years later, I remember the indignant letter it provoked, and the name of its writer, a man I never met, a name I never saw again until his obituary—death at 75—ran in the Bloomington newspaper in March 2014 and I read enough to confirm that yes, this resident of Noblesville who died was the Neil Eisenhut who graduated from Roanoke High School in Huntington County—the Neil Eisenhut who, though young himself, in 1958 took a cleaver to my cleverness in a justifiably nasty Letter to the Editor. I couldn't even argue; he was right. Never again did I consider cuteness more valuable than propriety. Which rendered me unfit for modern sports journalism, but life has its costs.

≈

I enjoyed my work. Besides sports, I was a lead news reporter, covering the police and fire departments, the city building, which included the mayor's office—and therein lies another tale . . .

In 1963, Huntington was electing a new mayor—a big thing on my "city" beat. Julie's family was strong Republican. That was her first year of voting eligibility, but I thought I had converted her to my side. On the way to the polls to cast our own primary-election votes, she told me, "I'm going to vote Republican." I wasn't shocked; one of the two Republican candidates for mayor was the owner-operator of Huntington's main movie theater, a genial fellow who sensed our economic plight and regularly waved us in as his unpaying guests when we showed up for a film, even sat with us a time or two, long before he was into politics at all. Her voting crossover was solely to support him in the mayor vote. I said, "Fine. Do it."

Our kids then were not quite 4 and 1, so she sat in the car with them while I voted, then she headed out to cast hers. She returned, obviously upset—not crying or close to it but fuming, and trying to hide it all.

Once we were in the car, I said, "What's wrong?"

"Nothing. Let's go."

"*Some*thing's wrong—what is it?"

"*Nothing* . . . dumb paper ballots . . ."

Turned out the lines were a little askew on her printed form and she accidentally put her X in the wrong candidate's box. I said, "That's no big deal, you just asked for another ballot, didn't you?"

"No . . . I was too embarrassed. I just put it in the box. It won't matter anyway. Dumb ballot . . ."

About 2 o'clock the next morning, I called her from the newspaper office and said, "Uh, honey, guess what?"

She didn't believe me until I brought home the newspaper with headlines that said our friend had lost, 1,003 to 1,002.

If she had stayed home, or voted Democrat, he'd have tied and there would have been some sort of run-off or party-financed recount. If she had asked for a new ballot and cast it, he would have won. Instead, she cast the accidental vote that beat her friend. The idea that every vote counts has one bitterly convinced believer.

Our nine Huntington years weren't uninterrupted. The summer of 1959 I got itchy. After five years I despaired of waiting for the grand offer I had felt was sure to come someday when one of the Bigs read my work. Nothing close to that happened, so I applied for and got a sports-only job at nearby Peru. The Peru *Daily Tribune* treated me superbly, sending me to Chicago in October to cover the three White Sox home games in the 1959 World Series. Three months after starting at Peru, before the bills arrived from the moving company that had relocated me and my family of three from Huntington to Peru, I resigned to go back to Huntington. Nightly, I had been coming home to a weeping wife, homesick with her months-old first child heightening her feelings of isolation from the grandmas who could guide her—my mother more than hers. Finally, I called the *Herald-Press* and asked managing editor George Frye, my longtime deskmate, if the job was still open. He said it was, I asked if I could go home again, and I returned. I did give my customary two-week notice before leaving. Ernie Mazzatenta, a very capable and usually pleasant news executive at Peru, was visibly and justifiably irked when I in effect handed him those moving bills as I was heading out the door. But he did pay them.

When I had left Huntington that summer, the high school football coach, Charles "Wave" Myers, was in just his second year there but already a valued friend of mine. Wave, whose career reached as high as head coach at Ball State, pulled me aside one day just before I left and said, "This is going to be the best thing that ever happened to you. You're good. The people reading you here will never really appreciate you—prophet without honor, that kind of thing. You grew up with them. They take you for granted. In Peru, they're going to think you're great." The idea was heady stuff and reinforcing, even if I never did give it a chance to work out.

I returned with a small sense of shame and a determination to appreciate what I had in Huntington, partly in resigned acceptance that my wings were clipped and my traveling apparently over. I got my old responsibilities back—I loved my police station-city building beat because it always included a coffee stop at my close friend Joe Etter's barber shop for coffee and wonderful chats with him and his regulars. Also, once I got the sports page done, I frequently was responsible for putting out the rest of the paper—laying out Page 1 and writing the headlines. I felt important to the operation and enjoyed the feeling. And I *was* important. The night before the early-morning birth of our second child (Jane, on June 6, 1962, joining 3-year-old Ricky), Huntington was hit by its worst fire in history. The city's biggest, oldest factory, Caswell-Runyan—built in 1906 as reputedly the first manufacturer of cedar chests in America—burned to the ground. I was up all night welcoming Jane in. Sleepy-eyed, I made it to the office in time to get sports out, then heard the news that no one else had taken on "the Caswell fire," so it was mine. I headed out at 9 a.m. to get a story by noon. A neighboring second factory had been consumed; the loss in 1962 dollars was estimated at $6 million. It's still Huntington's biggest fire disaster, ever. Groggy and punchy, I put out a headlined story that I'm still proud of. I don't remember the lede, but I have always remembered the date, because of that blessed baby girl who accompanied it.

Sports remained my staple, and it was what opened the door to regional friendships for me. The best was with a writer 20 miles "down-river"—Tom Schumaker of the Wabash *Plain Dealer*. Tom was a little younger than me, and a lot more athletic. Our paths first crossed, though I didn't know it, when he was an outstanding senior basketball player at Chester Township High just across the Huntington-Wabash county line and thus out of our coverage area. I had no idea he existed. Near the end of my first year, I was following a center from Andrews, Gerald Yentes, who—personal research had convinced me—was about to be the first player in Huntington County history to score 1,000 career points. As the countdown got close, I made him the featured item in every Andrews game story, as when he scored 35 points—big night— but his team lost to Chester, which had a guy named Schumaker who scored 43. A Wabash County record, I learned later—didn't know and didn't really care then. I thought it generous of me to mention him at all, as I did in the last paragraph of the story, and even give him a first name: "Jack Schumaker scored 43 for Chester."

The Schumakers lived barely outside Huntington County, so close to the western borders of the Huntington County town of Bippus that they were among the few in their county who actually subscribed to the Huntington newspaper. Young Tom was understandably excited by his record night and couldn't wait to see what the Huntington paper had done with it. He read: "Jack Schumaker scored 43 for Chester."

Years later, after he had played at Huntington College and gone to work at the Wabash *Plain Dealer* and we had developed a friendship, we were covering an event together when Tom casually reached into his billfold, pulled out a clipping, and wordlessly handed it to me. "Jack Schumaker scored 43 for Chester."

I never made up a first name again. And to this day he has never sent a note to me signed anything but "Jack."

We did stay friends. Huntington and Wabash were in the same athletic conference, and one football weekend they were playing on different nights. Wabash was at home against strong Marion on Wednesday; Huntington was to play someone on Friday and Marion the next week. So, with an open Wednesday, I went to Wabash to see the game and walk the sidelines with my pal "Jack." Marion scored and scored and scored and scored, so we were unprepared when a photographer for Tom's paper came running up screaming, "Did you see that! Did you see that! They called that good!"

"That" was the extra-point kick after one of those touchdowns. It really didn't matter if it was or wasn't, but I said, "It looked good to me."

"Good?" Tom's man screamed. "It was too *high*!"

Hoosiers always have understood basketball better than football.

The newswriting part of my job provided some special access, and memories. For example, at age 22, before election laws had let me cast my first presidential vote, I sat on a hotel mezzanine couch with Harry Truman and had an interview-conversation.

In the election of 1958, Democrat Vance Hartke was running for Senate, and Mr. Truman, not quite six years after he had left the presidency in general disfavor, came to Fort Wayne to back Hartke. Fort Wayne was just twenty-five miles from Huntington. I arranged credentials for a press conference at the downtown hotel where Mr. Truman was to appear. He did, to a turnout of four, I the only out-of-towner—imagine that, a president of the '50s, a man of history for succeeding FDR and dropping the A-bombs that ended a long, bloody war, a man today commonly ranked with the all-time greatest presidents, so unpopular in the very decade he left office that he had a press conference and only four people showed up. I sat on one end of a small couch, taking notes and asking questions, Mr. Truman a few feet away on the other end—chatting, smiling, answering everything asked, shaking hands afterward. I felt big-time, and still treasure the moment.

I had another moment like that—*feeling* big-time, though no one else noticed—through a freshman Democrat congressman, Huntington attorney J. Edward Roush, for whom I had moonlighted quite secretly to help with news releases and such during his winning 1958 campaign. When Representative Roush came home during a break, I interviewed him. He said some things about how unsettled Washington was with Secretary of State John Foster Dulles so ill he was immobilized and his assistant, former Massachusetts governor Christian Herter, filling in but unempowered to do anything while the usual world crises were calling for attention. Roush made no big issue of it, nor did my story, but a Washington network correspondent—Richard C. Hottelet—saw the interview and gave it major play on his nightly radio broadcast: a Midwestern congressman speaking out on a near crisis of government that had inside Washington nervous but discreetly silent. Big things didn't often emanate from the Huntington *Herald-Press* newsroom, where the vest-pocket-notepad interview was done, but this one got *some* stature and me a tiny measure of Andy Warhol's version of fame.

In the spring of 1963, Arizona senator Barry Goldwater, just starting to make political waves on his way to ultimate selection as the 1964 Republican presidential candidate, spoke in the 9,400-seat "world's largest high school gymnasium" at New Castle, Indiana, about 50 miles from Huntington. I covered the event column-style, which freed me for some loose, opinionated fun. I looked at New Castle's star-spangled décor, thought about Mr. Goldwater's old guard, ultraconservative reputation, and suggested in my report that if this newcomer-outsider from

Arizona hoped to shake a stodgy, stuck-in-the-past image he shouldn't be speaking in front of 48-star flags. Great line, I thought, because it was true—more than a decade after Hawaii and Alaska had swelled the nation's total and forced a redesigned flag, the old 48-star version backdropped him at New Castle. One problem: my newspaper wasn't looking for reasons to laugh at Barry Goldwater or his rigid conservatism. It was owned by archconservative Eugene C. Pulliam, whose more noted and influential holdings were the pronouncedly right-wing Indianapolis *Star*, Indianapolis *News*, and both newspapers in Phoenix—Goldwater's base, its newspapers Goldwater's biggest early boosters. "Judge" Houghton didn't catch my line before it was in print, but he caught up with me shortly after. He wasn't amused.

Among the biggest Goldwater boosters at the Phoenix newspapers was James C. Quayle, who had been business manager of the Huntington newspaper when I was hired in 1954 and signed my first paychecks. Jim took a job soon after in promotions for the Phoenix papers and moved his family there, including young son Danny, familiar around the office in my first year as an active little guy of 8 or so. Danny was Eugene C. Pulliam's grandson, his mother, Corinne, the daughter of Pulliam. Danny was a junior in high school when his dad came back to take full control of the *Herald-Press*. Danny tried out in basketball his senior year, 1963–64, when the roster was loaded with the best team Huntington ever had. Young Quayle was cut. It's the Dan Quayle who became a lawyer, then a US congressman, unseating my friend, five-term veteran J. Edward Roush (who, while in office, with the help of Police Chief Wally Smith had made Huntington the pioneer city for eventual national implementation of the 911 emergency telephone system).

Four years after beating Roush, two-term representative Quayle upset three-term Indiana senator Birch Bayh. That made him a national name, because Bayh was one: the first since the Founding Fathers to author two Constitutional amendments (presidential succession and 18-year-old voting) as well as the earth-shaking educational act Title IX. During that 1980 senatorial campaign, Quayle stopped in at the *Herald-Telephone* to court editor Bill Schrader, whose office door opened to my desk area. I didn't know he was in the building, so when I looked up and our eyes connected as he and Schrader loomed suddenly a few feet away I blurted, "Danny!" It dawned on me quickly that I hadn't chosen a very respectful way of addressing a congressman running for Senate. A colleague brought my gaffe up when interviewing Vice President Quayle years later, and he laughed. "To him I'll always be Danny," he said.

When George H. W. Bush picked Dan Quayle as his running mate, it was a huge surprise—and the biggest news story ever in Huntington. A day after the convention, their successful 1988 campaign started on the courthouse steps in Huntington. And not very much later, there was the Lloyd Bentsen debate line ("Senator, I knew John Kennedy, and you're no John Kennedy") and the Quayle jokes began. But there is, only in Huntington, a Vice Presidential Museum, honoring all the number twos in American history, and on proud, conservative Huntington's city limits are signs that say, "Huntington, Home of Vice President Dan Quayle."

In April 1963, the major league baseball season was about to begin. The day before the season opener, Chicago White Sox owner Bill Veeck annually opened a team workout to the regional press to introduce and publicize the new team. Huntington wasn't really very "regional," but I always drove up to attend that briefing. In 1963, Jim Quayle—almost as fervent a White Sox fan as me—asked to go along. Somewhere on the four-hour drive home he asked a conversational question I wasn't ready for:

"What *are* your long-range plans?"

I realized I was 26 and I had none.

I enjoyed what I was doing, had become pretty good at it, and told him I had very broadly assumed my career would be the job I had in my hometown.

"Don't get me wrong, I think you're terrific at what you do," he said. "But you surely know you're already as high as you can go with us. You can't be my editor—not as liberal as you are. You wouldn't like writing for me, and *I* wouldn't like it. If I were you, for your own future, I think I'd start looking around. I don't think you have any idea where you could wind up."

No shoves, no kicks, just the gentlest of pushes out of the nest. In about three months, I was gone.

And close to 30 years later, I got a letter. From Huntington. Enclosed was a proofed reprint of my first sports column head, and the lead engraving that had been made for daily usage. Included was a brief note:

> *Someday when you are writing your memoirs you might want this.*
> *Jim Q.*

FOUR SCHOOLS, FOUR TOWNS, SECOND GRADE

I didn't jump out of the car that day with Jim Quayle and start job-hunting. A few months later, I called Charlie Keefer, city editor of the Fort Wayne *News-Sentinel*, a Huntington native and *Herald-Press* alumnus who had told me over the years to let him know if I ever was interested in leaving. He had no jobs open but said he'd see what he could do. He called back in about an hour, and he had created a deskless, titleless, nonwriting position that rotated me into day-off positions around the copy desks. I took it.

It turned out to be a job I loved and hated. It gave me a chance to learn and improve in copy editing, headline writing, and page layout under tight deadlines; it boosted my confidence in myself as a professional journalist. The hate part: the job included almost no writing opportunities. I spent two days a week on the wire desk, the number-two man in editing wire copy and writing headlines; two days similarly processing local copy; and one day in "the slot," actually supervising the whole news product for that edition and designing Page 1. Each employee's day off advanced each week: Tuesday this week, Wednesday the next. That meant every fifth week brought a big three-day holiday-like weekend, off Saturday and the next Monday, with no paper on Sunday. If called into work on your day off, you received overtime pay—the "Big Eight," employees called those eight time-and-a-half hours. On a Friday in late November 1963, leading up to one of those three-day weekends for me, at breakfast before my 7 a.m. report time I thought of our mounting bills and limited income and told Julie, "I'd give anything if something would happen that I'd have to work these two days (Saturday and Monday)."

Something happened.

I was on the wire desk that Friday, November 22, 1963, and as we were closing our edition for 1 p.m. press time, the wire machines began to scream. I was used to two types of bells on those machines demanding special attention: one tone for breaking news labeled URGENT, a louder one for the next step up, BULLETIN. The first bulletin said, "Shots have been fired at President Kennedy's motorcade in downtown Dallas." Seconds later came the harsh ring of a new level I'd never heard: FLASH. In the next few minutes of that stunning time, FLASH became familiar, starting with a report that the president had been hit by the shots and—short but tense minutes and several FLASHes later—confirmation that the president indeed was dead.

There was no TV set in the newsroom. With the first FLASH an immediate call went out to hold up on starting the presses. The assassination confirmed, a quick decision was made to change just Page 1, so only two people in the long newsroom had work to do: wire editor George Tetherly and I. George assessed quickly which stories and pictures could be pulled from the page, we remade it as simply but powerfully as possible, and sent edited copy, headlines, and layout on the way within minimal minutes, maybe 15, after official confirmation.

That was done amid pandemonium in the shocked newsroom—loud shouting, even screaming, some sobbing. Into that maelstrom walked the circulation director of Fort Wayne Newspapers, Inc., Ralph Heckman, whose job it was to hurry packages of freshly run papers off to buses and trains that maintained precise schedules. Ralph strode through the milling frenzy to find managing editor Bud Manth, and above it all I heard him bellow, "You're going to hold for *that*!"

Now, I was every bit the young liberal that Jim Quayle thought I was, a huge Kennedy fan. In retrospect, *I'm* amazed that my grief over the news itself was suspended during the demands of the moment—so much so that when I heard Heckman's comment, I broke out in laughter thinking, *If not for this, what would we ever hold for?*

We held.

And I worked a Big Eight Saturday, and another one Monday.

What I remember of Saturday is being handed a United Press story with a terse command from George Tetherly: "It's too long. Cut it to 16 inches." Routine, usually. I went to work on it, looking for expendable stuff, got halfway through, and did what a number-two desk man never does: argued. "We can't cut this. This is a Pulitzer." I was right. Merriman Smith's splendid you-are-there account of that day of tragic chaos—for United Press, in competition with all the remarkable writing that came out that historic weekend and everything else written in newspapers that climactic year—did win the 1963 Pulitzer Prize. Tetherly wasn't dictatorial; we ended up running about 22 inches of Mr. Smith's classic piece, and my dagger that cut off those other inches felt as bloodied as Macbeth's.

Charlie Keefer sensed my discomfort with a lack of writing assignments and did his best to steer some overtime reporting jobs to me, but there wasn't much—a horse show, a speech or two, Frank Beckwith's appearance. Summer came, and a new newspaper popped up in Kokomo, about 60 miles from Fort Wayne. By then editor of the Wabash *Plain Dealer*, Tom (my friend "Jack") Schumaker was offered the Kokomo sports editor job but said he wasn't interested—no one of sound mind and sound job in the newspaper industry would have been, given the expectable short life span of new papers. But Tom knew of my discomfort and gave them my contact information. The temptation to write again overrode discretion. Kokomo called, I went for an interview, and about a year to the day after I left Huntington for Fort Wayne, I started at the Kokomo *Morning Times*.

The move wasn't easy, and neither were the last days leading up to it. I told Charlie Keefer I was quitting. An exceptionally nice person who genuinely cared about me, Charlie asked me to talk with editor Cliff Ward first. I found Ward neither genuine nor nice. I'm sure he had never heard the name Bob Hammel up to then, but after Charlie briefed him before our talk, he was all smiles as he told me one-on-one what a great future I had at the *News-Sentinel* because of my . . . that kind of thing. He asked me to stay; I said I had decided to go. Then he turned cold, telling me I was a rotten husband and father, risking my family's livelihood for a move so obviously doomed. I heard but didn't change. I left to go back to that day's work, resolute but in truth shaken. I did know I was gambling, and mine wasn't the only fate involved. There were four of us riding on my gamble.

The Kokomo paper had started publication, and the first copies arrived for me that day. When I got home in late afternoon, Julie handed me two mailed issues. I took them to our upstairs bedroom, sat on the side of our bed, and eagerly tore off the wrappings . . . and read the two most amateurish newspaper productions I had ever seen: in writing, in headlines, *ohmygod!*

My rationalizing reassurance to myself in fending off the realities that Ward laid out stemmed from my Huntington years: all those times of what I felt was pretty good work with no job offers. I told myself, "This paper probably won't last, but unlike Huntington, this time *everyone* in the business will be watching. If I do well, I *will* be noticed. Whatever happens, I should come out with at least as good a job as I have now."

Then these copies of the new paper I was joining arrived. As I read, my head sank, I felt stunned, I let those Kokomo papers fall to the floor. *My God*, I thought, *this paper might fold before I get there. I'm going to have to swallow every bit of pride I have and go back in there tomorrow morning and ask crusty, arrogant Cliff Ward if I can have my job back.*

I couldn't do it. August 4, 1964, I started in Kokomo. It was a career-making move.

⁓

I thought when I considered the job that Kokomo would be a great place to be a sportswriter because the town loved its high school sports. If anything I underestimated that. Within a few days and after a few columns, I was a public figure in town, my name and my face quickly familiar. And, at this undermanned, overmatched little paper, getting out every day's edition was an adventure—high-voltage emergency mode, a daylong sprint, but energizing, stimulating fun! I loved my colleagues. We celebrated every small victory we scored, or imagined we scored, in battling the established, haughty Kokomo *Tribune*.

The investors who ran the *Times* wanted to compete. They found the money to send me to St. Louis for the Cardinals' home games in that 1964 World Series with the Yankees. They gave me time to do my best; if our midnight deadline had to be pushed back a little to let me squeeze in something more, it moved—sometimes to as late as 3 a.m. Occasionally management got on a make-the-deadlines kick and on one of those mornings, chief financial officer Bill Beck stomped into the newsroom with our newest edition in hand. He went up to news editor Lee Nance and pointed to a Page 1 picture of a postmidnight home fire: "With our deadline, how in the *hell* did this get in?" I walked over and said, "Bill, I was running late in sports and I told them they might as well get that fire story and beat the *Tribune*." He looked at me, smiled, and said, "Oh— that's great, Bob! Good thinking!" He left, calmed. Less pleased was the man I had taken off the hook. IU journalism graduate Lee Nance was not a sports fan or an Indiana native, and he was incensed by Hoosier priorities that got him rebuked and me congratulated—for missing the same deadline. A *great* place to be a sportswriter.

I was right about something else, too. For the first time, I was being watched within my industry. After only a few editions, hardly a two- or three-day stretch went by that I didn't get a call from some editor offering me a job. The day I went to St. Louis for the 1964 World Series opener, I had my topcoat on all set to leave the office when my phone rang. The confident voice on the other end said in a voice-of-God introduction, and a singsongy, hard-hitting cadence I've never forgotten:

"Bob, *this*... is *Irving Leibowitz*... of The *In*-dia-*nap*-olis *Times. How* would you *like* to go to *work* for a metro-*pol*-itan paper?"

Leibowitz epitomized Indiana journalism, nationally known as a columnist. And his newspaper had a tradition-rich history, a Scripps-Howard paper esteemed in Indiana for its own Pulitzer rewards for taking on the Ku Klux Klan in the 1920s and '30s. At Huntington, I'd have leaped at the invitation. This time I said, "Gee, thanks, Mr. Leibowitz, I really appreciate your call, but right now I have to get going to St. Louis to cover the World Series." Mine is a life of irony and pure luck. Knowing the frailty of my Kokomo newspaper's existence, I could—maybe should—have snapped up that offer. If I had, I would have been there when, well before the *Morning Times* folded, the *Indianapolis Times* did. And then, instead of being, as my scenario imagined, a Kokomo fish suddenly available to better-paying birds of prey, I'd have been an Indianapolis unknown bobbing out there in the unemployment sea along with many much more familiar names.

And Kokomo *was* exciting. My chance "to go to *work* for a metropol-itan paper" was unhesitatingly rejected mainly because I was too enchanted with the excitement of day-to-day competition and fond of the people around me to think about leaving. It was the greatest bonding experience of my newspaper life. I started there in August and four months later came back from a short Christmas break to join editor Jerry Pfarr—a former Kenosha, Wisconsin, sports editor and *Golf Digest* writer who was an outstanding talent and my most qualified in-house fan—in being invited into publisher Frank Gregory's office. With a wide grin, gregarious Frank said, "You two bastards are great! I just want you to know we almost folded this place just before Christmas but you two are the main reason we're going on."

Poof!

I had no inkling things were *that* precarious. The next call I got was from sports editor Wayne Fuson at the Indianapolis *News*, and I accepted it. My delightful, exciting, ego-restoring Kokomo adventure was over six months after it started.

The *Star* was Indianapolis's most popular paper. The *News*, its sister publication, particularly for older Indianapolis, was the afternoon paper bought to be read in unhurried study, not morning haste.

I came in as tenth man on a ten-man sports staff and resented my low position not at all. The other nine were very good, much more experienced, and warmly helpful to the new guy. When I left 18 months later, I was still tenth man and unresentful—and much more polished and confident for my time with professionals topped by the best columnist and writer on the staff, Corky Lamm. I had been reading and loving the wit and phrasing of Corky since my high school days working in the circulation department at the Huntington *Herald-Press*. When I got to know him as a cohort and friend, I found him as likeable as he was journalistically admirable. Five of us in that department, including Corky, became close; we golfed together, played poker together, and competed together for the $2 bills managing editor Eugene S. Pulliam liked to give out for what he considered exceptionally good headlines, cutlines, or ledes. Bob Renner, Dick Denny, Lyle Mannweiler, and Corky became my friends for life.

In late summer 1966, rumblings were being heard even in Indianapolis of another new newspaper in the offing—in Bloomington. Wealthy industrialist Sarkes Tarzian, an inventor and pioneer in color television, decided his hometown paper, the *Herald-Telephone*, was ripe for replacement. Tarzian and a disenchanted former *Herald-Telephone* editor, Bruce Temple, began putting together a new staff, which included Temple's whole six-man *Herald-Telephone* sports staff. In September 1966, the Bloomington *Courier-Tribune* went into business head-on against the *Herald-Telephone*—like Kokomo, another situation bound to end with just one survivor, these combatants much more evenly financed.

Speculation in Indiana journalism involved who would replace longtime *Herald-Telephone* sports editor Bob Owens, who had led the migration to the *Courier-Tribune*. The *Star* and *News* sports departments were on the same floor at 307 North Pennsylvania, only a few steps apart. The two departments' writers were competitive but friendly. About 3 in the afternoon, when the *News* staff's work was ending and the *Star*'s was about to begin, *Star* guys frequently stopped by for back-of-our-office conversation. The Bloomington opening became the frequent topic.

One day the *Star*'s Ray Marquette, best known for his auto-racing coverage but also one of America's leading college basketball writers, dropped the word that he had been interviewed in Bloomington and offered the job. New *Herald-Telephone* editor and publisher Perry Stewart impressed Ray. Everyone—including me—chipped in with opinions; the consensus, with which Ray ultimately agreed, was that you don't leave a good job with the Indianapolis *Star* to go to the Bloomington *Herald-Telephone*. He told Mr. Stewart no. Soon after that, writer-columnist John Bansch of the *Star* had the offer. John was impressed enough that he and wife Joyce did some real-estate scouting in Bloomington. But, the counsel he got from us and his decision were the same as with Ray: you don't leave the Indianapolis *Star* to go to the Bloomington *Herald-Telephone*. In Louisville, young *Courier-Journal* sportswriter Dave Kindred somewhere in the sequence got the same offer, got a quick counteroffer from the *Courier-Journal* that included a chance to write a column for a man who wound up America's best at that, and reached the same decision: can't step down.

How many more guys had and rejected the Bloomington job I don't know, but I'm guessing there were some and that Perry Stewart was exasperated that he couldn't attract *somebody* to come in and compete. Lee Nance, the non-sports-fan I miffed that night of the house fire in Kokomo, had moved to the *Herald-Telephone* as a news reporter. Seeing Perry's growing frustration, Lee dropped my name to him, mostly for my familiarity with two-newspaper competition. Indianapolis unknown Bob Hammel got a Perry Stewart call.

On the hour's drive to Bloomington for the job interview, I felt flattered but unexcited. Those afternoon *News-Star* sportswriters' huddles of course hung in my mind, as did their conclusions: *you don't leave Indianapolis to go to the Bloomington Herald-Telephone.* But, I told myself on the drive, the interview will be good experience for when a really attractive job comes along.

Five minutes into conversation with Perry Stewart, my casual diffidence was gone. Perry shocked me, in many ways. No one had told me that, only a few weeks before I met him, he had gone blind, victim of severe diabetes. He was a young man, late 30s, average-to-small in height, trim and fit, crewcut, compelling—inspiring. He wanted me, wanted *somebody*, to get going, competing. Bill Schrader, who went into

1.9. Family time at McCormick's Creek State Park in early Bloomington days for Rick, Jane, Julie, and pet dog Gus.

the Indiana Journalism Hall of Fame a few decades later, had come up from Evansville to replace Owens, but Perry had the productive, inexhaustible Schrader earmarked for a news role. In less of an interview than a let's-get-started pitch, Perry told me his grand plans for the sports job: this won't be an average small-town newspaper, you'll go to every IU game, home and road, you'll go to the NCAA Final Four, you'll cover the Olympics . . .

The *Olympics?*

That possibility had never occurred to me, never even been a dream.

He made it clear the job was mine, if I wanted it. He pressed for a starting date. I was close to setting one but felt I should discuss it with Julie. He agreed. I was to call him the next day with my decision. I waffled all the way home, all the next day. . . . *You don't leave Indianapolis to go to Bloomington* kept whirring in my mind, answered by another inner-me reality alert that said, "Hey, you aren't Ray Marquette or John Bansch. You're number ten on a very good ten-man staff, and none of those guys is likely to move. You don't deserve to move up here very fast, but somewhere else, with the ball in *your* hands . . . ?" The afternoon drifted by and I didn't call Perry. In late afternoon, he called *me*, borderline angry. "Are you *coming*?" Darned guy overpowered me. I said, "Uh . . . sure!"

Just about dawn on Monday, October 24, 1966, I walked in the front door of the Bloomington *Herald-Telephone* to begin my newest life. And my best life.

It took a few months to sell our Indianapolis home and buy one in Bloomington. My first six months as sports editor in Bloomington, I lived in an apartment in the newspaper building, going home to Indianapolis on weekends. In March, Julie and our two kids—Rick, 7, and Jane, 7—moved to Bloomington (fig. 1.9). Rick enrolled in the second semester of second grade at University Elementary School. It dawned on me: this was little Rick's fourth school in four different towns. By second grade. Thoughts of bad-father-me and Cliff Ward's irresponsibility rebuke haunted me. But only briefly. Life got fun fast.

THE HERALD- . . . TELEPHONE?

I have to be honest: what I had seen of the local newspaper during my student year in Bloomington made it a stop I never wanted to have to make in my career. In my mind it typified backwoods, small-town, dead-end journalism—pages with a 1920s look, nine columns wide, with long, endless type, one-column headlines, and an occasional gray picture: a total package that defined stereotype. And that was without considering the bucolic name.

That frozen image was from a decade before Perry Stewart and didn't consider the effect one dynamic leader could have.

In a fair world, I would not have to be introducing Perry Stewart here (fig. 1.10). He should have grown in recognition and reputation into a noted paragon of American journalism. Health forestalled that. The diabetes that blinded him in his 30s killed him just after he turned 40.

1.10. Perry Stewart—friend, big brother, counselor, visionary. Photo courtesy of the Stewart family.

My great break was sharing his last three years with him, talking with him, laughing with him, learning from him. I can't cite one insight I took away from any of our chats. I do know I matured, I sharpened my career focus, I elevated my determination to do better, to get better, to *be* better.

Perry had been a schoolboy athlete, diabetes and physical size and all—I'd guess five feet seven and not slight but trim. Andy Phillip of the 1940s Illinois basketball "Whiz Kids" was his idol. Home for him was in upstate Illinois, at Forrest, the northern point of a near-equilateral triangle with Champaign-Urbana, site of the University of Illinois, and Bloomington, Illinois, where Illinois Wesleyan University—Perry's ultimate college choice—was based. And there he met, dated, and eventually married his future partner in his professional and family life, Ellen Swartz. Their five children were all daughters, and all Perry-and-Ellen: smart, alert, great.

Perry started in the newspaper business as a sportswriter at the Bloomington, Illinois, *Pantagraph*—the Adlai Stevenson family's operation. Perry's career evolved into management, ultimately as an editor and publisher. Unlike too many in such positions, he never forgot that true, lasting profit comes from putting out a *news*paper. And I came along to be the greatest beneficiary of that acquired wisdom, because Perry brought me in to be a point man in an obvious two-newspaper duel to the death—sports a primary battlefield, a Gettysburg.

There was some stubbornness, and cocky anticipation of a quick knockout victory, in the decision of owner-publisher Tarzian and editor Temple to confront the established *Herald-Telephone* on its own time cycle—afternoon edition—rather than coming out with a morning newspaper. They did make one daring exception. Throughout its somnolent, unchallenged, pre-Perry Stewart years, the *Herald-Telephone* published six afternoons a week, with no Sunday edition. Saturday Indiana University football and basketball games were covered in the Monday *H-T*. The *Courier-Tribune* announced at its birth in September 1966 that it would have a Sunday edition. The *Herald-Telephone* responded by creating one, too. The week I began, on Monday, October 24, was capped by the fourth Sunday edition in *H-T* history.

I almost died with that thing.

It made sense to leave Schrader with IU football coverage through the last four games of that 1966 season. So, on Saturday, October 29, my sixth day in Bloomington, he was at Iowa City covering Indiana's football game and I had the job of laying out and filling my first Sunday edition.

Ohmygod!

All the usual rules of allotted news space I had known before—an ad space/news space percentage around fifty-fifty for the whole newspaper,

the number of pages determined by the space needed for all those in-
come-producing, profit-making ads—were suspended for sports in
both of the warring Bloomington Sunday editions. My first Friday afternoon I looked at the Sunday-paper "dummy"—the page-by-page
explanation of what portion of each page would be occupied by ads
and what was left for me to fill with sports stories and pictures—and
felt terrified. With one assistant, three part-time writers, and the full
availability of the Associated Press and United Press national and state
sports wires and photo services, I had page after page after page—a
staggering ten of them, each nine columns wide and almost void of
ads—to fill that night.

I started my work day at about 5 a.m. with a Saturday afternoon paper
to get out first. Finished with that around 10 a.m., I immediately went
to work on that massive Sunday hole. I wrote a few stories and found
national wire copy and pictures to fill one of those pages, then another.
I stayed at it hour after hour into the afternoon, then into evening,
then night, leading up to a 12:30 a.m. deadline. It was a college football
Saturday so there were regional and national stories. I used them all.
I blew up small pictures into huge, snatched up everything the two
wire services had to offer—*everything*. Schrader introduced to Indiana
sportswriting covering games with more than one story—at least two
or three, plus a column. I played everything he sent me from Iowa City
big, and longed for more. We had an excellent photographer, Larry
Crewell, at the game and I used every picture he sent back—blown up
big. I shoveled and shoveled into this infinite news hole but kept finishing one page dummy and looking at another empty one. Hours flew by.
I staggered to the deadline and felt an exhausted form of relief when the
very last pieces I had to offer fit snugly into my last page. I had one 1-inch
"short" left over when my last page was wheeled away, a little beyond
the established deadline.

Totally drained, I felt I had escaped. Then I rounded a composing
room corner on the way back to my desk and saw a completely open
"turtle"—the term for the metal form on which all the type and headline blocks and picture bases were fit together to form the page that
went from there to the press room. The turtle sat there, naked, all of its
nine 22-inch columns waiting for type to put in, and I had nothing left.

I slinked away to my desk without saying a word to anybody. I sat there in shock, waiting on the moment when someone would come charging in from the pressroom to say, "Hey! There's still a page to go in Sports!" Nobody came, so I envisioned worse: the paper coming out, with one blank page. The presses rolled, someone put a copy in my hand for quick checking, I peeked fearfully inside . . . and the section was full. The turtle I had run across was just an extra, a standby, not in use this day.

I had survived . . . the longest, hardest, most horrifying day of my entire newspaper life.

Every day after that got a little bit easier, because I met more and more people who were vital to my sports-editor existence. I had spotted my direct rival Bob Owens a gigantic edge: he had an experienced competency that had made him a key part of Bloomington's culture for longer than I had been in the newspaper business—solid with recent IU sports history, and first-name familiarity with every news source on campus and in the community. In my first days, I knew—and was known by—just two people in the entire IU sports operation: sports information director Tom Miller, whom I had written for game credentials several times in my Huntington, Kokomo, and Indianapolis days; and basketball coach Lou Watson, whose only head coaching experience prior to succeeding IU legend Branch McCracken had been three years at Huntington High School: my senior year, my year on campus at IU, and my first year at the *Herald-Press*. Contact with everybody else in the IU athletic family required an introduction.

Fortune favors the . . . in my case, lucky.

Schrader left sports with the end of football, and I began my full-scale IU coverage with basketball. In 1965–66, Watson's first post-McCracken team had finished last in the Big Ten. His first team I covered, in the 1966–67 season, made history by being the first Big Ten basketball team ever to go from last to first. Bloomington and all Indiana love their basketball. With the IU team winning, I couldn't put out enough copy to satiate those Hoosier-adoring fans. The novel achievement and

Interview Room Pass

ADMIT ONE

January 1, 1968 Rose Bowl Game

1.11. At pre-Rose Bowl Pasadena luncheon: quarterback Harry Gonso and captain Doug Crusan with Bob Hammel, and credentials from a historic time (Bloomington *Herald-Telephone* photo by Larry Crewell).

popularity of that first team's surprise success introduced me to those newspaper-grabbing fans.

Then the next fall my first IU football season was the greatest in modern Hoosier history.

Indiana, presumed in preseason to finish its usual last or next-last in the Big Ten, began the 1967 schedule by winning close game after close game to get attention as the nation's novelty story of early season, then kept winning games in imaginative and exciting ways to be The National College Football Story of the Year. When the Hoosiers upset maybe the best team archrival Purdue ever had in the climactic Old Oaken Bucket game, 19–14, they were 9–1, tri-champions of the Big Ten (with Minnesota and Purdue), and the league's choice to represent it for the first time in the Rose Bowl. Coach John Pont was national Coach of the Year. Indiana—*Indiana*—finished No. 4 in the national polls, matching its highest ranking ever.

That 19–14 victory over Purdue more than 40 years later was voted the best in Hoosier football history. The Rose Bowl trip still is Indiana's only one. That Rose Bowl season—the Saturday-to-Saturday upsets and escapes, the rise from nowhere to national notice and eventually unimagined presence in the national Top 10, its colorful characters and improbable moments, its precise game scores—all are indelible in the memories of fans who wild-eyed their way through it, a Once Upon a Time that out-Cinderella-ed the fairiest of tales (fig. 1.11).

And I got to tell those tales. The wave I as the new guy in town rode in that miraculous season was tidal. I never felt like an outsider again.

Though basketball was to be my primary identification in national sports coverage, and particularly swimming but also track in IU-related Olympic contexts, football in any major college town is huge.

Historically in the Big Ten, IU football is the polar opposite of basketball, Indiana's all-time won-lost record the league's worst, as opposed to basketball's contention for No. 1. And still it was colorful, still it was the wellspring for great story ideas and opportunities over my 30 years of coverage. And it gave me some of my dearest, closest friends— coaches John Pont and Bill Mallory up there high on that list, colorful Lee Corso certainly in there, others close.

Pont's storybook 1967 season was my introduction to the national, even global IU athletics family, but the man himself maintained a letter-writing relationship with me that carried to his death more than 30 years after his dream season. While he was in Bloomington, Julie baked John a birthday cake every November 13 from that Rose Bowl season on. He was a wonderful man, at Indiana the achiever of "The Impossible Dream" when that song was playing nightly on Broadway. John died of cancer at 80, seven months after celebrating the fortieth anniversary of the Rose Bowl season with his players.

Mallory, captain of the first team Pont coached as a young man at his alma mater, Miami of Ohio, came along at IU 20 years after Pont. He never got Indiana back to the Rose Bowl, but he did a Hall of Fame–worthy job as the most successful of all IU coaches from 1950 on. He alone among more than a dozen post–World War II Indiana coaches built a floor under the football program to make winning seasons and bowl trips commonplace at a school where they never were before and haven't been since.

Lifetime friendships also sprang from a number of outstanding players covered during those years, starting with those captivating Rose Bowlers. The best of all my years was two-time All-America running back Anthony Thompson, a great person and friend who—I'll always feel—lost the 1989 Heisman Trophy not because of anything he did or didn't do but because a last-game upset by rival Purdue dropped IU to a losing record (5–6). In the trophy's 70-plus years, only one player—charismatic Paul Hornung of the football opposite of IU: Notre Dame—won it while playing on a losing team.

The only edge I had over Bob Owens in those early head-to-head rivalry years was that I genuinely enjoyed covering most sports. Bob loved football, knew that in a state crazy about the sport he had to tolerate basketball, respected the brilliance of IU swimming coach James "Doc" Counsilman but didn't care for personal involvement in live coverage of Doc's meets, or IU track meets, or about anything else. All year was football season for Bob.

And swimming became a major breakthrough opening for me with my new audience.

I'm about to employ a word I dodge because I feel it's way overused in sports: Doc Counsilman was a coaching genius, the greatest swimming coach of his time or any other time. A peer of his told me, "All these years, swimming has advanced by trial and error. With what he knows about physiology and physics and psychology and the way he applies them to improving technique, Doc has advanced the sport one hundred years beyond where it would have been with trial and error."

Gary Hall, one of Doc's (and swimming's) all-time best, wrote a memoir and included an anecdote that showed Counsilman as more than a coach, truly a man qualified to write the swimming bible he did and title it *The Science of Swimming*. As a collegian headed for his own distinguished medical career, Hall experienced a day that he told of in his memoirs, the day when Doc's intense powers of observation made something as simple as Mark Spitz's natural hand action in his stroke change everything in the sport.

> Doc popped through the door of the pool office before practice, smiling like a kid on Christmas morning as he told about fifteen of us: "I made a startling discovery!"
>
> He pulled out some diagrams that looked like a connect-the-dash, connect-the-dot picture of butterfly wings. He rolled the paper out.
>
> "I spent hours last night mapping out the arm stroke of Spitz with my underwater shots. Look what I discovered!
>
> "You know we used to believe the basic law of swimming motion came from Newton's mechanics—that for every action, there is an equal but opposite reaction. . . . We thought we move our bodies through the water by moving our hands backward, like a paddle or an oar in the water.
>
> "In fact, we *used* to believe the hand was pulled straight back. As soon as I took my first underwater movies, I knew that was a bunch of garbage. Every one of you guys swim by moving your hand out to the side and then back underneath your belly."
>
> He was lecturing, and we crowded around the desk to listen.
>
> "Last night I discovered something even *more* important. You don't move your hand backwards at all!
>
> "Look at this!"
>
> Pointing to his diagram: "This is a plot of Mark's hand as he moves through the water. See, his hand actually leaves the water on the recovery ahead of where he put it into the water to start his pull. The only thing his hand has done is move from side to side and up and down a little bit.
>
> "Can you imagine that!"
>
> He was getting more excited.
>
> "His hand is moving from side to side while his body moves through the water. There is no paddle effect at all! He's sculling! He's using his hand like an airfoil. It's not Newton's Third Law, it's Bernoulli's Principle: the force created by the hand causing the propulsion for you guys to swim faster!
>
> "It's not drag, it's lift. We're dealing with airplanes, not boats!"

Forever after, eighteenth-century Swiss mathematician Daniel Bernoulli, through a self-taught twentieth-century physics wizard named Counsilman, had a hand in the way Indiana swimmers—and, very soon, the world's—went after speed.

Counsilman, an NCAA champion while getting his undergraduate degree from Ohio State, earned the doctorate while an assistant coach at Iowa. His swimmers called him Jim until higher-ups at his first head coaching job, Cortland State in New York, pushed for Mr. Counsilman, or Coach. "Doc" was the compromise, and it stuck—and fit. For years at Indiana he taught a graduate-level course that brought anatomy, physiology, and psychology into a coaching focus. Coaches of all sports took it. One of Indiana's top high school coaches told me it was the most valuable course he ever took—and his sport was wrestling.

Counsilman arrived at IU in 1957 and quickly made Indiana a nationally competitive program. Counsilman made Indiana the most visible and most admired swimming program in the country. But, he was snakebitten in pursuit of his first NCAA championship. He arrived at IU in 1957, quickly built a nationally competitive program, but just when he had Olympians and gold medalists in place and, under his Ohio State teammate Hobie Billingsley, a diving program on its way to being the best in the sport, football cut him down. Recruiting violations by coach Phil Dickens and his staff got Indiana penalized and Dickens suspended for a year by the Big Ten. Then, when the football rules-breaking continued while on probation, the plainly angry NCAA, citing every member university's responsibility for keeping its own program in adherence to rules, hit Indiana with—to this day—the most severe penalty ever exacted against an institution: suspension from postseason eligibility in *all* sports. For four years, April 27, 1960, to April 27, 1964. The Big Ten commissioner at the time, Kenneth L. "Tug" Wilson, said in the 1967 book *The Big Ten*:

> The NCAA Infractions Committee placed Indiana on probation (and) denied them any participation in TV programs, but one other stipulation was the toughest: it declared that for this four-year period, Indiana University would be ineligible to enter its teams or athletes in NCAA championship competition. I felt myself that the last probationary measure was an extremely rough one. In all the sweeping investigations of all athletes at Indiana University, I had never found irregularities in the recruiting or subsidizing of any group except football players. It meant that Indiana, which had the best swimming team in the country, would be denied a crack at the NCAA championship, always the top goal. It also banned any chance for their basketball team to compete in the NCAA championship. I felt so keenly about this that along with President Wells I appeared before the NCAA Infractions Committee

in Atlanta, Georgia, to see if the penalty might be modified in the other sports.... The NCAA council was adamant in their decision and felt that inasmuch as some of these rule violations had occurred while Indiana had been on probation, that the penalty should be very drastic, across the board on all sports.

I wasn't in Bloomington when that happened. Years later when I was there, I wrote that Indiana—as an institution—deserved the harsh penalty for refusing to clean up its illegal (and ludicrously clumsy, not to mention ineffective) football act. But, anyone had to feel as Commissioner Wilson did: that the undeserving loser was Counsilman. Under that suspension in the early-1960s probationary years, Doc's roster of Olympic medalists and world-record holders dominated Big Ten swimming, and teams thoroughly beaten by Indiana in the conference meet twice won the NCAA championship. When his teams were eligible again in 1964, they kept losing in the NCAA meet by agonizingly close margins, their ranks—though strong—undoubtedly reduced by athletes who during those probation years would have come to Counsilman but because of the NCAA ban went elsewhere. Just one of those elite swimmers who got away could have supplied the very few points that separated IU from three straight national championships in its immediate return to NCAA eligibility.

In March of 1968, chances looked good—finally!—for a breakthrough championship. Perry Stewart approved my request to go to Hanover, New Hampshire, to cover the NCAA meet. In Dartmouth College's pool, that elusive first IU-Counsilman-Billingsley championship came. That one started a still-unmatched 6-year run of national titles, during which the century's greatest swimmer, Spitz, came from California to Bloomington to lead the way in the middle four of those titles.

Spitz had dumbfounding accompaniment. At one point in 1971, when international swimming recognized world records in twelve commonly contested individual events, holders of most of those world records worked together daily as part of Doc's Indiana University team. As a stopwatch sport, swimming does not require any kind of speculative judgment to rank its athletes or teams nationally and internationally. So, I gathered data and compared the best career performances by IU's swimmers against the best by all other swimmers in the world, including the rest of the US—every active swimmer who wasn't on that team in Doc Counsilman's varsity pool in Bloomington. Comparing the best times in each event and scoring it as a dual meet—IU against The World—the stopwatch meet came down to the last relay to decide who would win.[5] I used that as the basis for calling that 1970–71 IU swimming team the best *team* ever—not best swimming team, not best college team, best ever in *all* sports, professional and amateur. Could even the 1927 Yankees, or the Bill Russell Celtics, or any other hallowed professional team champion have beaten a combination of all the other great players in their sport? There's room for debate, but I decided no and wrote that.

Sports Illustrated picked up the theme and, through writer Billy Reed, pretty much agreed in a feature story: IU's team could by itself beat the world, ipso facto it (*SI* scaled it down a bit) had a claim to being the best *college* sports team of all time. That IU team had John Kinsella, named the Sullivan Award winner as America's top amateur athlete in 1970, and Spitz, the Sullivan Award winner in 1971. It had two-time World Swimmer of the Year Gary Hall (1970 and '71) and two-time World Swimmer of the Year Spitz (1969 and '72). In one event, the 100-meter backstroke, that IU team was five-deep in US national champions or Olympians. And it had Doc Counsilman, genius, whose book *The Science of Swimming* was the worldwide Bible on the sport.

IU swimming had a lot to do with taking me to the Olympic Games at Munich. The promise Perry Stewart had made in 1966 was lived up to—two years after his death—by successors Scott Schurz (publisher) and Bill Schrader (editor). I was at Munich, representing easily the smallest credentialed American newspaper, when Spitz was the sports story of the year: seven gold medals, seven world records.

But he wasn't The Story at Munich.

---

5. In Hobie Billingsley, IU also had the world's top-ranked diving coach and his annual stable of Big Ten/NCAA champions and Olympians who would have held their own. But diving—with its subjective judging—couldn't be figured into my stopwatch meet.

Book Two

OLYMPIAN TALES

Five times I spent 3½ weeks covering the Olympic Games. That's 17½ weeks total, basically four months, considerably less than 1 percent of my 52-year newspaper career.

They're much more prominent than that in my store of memories and experiences.

My first one, Munich in 1972 . . .

was almost a book in itself.

WHAT A DIFFERENT WORLD IT WAS IN AUGUST 1972 WHEN I did my last packing in Bloomington before boarding an Indianapolis-to-New York flight to start my first trip out of the country. I checked and rechecked: yes, I had my first passport, my Icelandic Airlines ticket and itinerary—New York to Reykjavik (where at that very time, American Bobby Fischer was beating the USSR's Boris Spassky for the world chess championship); refueling; Reykjavik to Luxembourg, from there on to Munich. My compact portable typewriter took up little space. Clothing: minimal for a 3½-week jaunt, all casual. Always, I managed space for background material, data, records: never enough but some. Sports stuff.

Turned out I could have used a little on world history, politics, religion.

Munich 1972 was the return of the Olympic Games to Germany, for the first time since the "Hitler Olympics" in Berlin in 1936. These Games were intended from the first planning session to show the world a new Germany, even though divided by the Cold War into East and West. Munich was on our side, the West. From the start, the emphasis was not on division but on peace. The prevailing color on all posters, all banners, was a soft blue. The blue of an Alpine, Munich sky. The blue of peace.

And I was green. The green of good luck.

My "luck" was never more beneficial than at the start of those historic days at Munich.

Doc Counsilman's international stature in swimming and the recommendation letter he provided gave my application for working press credentials legitimacy with the United States Olympic Committee and, with USOC endorsement, the International Olympic Committee's media sanctioning officials. Approval came, and my newspaper spent more than its usual full-year's news travel budget to get me there for 3½ expensive weeks.

I arrived a few days ahead of opening competition as untrained in that type of duty as I had been that first day as a 17-year-old sports editor. Now I was twice that age, outside American borders for the first time in my life. A Big Ten colleague, Maury White of the Des Moines, Iowa, *Register*, was assigned to the same housing suite as I was, and he had covered the 1968 Mexico City Olympics. First thing you do, Maury counseled me, is check in at the US press office—make sure they know you, and go there first thing every morning to be up to date on interviews, press conferences, news bulletins, etc. I did, and the day before opening ceremonies, I and the hundred or so others in the 1972 US press corps were summoned to that office for an announcement.

Swimming had rarely been a premier coverage event at the Olympics—track and field much bigger, other events including basketball far more American-noted. This time was different, we were told. Worldwide, all sports considered, Spitz was the unquestioned headline performer going in, fresh from showing at the US swimming trials three weeks earlier that he was a threat to win all seven events in which he was entered. No one before had even approached seven gold medals. Four was the record. Suddenly, everyone wanted to cover swimming. And, US Olympic Committee press chairman Bob Paul bluntly told that quickly summoned gathering, "not everyone can"—the US was granted only enough press spots to handle a fraction of the unusual American demand that Spitz generated. Paul's reluctant solution: a lottery each morning would pick the lucky recipients of the American press positions for coverage of events *that day*. The rest would have to watch TV to get their swimming that day and hope for better luck the next.

I was crestfallen. My newspaper had anted up budget-busting money to get me there, and odds suddenly were that I'd be doing what I could have done at home: watch the Spitz spectacular on TV.

". . . with four exceptions," Paul went on in a voice that barely penetrated my gloom. "We will have permanent credentials every day for the *New York Times*, the *Los Angeles Times*, the *Washington Post*, and the Bloomington *Herald-Telephone*."

The . . . what? My eyes had been down, I was barely hearing, but . . .

The Bloomington *Herald-Telephone*?

I realized I wasn't delusionary, he really had said that, because incredulous faces were turning toward me—guys I recognized from the *Chicago Tribune, Boston Globe, Atlanta Journal, Dallas Morning News*, little places like that—and wondering the same thing I was: the Bloomington *Herald-Telephone*?

The Olympics' credentials process had begun more than a year in advance. Applicants were asked to rank the sports they were most interested in covering. Apparently, that far out, I was the only one to rank swimming first. That, and Doc Counsilman, and Mark Spitz, made Bloomington privileged.

How the *Post* and the two *Times* got their spots I can't say.

Swimming began on the first day of competition, and its first gold-medal event was men's 200-meter butterfly, where the two biggest stars of the Indiana swimming program, Spitz and Gary Hall, headed the field. Both were so multiskilled that Counsilman was able to win every meet he was in and still pointedly keep them from competing against each other throughout their college careers. Each won dozens of championships, set lots of world records, egos never at risk because Counsilman steered them away from head-on competition. In the Olympics, the choice of events was theirs, and both had set world records in the 200 butterfly—by happenstance Munich's first swimming event. Each wanted *that* gold medal.

Spitz won it. He took almost a second off the world record he had set three weeks earlier in the US trials. Hall, 2.16 seconds back, beat everybody else to take the silver medal. Two minutes into swimming competition, I had a tremendous local story: a 1-2 IU finish at Munich!

Munich was six hours ahead of Bloomington time. From that night session, I was able to call back a bulletin and get it in our Monday-afternoon edition. So, when ABC led off its "live from Munich" first-night coverage with its delayed telecast of the Spitz-Hall race, *H-T* readers already had in their hands a boldface bulletin from me in Munich telling them the outcome of what they were about to watch:

BULLETIN

Indiana University's Mark Spitz, the "goat" of the 1968 Olympic Games, became the first swimming gold medalist of the '72 Games by winning the 200-meter butterfly today. Spitz won in 2:00.70, breaking the world record of 2:01.5 he set just three weeks ago in Chicago. His IU teammate, Gary Hall, finished second in 2:02.86.

It was the end of a vanishing era, probably the last time one of my event stories got news to readers before TV did.

Already by then, I had been a "greenhorn" again at Munich. And lucky again.

Swimming events were conducted at the handsome, newly built Schwimmhalle, outdoors but under a shading roof. In Olympic swimming, each day is separate: preliminaries in a few men's and women's events in the morning, trimming each event's field to the finalists who race again that night for championships and medals—same with four or five totally different events the next day, on through eight days of competition.

I showed up for the first day's preliminaries and had to pull out my prescription sunglasses because from my privileged perch I was staring into fierce low-angle morning sunshine and bright TV lights. I watched Spitz and Hall win their separate preliminary swims, then changed to my regular glasses and headed for the locker rooms to interview the two—as I always had done back home.

Whoa! Doesn't work that way at the Olympics. Locker rooms are barred to the press—the only interviews allowed, I was informed by an armed military officer in front of the locker-room door, would be in brief group exposure to the medal winners after the evening events. Gotta play the game, I realized, and went back to my seat.

Disaster. My sunglasses were missing from my desk.

Fairly expensive, yes, but the big problem I faced was three weeks of headaches, glaring into that sun and those lights. I presumed they were stolen but asked where Lost and Found was, just in case. I followed directions and came up to the same locker room door and same military officer who had barred me before. I explained my plight and he opened the door. The Lost and Found desk was inside that locker room, behind the protected door. The armed guard told me how to get to it, around a corner, and left me to go back to his post outside.

I realized exactly where I was! Only yards away I saw not just Spitz and Hall but the other IU swimmers who were there, and I was past security, no one was restraining me. I checked about the glasses, to no satisfaction, then on the way out ambled by, said hello to the Indiana swimmers . . . and acquired some quotes and notes.

It was ridiculously risky. I could have been sent home for violating my credentials' plainly stated restrictions. I yielded to temptation—and not just then. Every morning the rest of competition, when qualifying races ended, I went to that door and to that officer to ask if I could see if my sunglasses showed up, he opened his door, and I had open season. After the third day, I didn't even have to make my request: I approached, he opened the door, and I went in—to check for glasses, on the way to invaluable, highly illegal interviews. Somewhere in Munich there is an aging soldier who probably remembers the cheapest American he ever met, the press guy who just wouldn't give up on trying to find a silly pair of sunglasses.

The ploy didn't work at night. I had to behave like all the other credentialed reporters and participate in the short, en masse, two- or three-question "interviews" of each day's medalists. Hence, each day I got from Spitz what everyone else was getting: a couple of bloodless one- or two-sentence answers to general questions. His gold medal count reached three, then on one night—a Thursday—he won the 100-meter butterfly, swam on the winning 4×200-meter relay team, and he had five golds: an Olympic record. In the mass interview that night, Spitz was magnanimous: "I've already been in here three times," he said to the massed press. "This is the first gold these other three guys on the relay team have won. Would you mind concentrating on them?"

One problem.

Mark had entered the 1968 Mexico City Games almost as trumpeted as at Munich. Remember my bulletined first-day lead from Munich— "the goat?" He was 18 at Mexico City, and brash. He didn't shy away from press predictions he would win six gold medals, break every record. His first individual test was the 100-meter butterfly. He was beaten in it, barely touched out, by American teammate Doug Russell. Spitz couldn't believe it. He *never* lost that race. A story I've heard but never confirmed with Mark: stunned by the development, he retreated to the locker room and, standing at a urinal, heard his fellow Americans jubilantly celebrating not just Russell's victory but that cocky Spitz kid's comeuppance. Whether the specifics are correct or not, clearly the defeat left him shattered and he couldn't recover. The rest of the '68 Olympics was disastrous for him. He didn't win an individual event. In the 200-meter butterfly, he finished last in the eight-man finals. Bet on it: from the first day he swam a meet, at 8 or 9 or whatever, Mark Spitz had *never* finished last in a race.

Spitz left Mexico City embarrassed and broken. A native Californian, he had planned to enter Long Beach State as a freshman in January 1969. Counsilman had no real hope of getting him to come to Indiana, but he had instructed his swimmers on the 1968 team—including three-gold winner Charlie Hickcox—to go out of their way to be friendly to Spitz. In the sneering atmosphere he encountered as his losses piled up at Mexico City, the IU swimmers' warmth obviously stood out to him. In December, when the Hoosier team was putting in its annual holiday training period at Fort Lauderdale, Spitz showed up on his own and asked Counsilman if he could come to Bloomington for a visit. The rebuilding of Mark Spitz's psyche by Freud-quoting master psychologist Counsilman began with his enrollment that January.

I sat down with Spitz in the back of an IU classroom after swimming practice one afternoon, and for the first time he talked about Mexico City, and the special devastation of losing the 100-meter butterfly—the event "I've been swimming the most, and winning it the longest, more than any other event. It's just like *my* event."

The shattered psyche he talked around that day. "I replayed the Olympics the year after, only for my use and my benefit. I believe in looking ahead, not behind," he told me. But:

I remember looking at Russell after the race. I knew how he felt. I had been there.

You can't describe to a person who hasn't known the feeling what it means to be No. 1. Once you've had it, you can't settle for anything else, and you'll scratch and work and do whatever you have to do to beat the man in the lane beside you to get there.

And if you were to ask me the same question after the Olympics, and I had won every race between now and then, I would probably answer the question the same way. Or if not, my biggest race would probably be in the same event at Munich.

So, that night of golds four and five for Mark—the 100-meter butterfly was the fourth—I thought of that 1970 interview and screamed to myself:

This was it! This was that race!

I had that memory in my brain and those notes in my briefcase! And Mark was giving bloodless answers.

When the postrace interviews ended, I approached an American coach and said, "I know Mark has tomorrow off. I realize he's not giving personal interviews [by Counsilman's direction], but I also know this win tonight meant a lot more than he is saying. Would you see if I could meet him [at a specified point in the Olympic Village] at 10 tomorrow morning and just talk about that for about 10 minutes?" The coach/manager said he couldn't promise anything but he'd see what he could do.

I showed up at the designated spot well before 10 and sat there, unjoined. The time came and passed. I waited a while longer. Maury White came up to me and said, "Aren't you waiting to see Spitz? I just saw him enter the hospital tent down there," pointing a few hundred yards away.

I went there immediately. At the tent reception desk I found nobody. I stood for a moment, a US assistant coach popped his head out from an opening inside the tent and asked what I wanted, and I said, "I understand Mark Spitz just came in here. I had an appointment to meet him at 10. (OK, I lied a little.) Would you ask him if I could set up another time later today?" He looked at me skeptically, retreated into the tent, and came back to say, "Are you Bob Hammel?" I nodded, he opened the tent flap, and I went in.

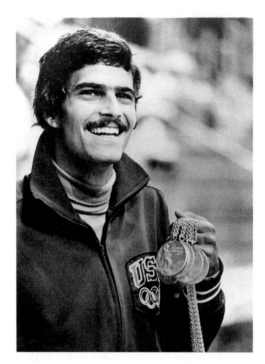

2.1. Mark Spitz—After fourth gold, and to him
biggest: 100-meter butterfly (photo courtesy
Indiana University Archives).

Mark was facedown on a rubbing table, a heat lamp baking his back.
I've never been altogether clear on exactly what happened, my best
guess that he had worked off some nervousness that morning by driving
a carnival-style recreation device—a simulated Formula-1 car in this,
the land of the Autobahn and Nürburgring—in the athletes' area of the
Village. Maybe as he was getting out of his car, another car bumped his,
and he lurched, twisting his back. He felt instant pain, instant shock,
instant horror. At the Olympics, world-class athletes are world-class
hypochondriacs, understandably. A reduction in efficiency by a fraction of a percent drops even a Mark Spitz within reach of the leaders of
the pursuing pack—at the one time on an Olympian's four-year clock
when it matters most. Hence, his trip to the tent and US doctors' all-
out attempts to limit carryover effects by putting him under the lamp.

Mark had 45 minutes to kill, and the idea of passing it with someone he knew took on a wholly different prospect than an interview request might have (fig. 2.1).

I filled several pages of a notebook with responses—including to this question: In, say, 20 or 25 years, how would you like Mark Spitz the 1972 Olympic swimmer to be remembered?

> I have no control over that. I could quit now and consider my Olympics a success. . . . Winning the fourth gold medal to tie Don Schollander's record and then winning the fifth to break it—that was the big thrill to me. Everything after that is downhill.
>
> I'd like for what I've done to be remembered, but who knows? I don't think the public remembers Don Schollander . . . but everybody remembers Jesse Owens and Jim Thorpe.

"Who knows?" he had said. He was more prescient than he imagined. The Palestinian terrorist group Black September was about to make Munich 1972 remembered for something far more historic than Spitz's remarkable run of golds.

Two nights after my story ran back home, Mark won his seventh gold as a member of the US 4×100 freestyle relay team.[1] Just hours after the

---

1. Mark Spitz's world-record performances at Munich have long since been eclipsed in a sport of constant improvement, but still in historical retrospect they stand out as special: for the exceptional longevity they did have. After Munich, I asked Doc Counsilman.to guess the order in which they would fall. He picked the exact order: first the 200 freestyle, then the 100 freestyle, 200 butterfly, and 100 butterfly.

Event	Record lasted
200 freestyle	724 days (a week short of 2 years)
100 freestyle	1,021 days (2 years, 9 months)
200 butterfly	1,375 days (3 years, 9 months)
100 butterfly	1,822 days (just under 5 years)

By international swimming standards, each had a long life: The average survival for all other men's swimming world records set at Munich was 565 days. The shortest-lived of Spitz's lasted 24 percent longer than that average; the longest more than tripled it.

celebrating had ended at Schwimmhalle, eight terrorists came over a wire fence surrounding the Village, made their way unchallenged to the building housing the Israeli Olympic team, and history changed.

The international press officers at the Olympics had followed Counsilman's suggestion and scheduled one tell-all Spitz press conference for 8 a.m. the morning after he finished. Mark came to it, fully aware of what most of us weren't: at that session, before about a thousand journalists crammed into a room built for maybe three hundred, came the first public announcement of the siege that was already ongoing, in Olympic Village, at Building 31, only a few blocks away.

The Palestinians were not sports savvy. Their target was the Israelis, but much more broadly Jews. They apparently were unaware that the most famous Jew in the world at that moment was not an Israeli but triumphant American swimmer Spitz. But that chaotic morning, no one, including Spitz, could be *sure* that he wasn't a target—that perhaps not all the invaders *were* in the Israeli building, that maybe one or two had fanned out and could be standing in among the mass of journalists surrounding the room, maybe with a gun, ready to step out at the right moment and . . .

Spitz was protected on all sides by security people. The questions he was asked he understandably answered in short, wooden words. His and his protectors' premium was on getting this obligation over and Spitz out of town.

Clearly, the press conference should have been called off, period. Clearly, all competition should have been suspended, immediately, but the world was getting its introduction to international terrorism and the part of it at Munich was operating in a dazed fog. Imagine: in this scene of horror, *sports events went on as scheduled all that next morning*, in venues all around the Village, around Building 31. I wrote from Munich:

> One can only wonder what thoughts went on in the minds of captured Israeli athletes Tuesday when they looked out their window and saw a blithe world playing games.
>
> With 10 human beings in the hands of trapped maniacs, their colleagues boxed and raced kayaks and played volleyball. Others

sun-bathed and went for strolls and even enjoyed convivial banter on the very lawn outside Building 31.

To keep informed on the played-down crisis, I was one of the American journalists—Red Smith was another—who sat that afternoon on the floor of the Associated Press office and stayed as up to date as possible by watching a TV monitor. ABC had cameras everywhere, showing everything: the focus on Building 31, and the floor where the hostages were being held, every now and then a head of one of the captors peering out to look around. On a balcony outside one of those upper floors, a masked man carrying an automatic weapon walked around brazenly, scanning what might be out there in the way of a possible threat, or the escape vehicle they had demanded—the iconic news photo that became this day's historic symbol.

An afternoon deadline was set: if the invaders were not provided with safe escape by 5 p.m., they would kill one of the hostages. That time passed, then another deadline at 6, another at 7. Peter Jennings, then just 34, was ABC News' man in charge. At the Olympics on vacation but rushed to the scene to take news-reporting command, he said of the set-and-reset deadlines words I've never forgotten: "That is the Arab mentality." They'll never carry out a threat, Peter was saying. The implication: Wait them out. Keep them sweating. They won't *do* anything.

Jennings was the first to say the identifying words "Black September" on the air. It was an informed guess. He knew enough about terrorism to know there was such a group. But his "Arab mentality" scoff indicated he—like the rest of us—didn't *really* know terrorism. In a *Sports Illustrated* interview 25 years later, the raid's chief architect said the "deadlines" all along were phony, designed to build tension around the world—back home in America, for example, where 5 p.m. was 11 a.m. in New York, then noon, then 1 p.m. And both tension, and gripping worldwide attention, did build.

I left the AP office in late afternoon and—considerably less astute about terrorism than Jennings—with a reporter's curiosity walked to the closest point to Building 31 outside the high fence the terrorists had scaled. It was a wire fence, see-through. I wasn't alone. People were all around, almost festive—*nowhere else to go*, they seemed to be saying, *might as well gather here and watch*. Never mind that, maybe four hundred yards away, that faceless man with the gun was walking around on that balcony. Big deal, they and I were saying with our casualness. *Think he'd just shoot randomly into a crowd? Think he's nuts?*

However naive my own actions, I did at least see the incongruity and wrote:

> Spectators by the thousands, their evening entertainment tickets no good because 12 hours after an act of murder and kidnapping somebody of authority decided to stop playing for a while, spent their idle time like picnickers in a park. They perched on the hillsides looking into Building 31, in such numbers they must have looked like a colorful wave of Alpine flowers to those frightened eyes inside the building . . . eyes that knew the waving color out there wasn't floral at all but clothing for human bodies with eyes that looked back at them and their plight as a dull evening's saving entertainment.
>
> A lot of conversational folks will go back to America and France and Brazil and tell their friends casually, "Yeah, I was right there . . . I saw Building 31 when they were in it." *Downright gay about it, they were. Carnival-like, I thought, All they need is the vendor with the cotton candy.*

Night came, so in the dark we all left, and went to bed, and heard during the night that the hostages had been released safely.

It was an optimistic premature public-relations-conscious announcement that turned out to be wrong. Dead-wrong. An hour or so later, on ABC in the middle of the evening back home but about 3 a.m. in Munich, exhausted and distraught Jim McKay said with despair in his voice:

"They're all gone."

All nine captive Israelis, and seven Palestinians: the human carnage from a Keystone Cops ambush police laid at the darkened Munich airport where all had been bused for a falsely promised "safe" flight out.

In late morning after the shoot-out, I took my copy to the Associated Press office for transport to my office. The receptionist who had taken my submissions without comment every day up to then saw my name and said, "Oh! You're Mr. Hammel. Mr. Johnson wants to see you."

A little catch-up here. My newspaper, which had busted its whole annual news budget just to get me there, naturally tried to cut corners where it could. One of the big challenges in the pre-computer era was getting stories back. *Herald-Telephone* editor Bill Schrader worked out a deal with eight much bigger US newspapers to lease a special Associated Press wire that transported those papers' reporters' work to the participating newspapers—cost worked out in advance, pro rata, per estimated number of words to be transmitted. Schrader paid at the rate of my sending 800 words a day from me. That's roughly the equivalent of one normal column. From the start, with Mark Spitz's splurge, I was running closer to 3,000 words daily—an 800-to-1,000-word column, and two, sometimes three stories of similar length besides. My suite-mate and one-time Indianapolis *News* colleague Lyle Mannweiler went with me to the AP desk most mornings as I dropped my stories off. Lyle knew of the deal and several times gave me a sly smile en route and said, "One of these days they're going to nail you." After that receptionist's "Oh! You're Mr. Hammel. Mr. Johnson wants to see you," Lyle's smile to me that morning said, "This is *it*!"

I thought so, too.

Bob Johnson, at one time the AP's Indianapolis bureau chief and an acquaintance of mine, was the head of the whole Associated Press operation at Munich. I went through a door to his office, he came out from behind a huge maple desk, extended a hand, and said, "Great to see you again, Bob!"

Didn't sound as if disaster loomed.

Johnson went on:

"We promised our clients (most newspapers in America and about every big one in the world) we'd have our major Spitz wrap-up tomorrow. We were going to base it on the press conference. You saw how that came out—nothing we can use. I saw the story you did for your paper over the weekend. Would you mind if we used some of the quotes from that? We'll attribute them to you and the *Herald-Telephone*, of course."

Mind? The London *Times* is going to be quoting the Bloomington *Herald-Telephone*? *LeMonde* in Paris? The Tokyo *Times*? Mind?

The next view my salivating friend Lyle got was Bob Johnson coming out through the door with his arm over my shoulder saying, "Bob, if there's anything I can do for *you* the rest of the way, just let me know."

Never worried about that 800-words-a-day limit again.

That afternoon was devoted to a solemn memorial service in the stadium where, just eleven days before, a festive crowd welcomed that Parade of Athletes, the day before competition began—and before these Games' own historic hell broke loose.

That Games-opening Parade of Nations had stirred personal emotions for me like no sports event I had covered. That opening day I had written:

> It sounds monotonous, this act of walking 8,000 people and 122 flags into a stadium, around the track, and parking them all in the grass. And then the thoughts start to flow:
>
> There's Ireland out there, and Vietnam, two bleeding nations that found time for sports . . .
>
> And there's Israel, getting a warm ovation and walking proudly into the land where its people once were brutalized . . .
>
> There's Japan, a crushed ally of the home team in a world war this Olympic generation has heard about in history class . . .
>
> War? A generation that has never seen a day without it put on this show that left more than one emotion-wrung spectator wondering: How can you hate anybody after seeing everybody like this?

This time my mood was 180 degrees different, funereal compared to that delight's-a-dawning day:

> The morning quiet was penetrated for mournful Beethoven tributes, played by the Munich Philharmonic Orchestra . . . for words of memory, by Olympic Organizations Director Willy Daume of West Germany, German President Gustav Heinemann, International Olympic Committee President Avery Brundage of the U.S., and Israel's Chief of Mission, Shmuel Lalkin.
>
> "A truly despicable crime," said President Heinemann . . . "A day of unspeakable sorrow," said Daume . . . "Every civilized person recoils in horror," said Brundage. Lalkin said: "Let the terror of the past hours finally awaken the consciences of the world."
>
> Into the forum of united grief, Brundage, autocratic and unyielding to the end of his reign as the self-anointed last true guardian of the amateur

spirit, injected an unrelated controversy that had to ruffle feelings. The
bigger the Olympics get, Brundage intoned, "the more they are opened
to commercial, political and now criminal pressures. We have lost two
battles here. We lost the Rhodesian battle to blatant political blackmail."
The equating of blacks' concern against government by segregation
and an act of murder surely occurred only to Brundage and made one
wonder:

"Why, Avery . . . why now?"[2]

But Brundage pronounced stridently, "The games must go on," and
they will. And in the future, there will be Israeli teams there again, a
solemn pledge Lalkin made of participation "in a spirit of brotherhood
and fairness."

"The Olympic ideal has not been contradicted," Heinemann said. And
indeed it hasn't, certainly not the idea that man should be able to gather
and compete in a harmony of races and beliefs. It has worked better here,
despite one horrifying aberration, than in the world outside Olympic
Village.

That makes the games worth continuing, with or without Brundage,
who used the morning to warn: "We must continue our efforts to keep
them clean, pure and honest."

And, maybe just a bit more human . . .

Today properly was a day to mourn. And Tuesday was no day to play.

They did go on and finish those Games, among the items of postdi-
saster history (on those Olympics' last Saturday night) the still-contro-
versial basketball victory by the Soviet Union over the United States.
Then, six nights after the raid, we were back in that stadium for the Closing Ceremonies, after which I wrote in my last dispatch from Munich.

> It's the Olympics the U.S. would prefer to forget—that section of the
> U.S. separated from direct association with Mark Spitz, who made the
> games his personal passport to all-time sports fame.

2. Four days before the opening ceremonies, the International Olympic
Committee voted 36–31 to ban Rhodesia's athletes after several African nations
threatened to boycott the Munich Games if Rhodesia competed. The dispute
was over the country's name. Within a few years, a national election changed
white-governed Rhodesia to independent Zimbabwe. In 1980, Zimbabwe competed at the Moscow Olympics and won a gold medal—in women's field hockey,
with ironically an all-white team.

Nothing in these games, or likely any that came before or will come later, touches the scope of Spitz's seven gold medals in swimming, the easy memory in a mental rerun of Munich happenings.

And nothing at these games, or certainly before or hopefully after, approaches the sorrow of the mass murders perpetrated here, leaving 16 people dead....

It's an Olympics that will be remembered for German efficiency and German misfortune at getting caught with its guard down in the very Olympics calculated to portray the country as newly non-military, a friendly sort of place. That face changed after bloody Tuesday, and the last five days no-nonsense guards patrolled the entire Olympic area, many of them armed and some blatantly walking patrol with sub-machine guns in hand.

Above all, it was an Olympics of people's achievements.

And people's failures.

THE PERRY STEWART EFFECT

In retrospect, my sportswriting Life After Munich was at a different level.

What Perry Stewart had talked to me about in my hiring interview six years before—how the Bloomington *Herald-Telephone* that he envisioned would not limit itself to typical small-town sports coverage but would be national and even international in scope—had started to happen. Two things had opened those doors: swimming, through Doc Counsilman, Mark Spitz et al from the Munich brilliance, and Bob Knight, though his impact was just beginning when I came back to my Bloomington desk in September 1972.

The tragedy to me—and I respect the word's precision and fully mean its heartbreak—was that Perry Stewart wasn't around to experience it, feel it, enjoy it.

Perry had been racked by diabetes since childhood. Though undersized, he was a fiercely competitive young basketball and baseball player. In his native Forrest, his father, Virgil, ran a grocery. Perry's heroes wore University of Illinois and St. Louis Cardinals uniforms. The Follmer brothers, Clive and Mack, starred as athletes for Forrest High, and Clive was a Fighting Illini basketball starter. Perry went to

Illinois State, near Bloomington, Illinois. There he started in newspapers as a sportswriter for the Bloomington *Pantagraph*, under a sports editor named Brick Young, who was a local institution. The *Pantagraph* had two major college basketball programs to cover: Illinois, 53 miles to its southeast, and Bradley, in Peoria, 40 miles west. In 1950, Bradley finished the college basketball season ranked No. 1 in the nation and in postseason was runner-up in both the NCAA and NIT—to unranked City College of New York, the only team ever to win both championships in one season. In 1951, both CCNY and Bradley, along with Kentucky, Long Island, Loyola of Chicago, and a few other programs of national stature, were pinpointed in a shocking New York–based college-basketball-gambling prosecution from that previous season. Young Perry got the assignment to go to Peoria and interview Bradley guard Gene "Squeaky" Melchiorre, a locally beloved first-team All-American who was implicated, his basketball life over.

Perry stayed in journalism and advanced not as a sportswriter but as an editor, then an editor and publisher. He had arrived in Bloomington, Indiana, just a few months before he hired me, but he had lost all appearances of a new guy on the job by then. He was in full command.

We weren't many years apart in age, but he became my friend, my big brother, my counselor. We went to press Monday through Saturday at 1 p.m. Most days Monday through Friday by 3 p.m. I was in his office, on a sofa across the room from him behind his desk, and we talked—about that day's paper, what was coming up the next day, what was happening in Bloomington and in major league baseball and in our building and in what we knew was our newspaper duel to the death with the crosstown *Courier Tribune*. Those afternoons were fun, laugh filled, educational, unforgettable. I doubt if they'd have been different if he hadn't been blind. He never seemed to miss anything.

Occasionally, his diabetes would hospitalize him for a day or two. Those interruptions became more frequent but not scarily so. I didn't really know the toll diabetes was taking on his heart. In mid-March 1970, my fourth year of IU basketball coverage over, my focus was on another personal passion: the Indiana state high school basketball tournament. On Wednesday night of finals week, I went to Indianapolis for the annual induction ceremony of the Indiana Basketball Hall of Fame. I stopped by the hospital where Perry had been taken a couple of days before, expecting to share a laugh or two while basically saying I was in town and wanted to say hello.

I wasn't prepared for what I saw on entering his room. Intravenous tubes were attached to him; he was heavily sedated, wan; the three youngest of his five daughters were huddled together in one chair in a corner of the room, frightened and softly weeping—the wife who was Perry's strong and crucial partner through his newspaper climb, Ellen, temporarily out of the room on an essential errand. He reached out to me and grabbed my hand, and I wasn't prepared for the weakness, the sense of desperation. I wasn't very manly. I squeezed the hand, said goodbye, told the tiny girls I had to go, and made it to the front steps of the hospital with my eyes flooded, walking down those steps thinking, "I might never see him again"—at most fifteen minutes after I had entered the hospital with cheerful thoughts, anticipating one more great exchange of bantering before heading out to a banquet.

Two nights later, I was in my hotel room at Indianapolis preparing for the next day's championship round when I got an after-midnight telephone call from the newspaper office telling me Perry had died. At 41. Because of what I had seen two days before, I wasn't shocked—just numbed, heartsick that what I had feared had happened so soon. We had a Saturday afternoon newspaper coming up. I said, "I'll be writing a column."

I set up my typewriter and began. I pulled from my clouded mind my merriest memories of our time together. I wrote with tears not welling—*streaming*, and falling onto the page, the only time in my life I remember writing like that. I finished and filed the column. I expected it to be in its regular spot in Sports. It ran on Page 1.

Through memories, men immortal

Remember the good times . . .

That was a Perry Stewart byword in times of grief. Remember the smiles, the funny times, the merry moments that showed people at the peak of being people, baring the best of personality and personableness.

Grand suggestion, but awfully hard to do. In a gloomy mind as in the eye, clouds make the sunshine tough to find.

So Perry Stewart is gone . . . on the first day of spring, the day of the state high school basketball tournament. The second seems abundantly more appropriate than the first, for Perry was the most intense sports fan I've ever known. It followed. He also was the most intense newspaper-man, the most intense competitor, the most intense man.

Perry grew up in central Illinois . . . not very far up, to maybe 5-7, maybe 140 pounds. He grew up in a sports-loving atmosphere, going with his Dad to Cardinal and Cub and White Sox baseball in high school before going on to college. Those days were never forgotten.

Dike Eddleman's name was in the news a month ago. "I'll never forget those Centralia teams Dike played on," he said, easing into a grin. "They used to tape themselves all the way up to their knees, then paint the rest of their leg with mercurochrome or iodine or something red.

"I was in junior high then, and before every game, I'd tape myself up—I'd get it so tight around my feet sometimes I could hardly walk. Never could bring myself to put that red stuff on, though."

When Pete Maravich first burst onto the 40-point plateau, topping that for an average his sophomore year, Perry remembered the night he saw Andy Phillip of Illinois' famed Whiz Kids set a Big Ten record with 40. "It almost killed him," he remembered. "They just kept feeding him the ball and he kept going for the basket. He was so tired at the end of the game they almost had to carry him off.

"Now this guy does it every game."

Perry was a superb sportswriter, but he grew out of it. He was a youngster writing in Peoria when the college basketball scandal broke in 1950. Peoria is the home of Bradley University, and it was Perry Stewart who was admitted to the locked apartment of Gene Melchiorre for an interview that told the sorrowful story of a college hero who blundered into ignominy.

If the focus on sports suggests a one-dimensional man, for a news-paper editor and publisher, please remember it is a one-dimensional look. The remarkable fact about Perry Stewart was that he was equally conversant, in depth, background knowledge and interest, in govern-ment, politics, community affairs, education, business . . . all of this by a vibrant, active man who absorbed the blow of blindness in his late 30s without breaking a stride.

I never knew the man when he wasn't blind, yet he knew day-to-day happenings better than any person I've met. His evenings were spent at radioside, dialing in St. Louis (where longtime Cardinal devotion was darned near severed last fall when Harry Caray was fired), Chicago, Atlanta, Philadelphia, Des Moines, New York, Boston . . .

And he knew every line that was in his newspaper, and others, and in Sports Illustrated, Time, Newsweek . . .

How? A fantastic family helped; Perry did the rest.

He had a knack few have, or care to develop—the willingness to say "congratulations" or "well done" or "thank you" when such are merited. Coaches around Bloomington-Bedford and IU knew Perry Stewart through letters, although most never met the man. Blind men, even intense ones, don't frequent arenas.

There wasn't a shrewder, tougher, more competitive $1 better around. Ask a man who's down a few.

And there wasn't a better master of the deft dart, the quick one-liner that tickles as it pierces. A personal favorite came in spring 1968, when he strolled by my desk and said quietly: "Nice column last night." He walked two more steps, turned back and said: "About time, too. It was the first really creative thing you've turned in since your Rose Bowl expense account."

Ask any newspaperman what he wants most and he'll probably answer, "More money." Human, those newspaper guys. Right behind for most, though, is the chance to do a good job. That was Perry Stewart's editorial contribution, an atmosphere encouraging enterprise and responsibleness. His best legacy would be a great newspaper, and his memory would be best served if readers would howl to high heaven, as he would, when it falls short.

Remember the good times . . . ?

Personally, that means remembering 3 years, 4 months and 28 days of them in association with Perry Stewart. A gratifying, rewarding, challenging profession is more of each because of those times and that man.

Two days later at the funeral, the minister read parts of my column. Those tears were close again, and for most of those few hard days.

We buried him in Forrest. His numb parents rode over in a car that I drove, each of us at times trying to force cheerful conversation and remember special moments, but Virgil and Mabel Stewart weren't ready for this ending. Not for their only child, at 41. There were long, quiet moments. They wept a lot. I couldn't. I had to drive. But I was close.

Nothing ever happened in the rest of my career that Perry Stewart wasn't a part of. When I retired from sportswriting in 1996, the Bloomington Press Club asked permission to put on a roast (fig. 2.2) as a fundraiser—the net profit from which to be split between the Press Club's intern project and an Indiana University scholarship fund I already had started. I figured there was a chance we both could come out with a

2.2. Wheelchair-bound Doc Counsilman and wife, Marge, arrive at a 1996 Bloomington Press Club roast honoring me. Given half the net income from the event, I was able to start a scholarship program that gives at least $1,000 to three incoming IU freshmen each year (Bloomington *Herald-Times* photo by Mark Hume).

few hundred dollars net profit. The prospect of Bob Knight as a roaster (and a few other people I covered along the way), donations that came in from some generous people, and amazingly aggressive selling by Bloomington community leader Lloyd Olcott and others in the Press Club netted $35,000 for each of us. I had planned one annual scholarship, which I already had named: the Bob Hammel–Perry Stewart Scholarship, intended for incoming IU journalism students but not limited to that field. With the new money, I added a second scholarship, to be given to an IU-bound senior from Huntington, with writing skills a requisite. I named that second one the Bob Hammel–Jennie B. Wilson Scholarship—another story that demands telling. Miss Wilson, who had taught my mother, was considered stern, harsh, demanding, a stickler for treating grammar's rules as commandments. Spelling was on a list of writing sins that dared not be committed; she called them "Gross Illiteracies," and a GI marked boldly on a submitted paper meant unacceptable—do it over. I took senior English Comp from her, and I chilled one day when she interrupted her lecturing to say firmly, "By the way, I want to see Bob Hammel after class." Heads spun toward me with an *Oh, boy!* look, and I know I blushed, as sure as they that this wasn't good. The bell rang, everyone left, and she walked toward me, unsmiling, with a rolled-up theme in her hand—one of mine. "I don't know what you plan to do," she said, her hand now gently twirling the theme to call my attention to it, "but in my opinion if you wanted to do this, you could. You can go now." Write for a living, she was saying. By then, that was my ambition, but what an enormous boost my self-confidence got that day, because she was so respected.

"Jennie B" passed away long before the roast, but our names are still together on that scholarship. And now, because the original fund has benefited from wise IU Foundation investments, there's a third equal grant, the Bob Hammel–Jane Hammel Priest Scholarship, honoring our daughter and her nearly 30 years as an elementary school teacher. Each gives an incoming freshman at least $1,000—more than $75,000 given out by now. Every selection time brings back memories of Perry Stewart, and Jennie B. Wilson, and pride in Jane.

One other thought that always comes back to me at scholarship time probably was the stimulus for the whole project.

I graduated from Huntington High School in the spring of 1953—number 26 academically in a class of 125. There wasn't such a thing as an SAT yet, a standardized national test, but a forerunner of that from Princeton gave me national test-score ranking that pinpointed me as (1) bright, but (2) a lazy, poorly prepared, academically undisciplined classic high school underachiever who (3) was probably headed for college classroom problems. However, those high test scores and my family's income qualified me for a few scholarships. The biggest, financially, was from a social Huntington sorority, Kappa Kappa Kappa, giving me $200. Today, that $200 would be equivalent to about $2,000, even more in college terms. In-state tuition then was $4 per credit hour—$136 for the 34 class hours I took. Today that cost would be $10,534—more than 77 times higher. In academic spending, that made my 200 Tri-Kappa dollars worth $15,491 today.

It was big enough then that the ladies of the Huntington sorority no doubt watched each year's recipient's academic progress carefully. Most of my predecessors had done great, made the ladies beam. Then came this Hammel guy. In my nine *Herald-Press* years when my name was in the paper so frequently I was always embarrassed that "Bob Hammel" represented to so many prominent ladies of Huntington such a misuse of their funds.

Each one of those $1,000-plus scholarships given today in my name somewhat assuages—at least a bit—the guilt I feel over my past irresponsibility. And to date, I haven't known of a Bob Hammel–level disappointment among my recipients. From reports I get, most have done extremely well.

Book Three

MY GIFT THAT KEPT GIVING

*Besides Mark Spitz, and the Israeli horror, at
Munich there was this basketball game . . .*

*And at Montreal, there was Jim Montgomery, and at Los
Angeles . . . and at Barcelona . . . and at Atlanta . . .*

Perry Stewart wasn't around . . .

but his effect was Olympian.

PERRY STEWART'S OLYMPIC PROMISE WAS PAID OFF FIVE times over, not just at Munich.

With me and my newspaper now on the approved list, I got credentials and covered the Summer Games at Montreal (1976), Los Angeles (1984), Barcelona (1992), and Atlanta (1996). I was cleared to go to Moscow in 1980, too, but the US boycott (because Soviet troops were in Afghanistan) kept me home. Of course world events trump games in importance, but subsequent happenings don't suggest much was gained or lessons learned by denying our 1980 athletes their quadrennial challenge.

None of my other four Olympics came close to Munich in memories. Neither was any of them unrewarding. Always, the wisdom of Perry's vision justified a little Indiana newspaper's being there. Always, there were stories to deliver of special interest in Bloomington—*always*, including some at Munich besides Spitz and the Israeli tragedy.

MUNICH 1972

Even at Schwimmhalle, All Wasn't Golden

Covering my first Olympics showed me how very much is out there at an Olympics to harvest, in a storytelling sense: to seek and find from involved young athletes their personal story of investment, of risk, of hopes, of dreams, of shock, of dismay. *Wide World of Sports'* "thrill of victory, agony of defeat" only hints at the parameters of a thousand individual stories at each Olympics.

Let me tell you one that launched my "Spitz Olympics" with a story not of triumph but of terrible disappointment, of an earned and deserved shot at a life's dream that didn't have a Spitz ending.

Cynthia "Cindy" Potter should have been one of Munich's triumphant queens. She went there as the best female diver in the world. Four weeks earlier in the US Olympic Trials at Park Ridge, Illinois, she overwhelmed her springboard competition—as she had in just about every national and international test since she emerged as a precocious 16-year-old threat at the 1968 Trials. Her talent and toughness, her bubbly will only got better in the Hobie Billingsley coaching crucible at IU, where she went not as a scholarship athlete—because no women were in those days—but as a family-financed student of academics, and of diving. At Munich, she was primed. Ready.

On her last dive of her last precompetition practice session at Munich's Schwimmhalle, she cut her trajectory a bit short and banged the top of her right foot against the board as she neared entry into the water. I was there. It was my first afternoon in Munich, my first hour in the loud and busy pool where there were all kinds of noises—but all the clamor seemed superseded by one discordant, fleshy *thwack!* In the water, on the deck, watching as I was from bleachers—it was a crowd of divers, coaches, and spectators wise to such a sound. There was a hush, heads turned, and all saw that the victim of that sound was the pretty little American, in the pool in pain. She was helped out, given a quick check, taken away. I had arrived there minutes before, my first afternoon in Munich, just getting a feel for things, hoping for a last-minute note or quote for a next-day story verifying to readers and management that I was there, working. My mind said, "Oh, *no! Surely* not!" I hoped that it wasn't the story that it turned out to be. Nothing was broken except Cindy Potter's heart.

Just a deep bruise, they told her. That's all. Just enough to make her limp awkwardly when walking. Imagine what it did to the precision, the timing, the strength, let alone the poise and champion's confidence needed in takeoff from a springboard at the Olympic Games. I wrote at the time it was a three- or four-day injury, in the very worst three or four days it could have come. She told me years later it was much worse than that, still painful weeks, even months afterward.

And still, somehow, she made it through preliminaries into the finals, buying another recovery day. It wasn't enough. She placed seventh, 36 points behind American Micki King—seventh in the world, when she limped just to walk, seventh to a great US teammate whom she had left well behind at those Park Ridge Trials.

Cynthia recovered to go back to winning everything available, a record 28 national championships in all, but her career had crested before her next Olympics. At Montreal, she competed hard but finished third, a bronze medal her best Olympic memory. She has remained for years an—maybe *the*—acknowledged queen of her sport. Regularly, through the 2016 Rio Olympics, she has been the expert commentator for network Olympic and national-championship diving events.

About That Basketball Game...

Swimming was my coverage priority at Munich, but basketball was my diversion there, and it still is—because of one historic game.

Not too many people still able to tap a keyboard were there covering the 51–50 Soviet Union victory over the US in—think about it—my nominee as the most famous basketball game of all time.

You say infamous, I say famous: we'll get into that.

Surely it is the most controversial basketball game ever played.

Let's get the fightin' words out right now: I felt then and I feel now the right team won.

For 40 years, I felt that even when it was accompanied by an anxiety about being out of step, about my maybe not knowing what *really* happened, about the possibility my bent for trying not to be an American "homer" in looking at Olympic happenings—in actually feeling good about occasional underdog triumphs in track, say, even when, maybe *especially* when, it meant me-me-me America had to let someone else from Trinidad-Tobago or some other less-blessed country win a gold medal, hear another anthem, see another flag hoisted—was affecting my judgment. Certainly Russia was never on my less-blessed list, but I did feel uneasy in being so very alone in thinking "we" weren't robbed, "we" lost. Was that determined neutrality part of me coloring my view?

At the root of my self-doubt was the role of Henry Iba, the US coach that night. In the years after Munich, I met Henry, was around him with Indiana and later US Olympic teams because of Indiana coach Bob Knight's reverence for the man. He was a man impossible *not* to respect, to admire. And Henry, as coach, I always linked with the post-game US decision not to accept the silver medal for second place—at the *Olympics*, the one place in big-time sports where genuine sportsmanship seems most likely to surface. Silver medalists, however keen their disappointment, don't duck the medal ceremony, don't reject their medals. I'd always felt that American decision at Munich was wrong, a reason to blush—except . . .

There was the Henry Iba factor, and for me it was huge.

I would tell myself, Henry—veteran of three Olympics, vastly more wise than I about what is de rigueur in competition as well as the ugly inside maneuvers that degloss Olympism's idealism—made that decision to tell Olympic basketball where to shove those silver medals. I saw what I saw on court, over and over I have reseen in telecasts what I thought I saw, and the overwhelming American we-wuz-robbed certainty didn't shake me. But Henry Iba and those snubbed medals—I *must* not have seen or known something that Henry saw or knew, I kept thinking, suspecting, fearing.

And then came a team reunion in Lexington, Kentucky, in 2012, where I learned Henry Iba did not make that silver-medal decision at all.

Going in to those 1972 Olympics at Munich, one story seemed a foregone conclusion: of course the United States would win the gold medal in men's basketball. Hey! It's our game! We're on one level, the whole rest of the world is on another, *way* below us, we felt. Americans were 63–0 in all-time Olympic competition, after thumping Italy 68–38 at Munich to advance to the gold medal game against the traditional runner-up, the Soviet Union, which strained to a 67–61 semifinal win over a Cuban team the US had beaten by 21.

Oh, the American team at Munich wasn't great. The world's best amateur player, Bill Walton, declined to go even after being promised a spot on the team without having to go through the usual Trials. An injury *was* involved. So were other things. There always was speculation that Walton's UCLA coach, John Wooden, was offended—how could he not have been?—that he wasn't selected as US coach after winning his and the school's first NCAA championship in 1964 ... nor for 1968 ... and now not 1972, by which time he was well into a seven-year run of NCAA titles. He *might* have discouraged his players' participation, and might not have. Whatever, Walton wasn't alone—no starters from the 1972 UCLA team that had just won its sixth national championship in a row tried out, and neither did some other '72 collegiate All-Americans.[1] If their cumulative mood had a competitive basis—"Why bother?"— who could blame them? The US men *always* won the Olympics in basketball. Why waste a good summer proving the obvious?

Munich's Olympic planners certainly didn't see historic things coming. Basketball was treated as a minor sport. In contrast to the new and elegant Schwimmhalle where Spitz had reigned, and the magnificent new stadium where the opening and closing ceremonies, the poignant memorial ceremony, and the track events all were staged, men's basketball—even that gold-medal game—was played in a downtown gym that would have been substandard in Indiana high schools.

Championship night wasn't a big deal even to *basketball* people there. In writing elegance and knowledge—even outright love—of the sport, the best basketball reporter at the Munich Games was Dave Kindred of the Louisville *Courier-Journal*. At Lexington in 2012, Kindred said that, his mind still preoccupied by the proprieties involved in restarting so scarred an Olympics, he elected to skip the gold-medal basketball game and stay in his room to do some deeper thinking, and writing.

---

1. American collegians on the 1972 Olympic team were Mike Bantom, La-Salle; Jim Brewer, Minnesota; Tom Burleson, North Carolina State; Doug Collins, Illinois State; James Forbes, UTEP; Tom Henderson, Hawaii; Bobby Jones, North Carolina; Dwight Jones, Houston; Kevin Joyce, South Carolina; Tom McMillen, Maryland; and Ed Ratleff, Long Beach State. The official NCAA consensus All-American team, a composite of all major selections, that year had an unusual seven-man "first five" because of team variances, and a consensus second-team five as well. Of the twelve consensus All-Americans, the only Olympian was Ratleff.

Like me, Dave was in Lexington in 2012 primarily because a colleague and longtime good friend, banquet chairman Billy Reed, invited him. I went in appreciation to Billy but also ready to be convinced that from my cramped courtside spot in Munich I had missed something that the all-seeing cameras had frozen for history, that players from that game could tell me about.

I stayed hopeful through a day of those players' passionate grievance expressed in a series of panel sessions, then through social mixture the next day that included a luncheon (I sat at a table and conversed with an engaging star of that team, Bobby Jones), and an emotional, climactic dinner that night. The banquet honored in its title and format more than the players, saluting foremost their "Courage" in refusing to accept their silver medals. Emblazoned on the program cover that Saturday night, August 25, 2012, at Marriott Griffin Gate in Lexington was:

The 40th anniversary celebration of the Courage in Munich 1972 USA Men's Basketball Team

God love those guys. They're an impressive bunch, likable and intelligent, Bobby Jones a good representative. Lawyer Tom McMillen, a six-foot-eleven All-American from Maryland, was a Rhodes Scholar, a three-term congressman after an 11-year NBA career, a Hall of Famer. Doug Collins, the game hero for the US, was a standout professional player and coach, subsequently an articulate and clear-thinking TV analyst, a really good guy. Jim Brewer, Kevin Joyce, Jim Forbes, Dwight Jones, Tom Burleson, Tommy Henderson, Mike Bantom, Ed Ratleff— all were big-college players and pros.

Kenny Davis was homegrown, a graduate of Lexington's Georgetown College, which hosted the event—Davis on the team representing the strong AAU program of the time. A three-time AAU All-American who later enjoyed lifetime success as a Converse sales executive, he and Billy Reed led in organizing the reunion. Kenny Davis is resolute; he has it in his will that even after his passing no one in his family should *ever* accept a 1972 silver medal. That's firm, and he has company.

At Lexington, the reassembled players one after another stood by their postgame decision not to take part in the medal ceremony.

McMillen at Lexington and before had suggested something of a rec-
onciliation, essentially calling both teams claimants to the Olympic
championship with gold medals for all. At Lexington that idea got no
support from his teammates, no vote needed because it essentially died
for lack of a second.

And the banquet crowd cheered the rejection.

That night, we all watched as films of the game's finish ran: the Soviets ahead and in possession of the ball, Collins's steal, the hard foul
he took that averted a last-seconds go-ahead basket (a foul could very
well have been called intentional and *really* changed history), the epic
free throws he sank while dazed, a feat as heroic as it was historic given
the pressure of the moment. Those foul shots lifted the US, behind all
night, to a 50–49 lead with three seconds left to play.

My press-row seat at Munich was just behind the scorer's bench. I
had seen the Soviet coach, Vladimir Kondrashin, come to the scorers'
bench while Collins was at the free-throw line to ask for time-out. The
horn blew as Collins shot—an attempted "icing" time-out try by Kondrashin that came too late, or the timer's mistimed intent to grant Kondrashin last-play planning time? Whatever, after Collins' undistracted
go-ahead shot, play started without a time-out.

The TV rerun showed a Soviet pass inbounds, then chaos—ball
knocked out of bounds, still in Soviet possession the clock now down
to 0:01 and the US team starting to celebrate.

A tall Briton, R. William Jones, had been watching the game as a
spectator in the bleachers several rows behind me to my left. He came
clambering down past me and entered the pandemonium. He was secretary general of the governing organization of international amateur
basketball, in effect amateur basketball's international commissioner,
and he had seen the time-out attempt, too. Whether rules and rank
gave him a right to intervene or not, he did, and the Soviet time-out
was granted—the clock presumably to be turned back to 0:03, and the
ball back at the end line, in effect a do-over. However, when play resumed, the clock was at 0:01 not 0:03, the ball was passed in not from
the end line but from the sideline spot where it had gone out of bounds,
no shot got launched, and the US—team and fans—whooped and
hollered.

No, no, said Jones—the ball *must* go back to the end line, and the clock to 0:03.

That third pass-in was floor-length, gathered in like a tight end going up in a crowd by burly Soviet forward Alexandr Belov, between Americans Jim Forbes and Kevin Joyce. Joyce fell back, hoping for a charging call, but none came as Belov laid the ball in the basket just ahead of the buzzer. 51–50. Forever.

Terrible, terrible game administration it was, unquestionably.

Unfair? Robbery?

In the thousands of high school, college, and even pro games I have covered, I've seen clocks turned back and in-bounds passes redone lots of times when, administratively, things hadn't been handled right. That's all it seemed to be to me at the time—and all over again at Lexington after watching what Americans had seen 40 years earlier on TV. They heard ABC's voices shouting "Robbery!" at the time; they've heard and felt it ever since; but it looked to me live that night in Munich like a do-over was the right thing to do—and again that night in 2012 when I seemed to be the only one in that Lexington banquet hall who saw it that way.

The prevailing argument for the growing college and professional sports trend to TV replays is "We just want to get it right." Whether Jones had authority to do what he did, under international game rules, I can't say (I had a fervent debate with lawyer/administrator/Big Ten commissioner Jim Delany about that point years later). But the doctrine that he seemed to me to be espousing and enacting was that same argument for replays: "Just get it right." I've never been convinced that the Soviets didn't deserve their time-out *and* their pass-in from the end line at 0:03. In America, I'm outvoted about 11 million to one, and I'm lined up supporting an imperious guy who didn't like America, I'm told—openly rooted for the Soviets against the US in the 1952 Olympic finals, 20 years before, they say. Pinko, they hint.

Color me likewise, I guess. I still think we got beat—and, for most of the night, outplayed.

≈

Then there's that bit of the unclaimed silver medals, still in an Olympic vault somewhere.

In all that time I spent in the 1980s and '90s around Henry Iba, because of his fondness for Bob Knight, I had chances to ask but never brought up Munich because of what I was sure I would hear. In 2012 I went to Lexington convinced that Henry, by then deceased, *must* have felt robbed at Munich if he—steeped as fully as any American in Olympism after two previous gold-medal ventures—went so far against Olympic protocol as to turn down silver medals for his team.

I learned one new thing at Lexington: that wasn't what happened.

The players told us they had Iba and his assistants leave the locker room—in effect, kicked them out—and on their own voted not to go out and accept the medals.

The idea of 20-, 21-, and 22-year-old "kids"—not their coach but the players who had lost a close game they were expected to win and hadn't really played very well—taking the unprecedented step of refusing their Olympic award made that an altogether different matter to me. That it wasn't Olympic veteran Iba making that stand swung my view of that act toward one of youthful petulance unbecoming national representatives of the United States, historically bad sportsmanship.

Now, this whole issue is not a point of agreement for Bob Knight and me. One of the millions who watched the game at home, Knight was so bitter about his friend Henry's "robbery" that in 1984, after Knight's own US Olympic team won the gold-medal game, before he would get on any shoulders himself he had his team pick up unofficial assistant Iba and carry him off the Los Angeles Arena court in triumph. Clearly, openly, Knight considered that an act of atonement, redressing a 12-year-old wrong by making Henry's last Olympic memory a merry one.

Changing his mind on the deserved winner I regard a lost cause. However, I suspect even Knight might rethink if not change his mind on the medal decision if aware that his friend Henry Iba had been asked or told to leave the room before the vote was taken and thus had no voice in it . . . that some of his players—Henderson the most outspoken, but not alone—openly said at Lexington that the main reason the Soviets led the game so long was Iba's fast-break-stifling coaching style, and the only reason the team rallied at the end was that the players on their own, cast off Iba's shackles and upped the tempo in those closing minutes. Bob Knight, if at Lexington, wouldn't have liked that. Iba's US assistant coach, John Bach, who *was* there at Munich and was expelled from the room with Iba when the postgame skip-the-medals ceremony decision was made, that night at Lexington quietly but firmly dissented from implications of a veritable in-game revolt and style change, that players won the game in spite of their coach. Bach has passed since, at 81 in 2016. Obviously, I can't speak for him, but his quiet support of Iba in the face of the banquet dissing made me think he would have agreed with my strong feeling: the decision-maker on accepting or rejecting rings should have been Iba. If it had been, I'm betting it would have been different.

MONTREAL 1976

Less than four months after the greatest basketball season in Indiana University history reached cutting-down-the-nets time in Philadelphia, the two senior stars of that team were doing it again.

Scott May had been the College Player of the Year for Indiana's 32–0 NCAA champions. Quinn Buckner was the team's four-year leader. They played the same roles for North Carolina coach Dean Smith's Olympic team, which—because of the after-Munich mélange of shock, anger, and bruised national pride—no longer had problems getting enlistments from the very best college talent. Dean and the selection committee chose a squad mostly made up of players from his team and his league, the Atlantic Coast Conference. Not at all undeservedly, four Tar Heels were on the team, with four other ACC players, but when it came time to pick a captain, Buckner—always a captain, always a leader, always a champion—was even this ACC-loaded team's choice. And May, as he had at Indiana, consistently led the team in scoring, or was right up there with Adrian Dantley of Notre Dame.

This was a team on a quest: to reestablish America's international basketball superiority, at the very least brought into question by that

Munich game. The US and the defending champion Soviets were in opposite brackets, guaranteeing there could be no rematch until the gold-medal game. It didn't come off. The Soviets were upended a game short: 89–84 by Yugoslavia. The only thing denied by that surprise was revenge. The Americans, 8–0 in their Olympic games, beat Yugoslavia for the gold, 95–74.

That made May and Buckner 40–0 for their farewell year as amateur basketball players—41–0 counting IU's preseason exhibition victory: 94–78, over the Soviet National team.

My other major interest at Montreal was in swimming, and it was considerable.

Nobody approached Mark Spitz's seven golds, but the biggest winner in the Montreal pool was another Hoosier, sprinter Jim Montgomery. He took home three golds, including a :49.99 victory in the 100-meter freestyle that US and IU coach Doc Counsilman pronounced swimming's last barrier breakthrough: sub-50 seconds in the sprint, the last one, Doc figured, because nobody will ever break 40.

Unlike Munich, where he had no bleacher seat, just standing-room-only views of Spitz's feats, Counsilman was the US men's coach at Montreal. Yes, it's an individual sport; yes, he was working with not just his own swimmers but lots of other coaches'. But, the master of physiology, anatomy, and psychology led that team to an unprecedented medal sweep: eleven for a possible thirteen in gold medals, nine-for-eleven in possible silvers, and seven-for-ten in possible bronzes. No team, US or otherwise, before or since, ever dominated swimming like that

For Doc and IU there was one touch of bittersweet, though really much more sweet than bitter. Gary Hall completed a best-in-the-world career without ever winning an Olympic gold. He won silvers as a high schooler at Mexico City in 1968, then the one at Munich in 1972 when he chased Spitz to the first of his golds in the 200-meter butterfly. With his IU graduation and entry into medical school, Hall's Olympic dreams seemed over, but he surprised the young pups by fitting swimming workouts into his difficult medical-school routine and made the 1976 US team in an event unusual for him: the 100-meter butterfly, a sprint event, not strength and endurance. At Montreal, the three American 100 'fly entries came to the wall in a blanket finish, but native Hoosier Matt Vogel, who swam for Tennessee, was ruled the touch-out winner and Hall was called third, three-tenths of a second from first.

It was a disappointment, of course, his last shot at a gold medal—at two, really, because Vogel as America's highest finisher in the 100 butterfly automatically got to swim that leg in the medley relay, where the Americans won easily.[2]

Gary Hall won elsewhere. Before the Games his swimming teammates voted him captain, and at a Montreal meeting of captains—including basketball's Buckner—Gary Hall of Indiana was picked to be the US flag bearer in the Opening Ceremonies parade. Perry Stewart would have smiled. Before-and-after quotes from Hall were priceless, another thing inaccessible for Bloomington if not there.

Montreal swimming gave me one other bright feature. Jennifer Hooker, daughter of the Bloomington mayor, was just two months past her fifteenth birthday when she lined up with the football-sized products of East Germany's laboratories in the finals of the 200-meter freestyle. Jennifer finished sixth and was so chagrined she shied away from a set-up postrace interview. She shouldn't have been. She was in an Olympics final when boys in her class were back in Bloomington playing Babe Ruth League baseball. She also swam a leg in qualifying for the US 4×100 freestyle relay team, which pulled off the biggest upset of Montreal swimming by beating the East Germans for that gold. Now, Jennifer would have received a gold medal, too, for her role in getting the US into the finals, but rules then gave golds only to the four finals participants. She went on to an outstanding career at hometown IU, stayed on to work there in compliance, and now is in her second swim-

2. As much as Hall's Montreal goal was to win a gold medal, after the third-place finish he radiated genuine joy, captivating everyone by carrying his infant son as he waved to the crowd from the pool deck. That infant son, Gary Jr., later joined his dad in swimming's Hall of Fame, winning golds as a freestyle sprinter at the 1996, 2000, and 2004 Olympics.

ming career as the mother of a bright star on the powerful-again IU men's varsity team, distance swimmer Michael Brinegar.

LOS ANGELES 1984

At the Los Angeles Olympics in 1984, my coverage focused on basketball: Bob Knight was the US coach, Indiana freshman Steve Alford was a starter, and the team had been picked and then developed at IU's Assembly Hall.

For Bob Knight, the 1984 Olympics began with a phone call in May 1982. I was at a track meet in Minneapolis when he got the word. I didn't know the decision was imminent. When I called in my meet story, I was told Bob had called and wanted me to call him at—and the guy at the office gave me the number. Bob's home number, which he *never* gave out to anyone but intimates. That told me the call was special.

There was no Caller ID then, but he didn't need it. He greeted me with "You're not going to believe this: I'm the 1984 Olympic coach."

In now close to 50 years of being around him, even by phone connection he came across to me that moment as the most moved I've ever known him about an honor given him, which is exactly what he considered the opportunity to coach an American team in the Olympic Games.

Pete Newell had notified him, as happy and emotional on his own end as Bob on his. That day, in May 1982, Bob Knight started making plans for finding the best available talent, going to whatever ends of the earth were necessary to scout possible opponents, and winning a gold medal in basketball competition two years later at Los Angeles. This one had nothing to do with his usual priorities: playing well, competing against not an opponent but the game. This was about winning, for the United States.

He had heard and sensed from his gurus, Newell (US Olympic coach in 1960) and Henry Iba (1964, '68, and '72), that nothing in basketball coaching approaches that Olympic chance. "You're not coaching for a state or a university, you're coaching for a country," he remembered Iba telling him—not of Bob's own chance, when it came, but when Iba said what coaching those three Olympic teams meant to him.

The competition at Los Angeles was the climax of a basketball spring and summer unlike anything Bloomington ever saw before or will again. In April, more than seventy players were brought in from all conceivable points for a week of Trials capped by two Assembly Hall doubleheaders matching teams made up of the final 48 candidates. On the floor that night, before full houses of more than 17,000 people, were several players who already have been inducted into the Naismith Basketball Hall of Fame, and some more who eventually will be.

Not all of those made the Olympic cut: not, for example, John Stockton, Joe Dumars, Karl Malone ... and Charles Barkley.

Barkley's was the loudest chop. The "Round Mound of Rebound" from Auburn clearly was a star of the Trials, exceeded in excellence by only the incomparable one of the camp: Michael Jordan, who with that summer was just beginning to emerge as the all-time great that he became. One fact shows Michael hadn't quite reached there before his Olympic experience. The NBA draft came after the Trials, and Michael Jordan went not No. 1 nor even 2 but No. 3 (behind Akeem Olajuwon and Sam Bowie). After his rookie year in the NBA, certainly after his career peaked with six championships, the selection order looked ludicrous. (For the record: Barkley went No. 5 in that draft, Jordan's North Carolina—and Olympic—teammate, Sam Perkins, in between.)

Jordan wasn't unsung; he was 1984 College Player of the Year. But in Bloomington that summer he came across as an unselfish, locked-in leader determined to win a gold medal—exactly what Knight was looking for in putting together, piece by piece, his Olympic team. Never did he promise or intend it to be the twelve best players from the Trials. Certainly, when Barkley was sent home, it wasn't.

That came after Barkley had survived the first-week cut. When he and 15 other finalists were dismissed for a few-weeks' break before reassembling for home-in time, Knight told him to lose some pounds before returning. When he came back with his weight not down but up, he was given a ticket home.

Nobody respected the toughness Barkley brought to a team more than Knight. No doubt in his two-year lead-up from selection as coach to actually putting the 1984 Olympic team together, Knight saw the Soviets as his number-one threat and Barkley—or a Barkley type—as his prototype counter to the bulky power game the Soviets played.

But nobody regarded commitment—to a team achievement, not individual—more than Knight. I wasn't there, so let me guess how Barkley's post-Trials challenge from Knight went: "You're 258. You can't be that heavy and play the way we want you to play. Come back at 248." When on his return the needle said 268, Barkley was handed that ticket.

Later, as his NBA success stamped him as a truly great player, Barkley was critical of Knight's cut, and he had media support. Knight's playing-weight assessment wasn't disproved. Barkley's freshman-year NBA success came as a visibly trimmer player, listed at 240 pounds.

Even at Los Angeles, Munich revenge against the Soviets wasn't gained on an Olympic court. Yugoslavia's surprise upset over the USSR had averted a meeting in 1976; the US boycotted the 1980 Moscow Games; and, to no surprise but Knight's huge disappointment, the Soviets boycotted the 1984 Los Angeles Games.

It was his only disappointment that summer. The twelve players he picked went 9–0 on a national tour against various NBA all-star teams, including a game that set an American basketball-crowd record of 67,596 as the first event in the new Indianapolis Hoosier Dome. Then it went 8–0 at Los Angeles, without anything really resembling a close call. The gold-medal game with Spain ended 96–65, the margin right at the US team's 32-point average for the Games. It's hard to believe, but my own records don't show perfectionist Knight calling even one time-out at Los Angeles.

Alford, the youngest player on the team, became a starter and led that great group in shooting at Los Angeles. Knight on gold-medal night said, a little bit hoarsely and clearly proudly, "Steve Alford carried his weight."

And Michael Jordan that summer was what was to become a term for the ages:

Jordanesque.[3]

Alford wasn't IU's only gold medalist at Los Angeles.

Hoosier track had a couple of outstanding representatives in Jim Spivey, the best American miler at the time, and Sunder Nix, outstanding at 400 meters.

Spivey ran the fastest Olympic 1,500-meter final in US history, 3:36.07, but wound up fifth. (Eight Olympics later it's still No. 2 by an American.)

Nix, in an international race filled with American collegians, came in fifth in a half-second, five-man blur at the finish of the 400 meters. He came back to win a gold with the US 4×400 relay team.

---

3. In Michael Jordan's breakout first NBA season, he put together a rookie-record string of forty-point performances and came to Indianapolis to play the Pacers with that streak going. I lined up press credentials and the afternoon of the game got a call from Bob Knight:

"Coming out to practice?"

"No, not tonight, Michael's playing against the Pacers and I'm going up."

Long pause, then: "Come out about 5. I'll go with you."

Bob Knight *never* cut into his practices. Like the football coach he admired, Paul Brown, he planned them precisely, stuck with them, and through the years kept every one on file for ready reference. This day, he cut practice short, we got in my car, and headed north. We weren't at the edge of Bloomington yet when he made a remark that told me . . . *whoops!*

Bob thought the Michael we were going to see was one of his favorite former IU players, Mike Woodson, not Jordan. And that's whom he had shortened practice for.

I kept driving and told him the true situation. We drove a good five miles more without a word back. Finally, he said:

"Okay. I'll go. And I'll enjoy it. I really like Jordan. But—from now on— *you* remember:

"In *this* program: *Michael* is *Woodson*."

BARCELONA 1992

I jeopardized my privileged status with the circulation-conscious US and International Olympic credentials granters in 1988 by telling them that—college football being what it is in America and the Seoul Olympics, because of South Korean heat, backed into a mid-September start—I couldn't justify spending September-October in Seoul and leaving IU football coverage to my small staff. Someone understood, so I stayed on the eligibility list and my fourth Olympics came in 1992, in beautiful Barcelona, Spain.

These were the "Dream Team" Games in men's basketball. Exasperated by being whipped again at Seoul—including an unprotested 82–76 semifinal loss to the USSR, those teams' first Olympic game since Munich—America abandoned amateurism and went to Barcelona with an all-NBA team: theoretically, our very best, our "dream" group of our very best available at every position.

Really, it wasn't. Things got a little ugly internally—and it had an IU touch. A true 1992 US Dream Team would have had to include former Hoosier Isiah Thomas, a two-time NBA champion and perennial All-Star—to me the best player ever at his size. Word leaked out that it wasn't an omission, that Michael Jordan, in particular, and maybe Larry Bird as well, detested Thomas so much that they said they wouldn't play if Thomas was on the team. Chuck Daly, Thomas's Detroit Pistons coach, was the US coach, but he went to Barcelona without his man and the US flexed its muscles impressively. That Dream Team did, correctly, include Charles Barkley, who got his gold medal after all (and got another four years later).

Whatever. The question, if there ever was one, of international basketball supremacy was resolved in the USA's favor once more.

My Bloomington focus at Barcelona was primarily on track, though my gold medalist emerged elsewhere—in a beautiful setting looking out over the gorgeous city, where Olympic diving was done. Mark Lenzi was the man of that hour.

In 1984, Mark was an outstanding high school wrestler in Pennsylvania when he watched American Greg Louganis win the Los Angeles Olympics with about the best display of springboard diving ever. Young Mark was so inspired he went right from TV-side to a nearby pool's diving board and, over his college scholarship-conscious dad's dismay, found himself a new sport.

He adapted so quickly as a high school diver that within a year he caught the attention of IU coach Hobie Billingsley. Lenzi's wrestling training made him unusual in his new sport: much shorter and more compact than Louganis, but barrel-chested with powerful legs. After recruiting him, Billingsley worked him into high-reward power-agility dives never tried before. When Louganis retired, the man who succeeded him as Olympic springboard champion was ex-wrestler Lenzi at Barcelona. His gold medal gave me my story of the Barcelona Games (fig. 3.1).

My track and field focus was on two great IU performers with different career arcs. Distance runner Bob Kennedy was climbing his greatness ladder, and pole vaulter Dave Volz was completing his.

Volz grew up in Bloomington, won a couple of state high school championships there, and then got really serious at the vaulting game as a young phenom at Indiana University. He won the NCAA outdoor championship as a freshman, and by then the young man who acquired a business degree and had an engineering mind was consciously on a quest: to be the first vaulter in the world to clear 20 feet. He hadn't made 19 yet, but 20 was the goal. He had it measured; he could see it out there, a year, maybe two away.

The vaulting world was starting to see it with him when, at 20, he raised the American record to 18 feet, 9¾ inches, then a few weeks later on the summer European tour improved it to 18 feet, 10¼ inches—as high as anyone in the world went that year. It turned out to be the highest Dave Volz was to get for a long, long while, because the very next day, with the tour moved on from Nice, France, where he set the record, to Cologne, West Germany, for the next scheduled meet, his career darkened in an instant. In practice, he stepped on a carelessly misplaced

3.1. A private salute—after winning men's springboard diving gold at Barcelona in 1992, IU's Mark Lenzi spotted me and my pointed camera in press row and gave a happy flag wave.

crossbar. Nerve damage to an ankle shut him down, required surgery. Before he was back from that, he reinjured his leg helping demonstrate in an IU physical education class. He never again was the same in speed and flexibility as the coverboy for the sport's American Bible, *Track & Field News*, as the man of whom a top competitor, Earl Bell, said, "If the guy wouldn't have been hurt, he could have been the best in the world for the next five years."

He went through surgeries, and rehabs, and grimly, determinedly attempted comebacks but didn't come close to making the team at the 1984 US Trials. In 1988, those Trials were at Indianapolis, but he wasn't even entered, wasn't qualified, wasn't vaulting. I covered those Trials, watched the US team filled with three vaulters who six years later weren't close to where 20-year-old Dave Volz had soared, and wrote what a shame it was that Volz wasn't there, the Volz of old, the Volz with 20-foot dreams, the Volz cut down by a hauntingly freakish injury.

I thought I was writing his vaulting obituary, shoveling respectful dirt on a once-bright career. I considered his career over and let my contacts slip. I had no idea he decided to give it one more go in 1992. I had my credentials and my flight ready for the US Trials at New Orleans that summer but targeted the last days of the Trials when Kennedy, Jim Spivey, and such would be running. The Sunday before I was to leave on Wednesday, a story came over the Associated Press wires and got me a call at home from our sports desk: "Did you know Volz was there—and he just made the team?"

No, I certainly did not.

This was before cell phones, but I made some immediate long-distance tries and finally worked my way into contact with Dave for a quick story. I learned that months earlier he and coach Sam Bell—another IU master coach with whom I enjoyed a lifetime friendship, up to his passing at 88 in 2016—had worked out an arrangement with Bloomington industrialist Bill Cook: Dave could work his Cook Co. hours on a tailored schedule that allowed all-out training to give him, at 30, one last grab at an Olympic berth. I missed knowing all that, missed seeing him vault in the Trials, but I was there at Barcelona when Volz qualified for the finals, and on the day when the world's best vaulter, Soviet Sergei Bubka, led the field in pursuit of height and gold.

It was a terrible vaulting day: cool, damp, and worst of all, very windy, a capricious wind, gusty, swirling, unfathomable. Bubka—the world-record holder, the reigning Olympic champion, the unquestioned king of the event—went out early: "no-heighted" is the vaulting term. Never even got started.

That threw the event wide open. But there was still the matter of beating that wind. The field shrank, and Volz stayed in. At 18 feet, 4½ inches, he was in trouble. Four cleared the height. Volz missed once. Missed twice. Volz had one try left. He knew the rules. Misses factor in for breaking ties, so even if he cleared 18 feet, 4½ inches on his third try, if no one made the next height he would finish fifth. Wile and guile came in. For his last try, he ordered the bar raised from 5.5 meters to 5.6—two inches, to 18 feet, 6½ inches. His thinking: if he cleared 18 feet,

3.2. Dave Volz—a dream realized as Olympian at Barcelona.

4½ inches, he'd probably be over 18 feet, 6½ inches. And if he did—and he did!—suddenly he had the edge, on *everybody* else. If the winds got nasty and nobody made another height, canny Dave Volz was the gold medalist.

Didn't happen. Conditions actually eased a bit, and Volz placed fifth. A happy fifth. He finally had made it to the Olympics, to an Olympic final. "I couldn't have scripted it better," he said later (fig. 3.2).

Kennedy was in one of those distance events Americans never win: happened in the 5,000 meters once (Bob Schul, Tokyo, 1964—the point when distance-running dominance was about to shift from Europeans to Africans). Kennedy, who had just turned 22, made the finals, finished twelfth, and took notes. He planned to be back.

Bloomington had one other 1992 Olympian: Dr. Larry Rink, my personal physician and longtime close friend, familiar to IU basketball fans as the Hoosiers' team doctor. Dr. Rink was one of seven US physicians whose "patients" at Barcelona were the 600-plus American athletes. Rink had primary responsibility for US track athletes and for divers. That put Volz, Kennedy, and gold medalist Lenzi in his care. Selection to an Olympic staff is an elite one-time-only honor, but Rink also served in similar roles for US teams at World University and Pan American games. Because, he said then, "there are not good studies on the cardiovascular systems of the really elite athletes," he capitalized on the access his 1992 Olympic role gave him to coordinate a mass study. Starting with the US Track and Field Trials and carrying through Barcelona, he said, "We did some very detailed cardiovascular exams with the track and field athletes." Those findings enriched international knowledge, and Dr. Rink also had worldwide impact in improving detection of use of banned drugs at national and international events.

ATLANTA 1996

For at least a year I had been counting down to this event: the self-selected end of my sportswriting trail. My health was good but I knew I was working too many hours at too hard a pace with too little sleep for some kind of breakdown—a stroke was what I feared most—*not* to be looming out there somewhere. Timing of the Atlanta Olympics (July 19–August 4) seemed perfect: the year I turned 60, coming when my successor could be picked and on the job when Indiana's football practice—much better for a transition than on my actual birthday (in October, midseason for football) or December 31 (midseason for basketball). Newspaper management agreed, and before I left for Atlanta, an outstanding young (compared to me) veteran writer, North Carolinian Gary McCann, was on his way to Bloomington and ready to begin.

At Atlanta I was green in a different sense, an old dog learning an altogether new trick: covering rowing. I had never seen a rowing event, never even *met* a rower. But I was about to. Melissa "Missy" Schwen, an all-round athlete in her Bloomington South high school days, had learned to row, found a harmonious working partner in Karen Kraft, and they rowed to the top of the US charts in women's pairs competition. All of that was done within two years, shockingly fast development for Missy from beginner to American Olympian. She became my biggest and best Bloomington story at Atlanta—not quite so happy as it might have been, because she and Karen, in an event in which the US had never even medaled, had to settle for a silver after being edged out by just a few feet in the closest finals race of the Games.

It was an astonishing achievement, but it brought tears. She and Karen wanted gold, and were so very close to getting it.[4]

At Atlanta I also saw another, much slower developing story reach a satisfying end. I had covered distance runner Bob Kennedy through

---

4. Missy's story didn't stop with Atlanta. Months later, she gave a kidney to her brother David, a major career risk for a world-class athlete with ambitions to keep competing. David thrived, Missy and Karen came back, and in 2000 at Sydney they won bronze. Then, in 2010, they were inducted into the National Rowing Hall of Fame. I wasn't at Sydney, but I did accept her invitation and attended her Bloomington wedding (to Tim Ryan). A framed picture of their close 1996 finish, with signature and a kind inscription, hangs on my wall. And I was there to give her a hug the 2011 night when she was a charter inductee into the Monroe County Sports Hall of Fame. My introduction to rowing obviously came at the sport's royalest level.

3.3. Bob Kennedy—The sport's "bible" names him a king. Magazine cover courtesy of *Track & Field News*; original photo by Gray Mortimore/ ALLSPORT.

five collegiate years, through his 20 Big Ten championships and three NCAA, and through his advancement to clear standing as America's best distance man—best ever, stopwatches at several distances said (fig. 3.3). Bob was a very good miler who became great by moving up in distance. He set American records at 3,000 meters, two miles, and 5,000 meters. *American* records, not close to the world-record times of the best African runners, most notably Kenyans. After Barcelona, Bob committed himself to training with Kenya's best in their homeland, at their altitude, and under an international coach who rather regularly had his athletes running sub-four-minute miles in workouts. The Bob Kennedy who came back took big chunks off the previous American records—his own. He went to Atlanta determined to hold nothing back. He ran with the African-loaded front pack at the pace they set and actually moved in front on the next-last lap. He finished a competitive sixth. Of course he wanted a medal; of course he wanted gold. But he left the track in Atlanta knowing he had exhausted every bit of will he had in him.

Missy Schwen and Bob Kennedy: two consummate competitors, two totally different experiences. And two excellent Bloomington stories that, one more time, made Perry Stewart look smart.

Another trail was ending there. Mark Lenzi decided to give springboard diving one more try and talked his old warhorse coach, Hobie Billingsley, into helping him make it. There they were at Atlanta—Lenzi a bit injured but Olympian, Billingsley at 70 making his own high-level exit by being picked to be the one to read the hallowed Olympic judges' creed at the Opening Ceremonies. Like Kennedy, Lenzi went out gallantly—finishing a strong third behind China teammates Xiong Ni (701.46 points) and Yu Zhuocheng (690.93). Limited by shoulder problems, and being 28, Lenzi finished just behind Yu (686.49) and 20 points ahead of anyone else in the field.

This was an Olympics where US men's basketball success came with minimal effort. Such wasn't the case in women's basketball. For a year, Stanford coach Tara VanDerveer had been working with the best American women's talent. She gave up a year with her great college

program to take the American women on a 60–0 drive that began in
November and culminated in gold at Atlanta—the very last event of
the Games, the very last sports event I covered. Perry Stewart would
have approved of its Bloomington tinge: Tara, Massachusetts-born and
named for the *Gone with the Wind* plantation, had transferred from a
New York college to play her last three years at IU, where her basketball
education included sitting high in the stands taking notes while Bob
Knight in 1975 was putting together the best team in Big Ten history.

She kept those notes. In one Olympic game, she explained her
team's considerable improvement in the second half by saying, "We
played good defense—good *Indiana* defense," shooting a smile toward
me. And, late on a Sunday night in Atlanta, under a headline reading
"Women Wrap Games with Golden Bow," I wrote:

> ATLANTA—They blazed from outside and they were slick and produc-
> tive inside. They drove, they passed, they shot, they ran and ran and ran.
> They won an Olympic gold medal with as golden a performance as
> their yearlong, 60-game quest, their work and their coach conceivably
> could have produced.
> It was dunkless basketball, it was fundamental basketball, and it gave
> the United States a 111–87 victory over Brazil Sunday night—not just an
> exhibition of good women's basketball but of excellent basketball, period.

And I finished:

> It represented just the second time the U.S. swept both men's and wom-
> en's basketball golds. The other was in 1984. For Brazil, it was history, the
> team's first Olympic women's basketball medal. Its only previous appear-
> ance was in 1992, when it finished seventh.

And *I* was history. My last line as a sportswriter.

Book Four

THE BOB KNIGHT EFFECT

You know him as the basketball coach who threw a chair . . .

*I saw him as a man who made the job of coaching
basketball seem grander than that . . .*

who made a tenure feel like an era . . .

because it was.

BY 1972, THE MOST CONSEQUENTIAL RELATIONSHIP OF MY professional life had begun. Bob Knight, four years younger than me, was in place as Indiana University's basketball coach.

My native state, Indiana, was known nationally and internationally for several things, not all of them bucolic—the Indianapolis 500-Mile Race, for example. And basketball. Just over 33 years after he invented the sport at Springfield, Massachusetts, Dr. James Naismith attended the 1925 state high school tournament in Indianapolis and said, "Basketball really had its origin in Indiana, which remains the center of the sport."

The sport fit a state of hundreds of communities hubbed around Indianapolis, its large but somnolent capital city. Naismith watched the fifteenth edition of a tournament that began in the same year as the internationally famed Indianapolis 500. At one time, 786 high schools—some with basketball teams proudly representing hamlets—played together, irrespective of enrollment size, for that one hugely important state championship. It was a four-stage, four-weekend tournament—sectionals, regionals, semistates, state—that engrossed Hoosiers to an extent outsiders couldn't imagine. Annually, the week before tournament games began, at 7 a.m. on a Wednesday, statewide news wires out of Indianapolis shut off the outside world and spent almost an hour announcing the hand-drawn pairings for the entire tournament. All of them—every game's matchup went out on radio, in the '50s to bigger, more breathless Indiana audiences than a decade earlier FDR's Fireside Chats had drawn. On the Saturday night when the 64 first-round "sectional" champions were crowned, it was impossible to drive in Indiana and not pick up play-by-play radio broadcasts of a game—probably 10 to 15 available on any dial anywhere in the state. Three Saturday nights later, when the state championship was determined, there wasn't a point in the state where radio broadcasts—and, later, telecasts—of the game couldn't be picked up. Zeal understates. Hoosiers loved their tournament.

I was no exception. I grew up with the tournament and wrote the most critical book of my life, *Hoosiers: Classified*, when infidels—the word's dictionary definition, "disbelievers in something specified or understood," justifies its usage for those people—voted in 1997 to de-unique Indiana's crown jewel and make it like everybody else's: four tournaments, separated into enrollment groups called classes, no longer one single State Champion. Within a few years, attendance and interest fell off massively, the air waves went almost basketball silent, state championship games became impossible to pick up on TV or radio in wide areas throughout the state. What that reflected was worst of all: people stopped caring. People who before 1997 could quickly tell you which team won "The State" 22 years or 33 years or 55 years before now look blank when asked "Who won last year?" Once-packed giant gyms— not long ago 14 of the 15 largest high school gymnasiums in America were in Indiana—now play to quarter-filled houses, some closed altogether. Because, in comparison with previous years, Hoosierland barely cares.

Now, Indiana still is a basketball state. Bob Knight, an Ohioan who arrived in Bloomington in 1971, did more than anyone else—than any non-infidel, anyway—to pull some of that Hoosier basketball attention to the college game. From the '70s through the end of the century, the Indiana University program that Knight built had border-to-border popularity throughout Indiana.

"IU" was a noted college basketball program long before Knight. The championship of the second NCAA basketball tournament was won in 1940 by Indiana. Branch McCracken, himself a small-town Indiana high school star and an IU All-American, coached that '40 championship team—at 31, still the youngest coach ever to win one. McCracken, at 44, won a second championship in 1953.

But Knight—young and fiery, 30 when he signed his first IU contract (for $20,000 a year) in March 1971—reshaped Indiana's basketball emphases into his own. Sixth man as a sophomore on the great 1960 Ohio State NCAA champion of coach Fred Taylor, Knight won games at a two-of-three clip in six years as head coach at West Point, where height was restricted and when basketball recruits came knowing a Vietnam War future was promised, not NBA riches. He arrived at Indiana after basketball had hit a modern low there, four last-place Big Ten finishes in the previous six years. The problem wasn't just a lack of talent. The reputation that got Knight the Indiana job was for discipline, bringing him into a program that almost had a players' boycott of the last road game before the coaching change to Knight was made. It was an un-usual calling card for a man whose Army teams played impeccably but whose own sideline conduct never was categorized as "disciplined." In the harsh East, even some of his press admirers gave the hot-tempered Knight the nickname of "Bobby T"—for technical fouls.

The technicals were overstated but the temper wasn't. Basketball fundamentalist-perfectionist Knight could blow, but IU fans loved that element along with—really because of—his coaching results. Assem-bly Hall, its seating capacity more than double the average IU game crowd before Knight arrived, soon had sold-out-every-night status. He was an attraction. For more than a generation, Assembly Hall crowds watched the game closely and still saw every move Knight made on the sidelines—and TV cameras always included one focused solely on him, lest an outburst be missed.

What universally was indisputable was that what was happening on court was as beautiful as team basketball could get.

In Bloomington, he came in as a coaching unknown—actually, maybe a little worse. In a state and on a campus where shooters were revered and high scoring brought ecstasy, what identity he had as the young coach at Army was for leading the nation in defense, which in Indiana translated to slowing the ball down so much both teams scored in the fifties. My brother Jim, already a high school coach by then, was the first to tell me what a jewel Indiana had found. "I've been going to his clinics for a couple of years," Jim said. "The guy's brilliant."

"He may be," I said, "but I don't know how those 52–50 games are going to go over around here."

At least a dozen times over the next several years, every big IU win under Bob brought a phone call to me from Jim: "How are those 52–50 games going over down there?" Touche.

Although we did score a clean beat on announcing him as the new coach, I had never met Bob Knight before he was formally introduced at a press conference at the Indianapolis airport. Afterward, I walked up, introduced myself, and asked a couple of quiet, one-on-one questions:

"What do you prefer, Bob or Bobby?" (Answer: "I don't really care." My response: "Then in our paper it's going to be Bob. I hated 'Bobby' when I was a kid." And:)

"What's your middle name?" (Answer: "Montgomery. But don't use it.")

My response to that? I'm not naturally contentious, but Robert Montgomery Knight did appear in the story—not in "I'll show *you*" defiance but because it fit as introductory, getting-to-know-you news for information-hungry Bloomington. He much later said the "don't use it" was not evasiveness, just a feeling the Robert Montgomery was too pompous a community introduction for a basketball coach named Bob.

He immediately began to recruit. When he landed someone—Steve Green of little Silver Creek, up to then weighing offers from Kentucky and Vanderbilt, was the first—our paper and the rival *Courier-Tribune* always got properly advised. We tended to dig a little more, write a little more, and play each recruit a little bigger than crosstown did. By the time he arrived, most of the state's stop stars were committed to places like UCLA, Louisville, and Purdue, but he sifted the uncommitted crop well and his priorities showed. His first three recruits—Green and guards Steve Ahlfeld of Northfield and John Kamstra of Rossville— were excellent scorers and players, yes, but also valedictorians or close, and they wound up being (1) a dentist, (2) a doctor/orthopedist, and (3) a chief financial officer of a global company. And, all were from Indiana, as was No. 4: John Laskowski of South Bend, a future Hoosier legend.

Bob was out of town most of the summer, working the basketball camp he had built up at West Point. I stopped off there and spent a day with him on my way to Munich. Fall started, we had some conversation time when he went on one of the IU football trips, and it was basketball time.

Unlike later, practice then was open to the press, but few bothered. I did get to most of the early practices and realized quickly things were different: a *lot*. Basketball was being taught, not played, in an atmosphere more classroom-quiet than fieldhouse-loose. And it was evident: those last-minute recruits Bob had landed picked up his offense and defense much quicker than the returning varsity players. That was not good news, because this was the last year of freshman ineligibility, so guys not eligible to play were regularly beating the bigger, more experienced, even more athletic guys who were going to be Knight's first team.

Partly to introduce himself around the state, Bob ended his first week of practice with a free coaching clinic. About 700 high school coaches from all over Indiana and around the Midwest came to Assembly Hall to hear what most knew was a great clinician. His plan was to cap two days of lectures with an open scrimmage. Those 700 coaches sat in Assembly Hall's plush seats and watched Bob's varsity repeatedly fail to execute what he wanted on offense, and on defense, and generally get outplayed by the guys he wouldn't be able to use. Throughout his career, perfectionist Knight liked to end every practice—even every segment within a practice—with a positive play, something well done. This day, time to end came, and passed, but bad plays kept happening. So the scrimmage kept going, and the bad plays continued, and finally Knight gave up, blew a whistle, and barked, "Go on in!" Go to the showers, practice over.

He stood on the emptied court by himself, wordless, as the clinic coaches filtered out. I thought, *I ought to have a word or two from him for tomorrow's story*, so I headed down. As I was about to step onto the court, Bob—looking down, oblivious to me and everyone else—grabbed a wheeled rack full with about nine basketballs and sent it scooting thirty, forty, maybe fifty yards off the end of the court, over a cemented area, and smashing violently into a distant wall. Balls flew in all directions. I watched that ball rack sail, watched the dispersal of its contents, and said inwardly, *On second thought . . .* and walked away. I thought the story read just fine without a quote.

Knight's official IU debut was the first game ever played in Assembly Hall: an 84–77 victory over Ball State. Even before that, in the real "first game" there, the Hoosiers previewed the season by winning an exhibition game against the Australian National team. It was lightly attended and even more lightly covered. Bob Owens didn't go, but J. W. Lewis, one of his aides, did for the rival Bloomington *Courier-Tribune*. He and I met outside the locker room with Knight for postgame comments that went all right until I—presuming an eight-month relationship that had gone pretty well allowed some mild needling—asked, I thought rather humorously, "Was that the first game you've ever coached without a technical?"

Whoosh!

The eyes flashed, some unremembered words spilled out, then he wheeled and went back into the locker room, press conference ended. Lewis looked at me and said, "Dumb shit." Life went on. Forty years later, Bob and I were onstage together at a Knight speaking appearance and out of the blue, in front of the audience, he said, "Do you remember the question you asked at the first press conference after a game?" We both did.

When games started, the natives in the stands did require some educating, and some began as reluctant learners. Knight's fondness for stalling out the last few minutes of even mildly close games to guarantee victory sometimes brought scattered but audible boos in point-loving Bloomington. Once, IU was ahead something like 52–47 as time was running out, ball in Hoosier hands, and the quiet night was pierced by a mathematician's desperate lament: "We want a hundred!" Even Bob laughed, later.

In one of the first Assembly Hall games, Knight's inherited lead guard, Bootsie White—the only Indiana player ever to call him anything but "Coach" —was dribbling out the clock, and a few slow-to-convert fans hollered in objection, "Shoot! Shoot!" Bootsie kept his eye on his man, dribbled slowly toward Knight's sideline spot, and out of the side of his mouth said, "Don't worry, Chief, I can't hear 'em."

The day of full-fledged fan conversion can be pinpointed. Knight's fourth game was a 90–89 double-overtime victory over Adolph Rupp and Hoosier-hated Kentucky. It was Easy Street with the fans for the new man in town after that.

He used that 17–8 first season to recruit from an Ohio-Indiana-Illinois hub the most successful class in college basketball history. That's saying a lot, but: five from that first full recruiting class, with center Kent Benson arriving the next year as the last essential piece, were the core for a lot of Indiana basketball fun in the next four years.

Knight was such a young coach, his was such a young program that nobody—including me, the self-styled historian and gauger of perspectives—at the time fully grasped the uniqueness of those four early-1970s winters.

Everything built toward the 1974–75 and 1975–76 seasons. Forty years have passed and now they have a dimension. Those teams' deeds seem Arthurian, a college basketball Camelot that didn't last long but—don't let it be forgot—did happen: two back-to-back unbeaten regular seasons, one ending in tears, the other in triumph unmatched to this day.

In those four years, those 1971–72 recruits—Quinn Buckner, Scott May, Bobby Wilkerson, Jim Crews, and Tom Abernethy—won 108 games, 4 Big Ten championships, an unheard-of, never-since-approached 37 straight Big Ten games, and spent 27 consecutive in-season weeks ranked No. 1 in the country. That era included Indiana's first College Player of the Year (Scott May), two starters on the gold-medal 1976 US Olympic team (May and Quinn Buckner), and three players taken in the first 11 selections of the NBA draft (May, Buckner, and Bobby Wilkerson—and Benson went No. 1 the next year). Knight's IU won-lost record was 125–20. The school in those recruits' four seasons won as many outright Big Ten championships (3) as in all its previous 70-year basketball history. And Indiana was firmly established among the college game's au courant elite.

By then, also, Bob Knight and Bob Hammel had become friends.

Not that there weren't rifts. Once we went seven months without speaking. No hot words exchanged. Or cold. It started in April 1977 and months passed. As a new season approached, I did wonder how he was going to handle postgame press conferences. He was ready. The 1976–77 season opened, IU thumped East Carolina, 75–59, and when the press gathered in its usual place for postgame comments, a new policy was announced: Coach Knight will not be having postgame press conferences this year, he knows the questions sure to be asked and he will dictate his answers to those questions for distribution by sports information director Kit Klingelhoffer. *I* knew I was the cause, but there was no mention of me as the reason, and I don't think colleagues read it that way. Just another quirky move by a quirky guy.

I wrote a normal game story and a column that, in not at all angry terms, opined that it was really not a great idea for him to omit postgame press conferences, because those were his one consistent link with fans and he controlled every one of those sessions anyway. So what it took away was his eyes—his flashing eyes when angry, his laughing eyes when teasing, his communicative eyes that sometimes said more than his lips did. Nothing in the column contested his right to do it, just its efficacy.

That was Sunday morning. Monday, I got that day's pages out, went to lunch, and came back to field a phone call: secretary Mary Ann Davis from Bob's office, saying, "Just a minute for Coach."

His first words, the first I'd heard from him since April:

"Do you want *war?*"

I laughed.

A genuine, instinctive laugh—not at all meant to be derisive or combative, just an honest reaction because, in the flash that his words registered in my mind, I thought of *me*, pretty much the polar opposite of a warrior. It *was* a funny picture. And then I heard:

"Because if you *do*, you sure as hell are going to *get* it!"

Bang. End of call. And no follow-up.

I saw no need for one. I read it as what it turned out to be: the start of a Knight-style thaw, a breakthrough. By the first road game I as usual sat up front with the coaches on the team plane. I paid a little price on the first trip, my ears scorched a bit as a greeting, that kind of thing. The whole traveling party went to dinner together as usual the night before the game and conversation was chilly. But the crisis was over. By mid-December, there was even a call now and then—and the silent

4.1. Bob Knight and Bob Hammel (Bloomington *Herald-Times* photo by David Snodgress).

period never again came up. Apologies eventually? Oh, of course not. Either way.

But the coach and the sportswriter were friends again (fig. 4.1).

Of course that's journalism heresy, neverland between journalist and news source. I've never been much for bloodless, inviolate, impractical tenets. I had friendships with almost every coach I ever covered, from Huntington *Herald-Press* days on . . . felt I and my readers benefited more from intimate knowledge of what really was going on in a program than from more filtered "news" released to a more "proper," less knowledgeable Journalist. This was the mid-1970s. My feeling was when the standing of by-then-sainted *Washington Post* editor Ben Bradlee is trashed for his vastly more important and potentially news-inhibiting before-and-during friendship with 1960s president John F. Kennedy, I will join Ben in banishment.

Still, 15 years later in that friendship, I admit I felt shock when on first reading of John Feinstein's *Season on the Brink* I saw myself identified as Bob Knight's best friend.

I saw that, read it again, and thought, *What?*

The very idea of ranking friends hadn't occurred to me, and certainly not from Bob's direction. I simply knew better. I knew how he felt about John Havlicek, and Gary Gearhart from his college days, about Dick Rhodes and Tony Yonto and Don Boop and a whole lot of his hometown Orrville friends, not to mention Pete Newell and Fred Taylor and Stu Inman and some other genuinely revered coaching colleagues.

Best friend . . . that's silly, that's high school-ish, that's . . .

About then, about 3 in the morning, in the middle of that mental rejection of a whole preposterous idea, a reality hit me:

"Silly" or not, that's going to change my own professional status forever.

And it did.

Until that phrasing, I don't recall ever being labeled a Knight apologist. The tendency among colleagues actually had been to go the other way—if one ever mentioned me in context with Bob, it was in the nature of what a tough job poor Bob Hammel has in having to deal with him.

That was equally off-base. What Bob Knight did to elevate—skyrocket might be a better verb—Indiana University basketball clearly gave my coverage enormously increased attention and greatly multiplied whatever intraprofession national status I had.

But that night as my eyes locked in on that phrase, *Bob Knight's best friend*, I knew times had changed. That term's immediate effect was to disqualify me as a critic of John Feinstein's work. It colored the testimony of the only other one who had been there when Bob Knight laid out to Feinstein a few ground rules for his participation in the book project, very specifically including no use of his favorite four-letter word—"because my mom's going to be reading that book and I don't want that word in there, understand?"

The three of us were walking down Assembly Hall's floor-level west corridor on the way to the team locker room before an afternoon practice when Knight specified that provision to John. I can't say I remember Feinstein saying yes; I am absolutely certain he didn't say no—"Can't do that, Bob," as in the justification he used later: "*Obb*viously, you can't do a Bob Knight book without using that word."

You *can't*? Even if, by silence, you implicitly agree to do that before the project begins?

It seems the same to me as when a journalist hears at the start of an interview, "This is off the record." The textbook response is either (rarely) "OK," and what follows is not printed . . . or (almost always) "No—can't do that," and then it's up to the speaker to decide whether to go on. I am certain the speaker named Bob Knight would not have gone any farther and *Season on the Brink* would never have gotten onto let alone off the launching pad if "Can't do that, Bob" had been the upfront response on that walk down an Assembly Hall corridor.

The book was by no means a hatchet job. If polarizing is a fair term for its effect, it also covers the high percentage of readers who thought more highly of Knight because of some stories Feinstein told of times when he gave strangers—IU-loving basketball fans but people really unknown to him—help or a boost when it meant most, at the best of those times giving lasting feelings of significance to lifelong insignificants. Those acts came always without his wanting or getting credit.

Feinstein anecdotes gave him some. Other revelations worked other ways.

The only point of bringing any of it up here is that the book itself wouldn't have happened if, to the obscenity-omission demand, John had said, no, I can't do it that way.

And that term: "Bob Knight's best friend"—I'd have to call admirably clever and insightful, if it was a thought-out advance defensive move, which it probably wasn't. All I remember is it didn't take much insight at all from my end to perceive instinctively the new personal standing, the sudden disqualification from credible-critic status, that came to me on the sofa that first night of reading the work that made a bright young metropolitan sportswriter famous, and wealthy.

The friendship between Bob Knight and me involved a lot of off-the-record conversation, much of it political or at least ideological. He considered our difference less Republican and Democrat than warrior and peacenik. He once told a member of my sports staff that he and I were the classic hawk and dove. And my guy said, "Which one's the dove?" (Bob's the one who told me about that exchange, ending his report with "Can you believe he actually *asked* that? Where the hell do you *get* these guys?")

The "hawk" came out surprisingly antiwar in the 2013 book we did together, *Power of Negative Thinking*. I'm pretty sure he'd alter an antiwar label for himself to "anti-stupid-goddam-decision-makers who get kids killed for unworthy gains." Remember, some of these at-high-risk kids are the kind he had and genuinely loved in his coaching days at West Point. In that book he said:

> From talks I have given and responses I have seen, I can tell you there are mothers and dads, grandmas and grandpas out there whose love of country is not at all in question but who hate seeing kids come back victims of a national commitment they don't understand for a purpose they can't conceive. Somebody in Washington should understand there's a nation out there that doesn't see the worth of what all we're investing in these unending wars that began with such positive assurances.

That is not antihawk, that is anti-reckless-troop-imperiling-military and governmental stupidity. It is the kind of heartfelt emotion that commonly came up when we talked in private, the kind Emerson had in mind when his definition of a friend was "Before him I can think out loud." In private, we both felt free to do it. And I suspect Ben Bradlee and John Kennedy did, too. If that be treason to the craft, make the most of it.

That friendship actually centered on a philosophy we share and didn't see practiced nearly enough in the sport he taught and I covered. He believed, and so did I, that in college athletics it was possible to follow all rules, graduate players, and win the biggest championships. Not only possible, but imperative—if winning and the "college" in "college basketball" were to mean anything at all.

We get angry—and, granted, Bob is better at that than I, though on this subject I am catching up—when people of authority in college athletics abandon their primary responsibility: to keep academics and athletics in achievable, indispensable balance. In basketball, those people—coaches, yes, and sportswriters, too, but more indictingly athletic directors, presidents, conference commissioners, NCAA executives—have stood by as modern-day Pontius Pilates, washing their hands of responsibility during 30 years now of tournaments and championships spotlighting "one-and-done" pros on the make in what is still called a college sport. There are some signs of imminent change but none nearly as separative—pro-centered on one side, college-centered on another—as I would prefer for a college game and college tournament.

At a coaching level, my close-up, warts-and-all appraisal of Bob Knight is that he did more than anyone in his profession to kick the hypocritical slats out from under anyone, coach or president, who countenances rules-breaking as understandable because "You *have* to do *some* of that to win" . . . because "Everybody does it."

Everybody doesn't, which is why in no way do I include in such company Dean Smith or Mike Krzyzewski, the two most successful fellow coaches with Knight in the duration of his career and leaders of their own highly admirable programs. When Smith succeeded Adolph Rupp of Kentucky as college basketball's winningest coach, Knight spoke out in tribute to a man who had done it the right way. When Knight's victory total passed Smith's, Smith was similarly complimentary, and gracious. And when early in the 2011–12 season Krzyzewski passed Knight, the compliments—though relationships between the two had cooled from once close to father-son—flew back and forth between record setter and record shedder.

Of that three, Knight made himself with his outspokenness the coach most vulnerable to probing for even borderline rules violations. Under that kind of media and cohort exposure, he won everything there was to win, graduated his players, and in a spotlighted 41-year career never faced even the first charge of cheating. Quite the opposite. In a 2008 Yahoo! Sports column entitled "He Cheated the Least and Won the Most," Dan Wetzel based that comment on an interview with Sonny Vaccaro, one of the first to bring shoe-company money into college athletics and, in Wetzel's words, "at the very least a sounding board for just about every dirty recruiting deed ever done." Wetzel's subject, cheating in college basketball recruiting, didn't bother Vaccaro ("Because of my role, I know those things. I've heard it all. I've been there for these things."). And when Wetzel asked him "How many of big-time, great [college basketball coaches] were really clean?" Vaccaro's response was:

> I guess three coaches, maybe four. I'm not 100 percent sure about one guy.
> And even among that group, Knight stands alone, stands above. I've never heard a single thing about him, never heard anything. Nothing. He's the cleanest one.
> You know, that's incredible. Really, that's the greatest thing you can say about him.

That—more than the championships and far more than the blow-ups—in my mind should be the primary identification of basketball coach Bob Knight. Meanwhile, I had a choice seat at a remarkable parade—game after game after game of basketball, played at an orchestral level. In Indiana, the Carnegie Hall for such. By players I knew and liked as people.

My primary intent in discussing him here is twofold: to acknowledge how covering that one coach magnified my own career, and to stress the considerably less obvious, that different as we were in such incidentals as temperament, word choices, and politics, in the area where our lives primarily overlapped—his as a college coach, mine at Bloomington in the main as a college reporter—our views on the worth and the only justification for continuance of major college athletics were our tightest bond. The hawk and the dove flew quite comfortably side by side on that.

Even more than my small-town sportswriter's life has included history-making events I have seen and places I have been, it has been enriched by people, star-spangled people, heralded and important and major-league people in numbers a guy from a low-circulation newspaper in Bloomington, Indiana, should never have known. I'm not talking about people I watched and wrote about, I mean people with whom I shook hands and enjoyed a conversation, often over a meal, people on the other end of a Bob Knight–attached relationship that permitted private phone calls and notes.

It didn't occur to me till I sat down to write about myself that not all but a preponderance of my galaxy was spun off to me *because* of association with Bob Knight, whose own such list was infinitely longer.

Let me illustrate both—my on-the-fringe exposures, his genuine acquaintances—with a 24-hour whirlwind in mid-2002, after the release of *Knight: My Story*, his autobiography for which I was the "As told to" guy.

A few years earlier, I was still sports editor for the Bloomington newspaper when Knight was invited to speak to the National Press Club in Washington. I went along in a reporting, even picture-taking role. My dual work appeared on Page 1 of the next morning's newspaper: high-profile basketball coach, always with "controversial" as a preceding adjective, going into a boastfully hard-questioning den and emerging with one more group taken aback that this reputed snarling monster of a man spoke with reason, intelligence, passion, and humor even. A few years after that speech he was fired by Indiana, to national uproar, got the contract to write his book, and sometime in the wake of all that he was invited back to the National Press Club. By then he was in Texas, and I was in limbo—in retirement with no newspaper to cover travel-expense money. But he said, "Get a flight out here, my expenses will take care of the hotel, it'll be good."

Midway through a Sunday afternoon, I was in the air, Indianapolis to Washington. Our flights arrived almost simultaneously. By 5 or so we were at our downtown hotel, in time to toilet a bit and get started on The Knight Circuit. We cabbed to meet Red Auerbach for dinner at his chosen DC steakhouse, the Capital Grille. For more than two hours, close to three, this paragon of professional-basketball-coaching success and his college basketball counterpart talked as longtime friends and mutual admirers do. They exchanged stories and laughs, opinions and rejoinders, as harmonious as barbershop quartets—the sort of thing about which people say, "I wish I had been a fly on the wall when . . ." I *was* the fly, too timid to pull out a pen and preserve the good stuff, except in mind.

A major topic was the upcoming 2008 Olympics, for which Knight's onetime Army player Mike Krzyzewski had been named US men's basketball coach, to head up another "Dream Team" of already established professional stars. It had worked the first time, in 1992, at Barcelona with Larry Bird and Magic Johnson, in their fadeout days, and Michael Jordan, at his peak. That group overwhelmed their international opponents, who were so dazzled by the assemblage that some—suited up and competing on court against them—played starry-eyed and afterward lined up for autographs.

That was the first time the US, embarrassed by being whipped in its one native sport with collegians in 1988 at Seoul, had gone to pros. The second time, in 1996 at Atlanta, it was called Dream Team II and, though golden, its on-court play hinted at the nightmare stuff that was to come for basketball connoisseurs. The US pros of that year, without the pride of the first-time professional group, clowned their way through to their easily won gold medals. Once back home, one of those '96 Olympians, second-year pro Grant Hill, in a *Detroit Free Press* interview with Charlie Vincent, spoke from the inside as I had felt as an outside observer.

> "A lot of negative stuff was written about our attitude and how we conducted ourselves, and almost everything that was written was accurate," Hill said. "In practices, guys weren't going hard and the focus wasn't on the game. It's unfortunate. The Olympics should be something special, something you cherish.
>
> "The Dream Team experience, battling those guys every day, showed me how hard some of them worked and how hard some of them didn't work. Every last one of the guys on the Dream Team felt they were the best player in the world. It was a disappointment because these were guys I'd looked up to and dreamed of playing against. Some of them had been idols of mine when I was younger."

The trend for US pros to go through the motions in the Olympics and other international competitions didn't take long to show up on the scoreboard. In 2000 at Sydney, Lithuania lost to the US Dream Team III in the semifinals, 85–83, when a 3-point shot in the air at the buzzer just missed. The US beat France in the finals, 85–75, but the Dream Team aura of invincibility was fading.

In the 2002 World Championships at Indianapolis, it was gone altogether. The American pros were beaten three times—by Argentina, Serbia, and Spain.

Then in the 2004 Olympics at Athens, the US pros—Dream Team IV—lost. Three times. Outhustled. Outworked. Outplayed. Start to finish. In the opening round, Puerto Rico routed the Americans, 92–73.

America's Athens basketball pratfall thoroughly offended Auerbach, on behalf of the pro game, and equally so Knight, from a different perspective. His own two years of lead-up, focused effort that had produced the 1984 gold medal for America—with collegians—instilled in him forever an Olympic zeal.

Both felt for Larry Brown, the 2004 US coach who had been given a team to lead that was virtually self-picked: stars who were invited, deigned or did not deign to accept, and arrived to Brown as The Team, and were anything but one. Those sons-o'-bitches should have to earn their way, in tryouts, the Auerbach-Knight duotone ran. And they've gotta live in the Olympic Village with the other athletes, not sleep in swank hotels and come in in limos. And . . .

Precious stuff. In and around the stories, and the warm hilarity.[1]

By then The Fly was pleasantly pooped, mellowed out for early bedtime. But, no, once back at the hotel for a quick pit stop, we reconnoitered in the lobby, then walked up the street two blocks to another hotel. There, the Dallas Cowboys were billeted for their Monday night TV game with the Washington Redskins. We entered the secured hotel, knowing nods passing Knight along without a challenge—in the lobby, at the elevator, on exit at the proper floor, and along the way to the room of Cowboys coach Bill Parcells. It was a vital game for the Cowboys, who did win it, but Parcells—already in sleep gear, lounging atop his folded-down bed, in game-eve conversation with his chosen confidantes—received us warmly. Of course he welcomed his longtime friend Knight in, but he was gracious to me, too—"How are you *feeling?*" Weeks earlier, I had collapsed at a Texas Tech basketball game, and he had heard about it. And, obviously, cared about it, which I definitely felt from his question and appreciated.

It wasn't a long stay, maybe 45 minutes. There's a coaching decorum about such things, when games are to be won, so Knight broke off the conversation to give Parcells breathing time and we left. We went back to our hotel, turned in for what was left of the evening, got up early the next morning for breakfast before meeting the director of the Smithsonian Institute, who escorted Bob and his tagalong on a tour of a brand new sports exhibit that he wanted the coach to see and comment on. We used up more than an hour there, made a swing to the Lincoln Memorial and the then-new World War II memorial, and got back in a supplied car to head for the Press Club's luncheon. There, Supreme Court Justice Clarence Thomas was a surprise attender. In his wallet was a

---

1. The Athens losses had the same galvanizing, wake-up effect the Munich defeat did on the US Olympic basketball effort. Knight's former Army captain Mike Krzyzewski, in recognition of where he had taken his Duke program, was picked by USA Basketball to head up a suddenly much more willing group of NBA stars. It worked for a return to gold in 2008, and Krzyzewski stayed on to head repeated Olympic championships in 2012 and 2016.

worn clipping that he said he had long carried, a quotation attributed to Knight: "Everybody has the will to win. What counts is the will to prepare to win." As much as he appreciated the Justice's compliment in retaining the clipping, Knight told Thomas the particular wording was his, but he had retooled the thought from words he remembered from a conversation with former Oklahoma football coach Bud Wilkinson.

The luncheon talk and questioning went entertainingly well. Knight's topic was college athletics' ills. For a demonstration, he had brought along two items. He raised eye-high, so all could see, a pamphlet that carried the entire US Constitution, amendments and all. He dropped the thin volume almost soundlessly onto the top of the podium. Then he raised the NCAA rulebook, a ponderous Webster-sized tome that landed with a loud thud. "We've run the whole country for more than two hundred years with this," Knight had said as he dropped the first, "and we try to run college athletics with this." *Thump!*

After the posttalk questions, he chatted one more time with Auerbach, and Thomas, and met some other friends in the Washington press group. Then it was time for both of us to get to the airport. I made my Indianapolis flight, and once in the air, settled back, breathed deeply, and pondered my whirlwind.

Knight. Auerbach. Parcells. Smithsonian. Lincoln Monument. World War II Memorial. Press Club. Thomas. This all happened in 24 hours. This was the way my life used to be.

I smiled, and one more time felt lucky.

And, in my 70s, pooped.

Bob Knight had a long list of contemporary coaching friends. Primarily, though, his greatest basketball influence came from other generations. More than any person I ever met, Bob consistently practiced a near reverence for older people in general—the product, I sensed, of spending some growing-up years with his maternal grandmother in his family's Orrville house. Bob was long and lanky in his high school years, but when his grandmother lost her husband and moved into her daughter and son-in-law's home, Bob gave her his room and slept on a living-room couch—all leggy, six foot four of him.

He and Grandma grew close. Over the years he has laughed in remembering a time when the two were alone in the Orrville living room, Grandma reading or knitting or doing something by herself when she said idly, "Sometimes God puts people on this Earth just to show us what *not* to do." He says, "I looked around, didn't see anyone else in that room, and figured she had to be talking about me." When as an Orrville High senior he drove to visit Miami University on a recruiting trip, Grandma—not railroader Dad or schoolteacher Mom—was able to go along, and did. After Bob had gone to Ohio State, he came home on a school break to be the one who discovered his grandmother slumped over in a chair, dead. Maybe it would have happened anyway, but Bob's patience and obvious fondness whenever older people are involved—and their reciprocated warmth for him, especially among older women—seem to me rooted in Robert Montgomery Knight's relationship with Grandma Montgomery.

For Knight, that visible respect also applied to older coaches, who tend to be forgotten by most young coaches caught up in today's game. Knight, as big an innovator as the game has ever seen, constantly denied such tags and said everything important in coaching the game was discovered long before him—that coaches ever since have done their whiz-bang new things with old principles.

His influences were many, but to me two stood out—and they were two, Fred Taylor and Pete Newell, whom because of Bob I got to know, too, as friends.

I also met, through him, two of his other revered mentors, Henry Iba and Clair Bee. I already knew Everett Dean and considered him the Father of Indiana University Basketball, because he was the school's first basketball All-American and first championship coach—in a state where before him the high schools were giving Hoosierland its basketball identity, and among college programs IU was languishing way below Purdue, behind Notre Dame and Butler, and bobbing somewhere in the waters with Wabash, DePauw, Indiana State, Franklin, Rose Poly, and Earlham. Dean never caught Purdue but he passed all the rest and got the fire lighted in what ultimately became Indiana Basketball. I knew Everett, but through Knight—40 years his junior—my own friendship with him became tighter.

And Dean Smith—Knight's one eye-to-eye contemporary in the '70s and '80s in winning championships and graduating citizens—became a friend of mine for life after daily contact at the Montreal Olympics. Dean's particular openness to me there no doubt was largely because of my linkage with Knight.

One especially treasured experience I had with Dean really didn't involve Knight. Indiana and North Carolina were in a tournament at New York, and a game-eve party at one of the Trade Center towers was open to press and the competing teams' officials. Knight rarely made those events and didn't this one, but Dean was there with assistants Eddie Fogler and Roy Williams. All three were around, as was I, when Indiana athletic director Ralph Floyd introduced his wife, Sue, to Dean and said, "You may not know this: Sue is from Emporia, too." Emporia, Kansas, the town of William Allen White, was where Dean Smith grew up, and Sue Floyd, trying to make a connection and realizing she was several years ahead of Dean in school said, "Now, who was your father?" Dean filled in a few blanks, including the church that it turned out both he and Sue attended, and her quizzical expression suddenly changed as she made the connection:

"Oh!

"You're little *Deanie!*"

He was, he blushed, and out of his sight behind him Fogler and Williams almost collapsed while trying not to howl.

Each of the older coaches, all Hall of Famers—Taylor, Newell, Iba, Bee, and Dean—influenced Knight.

Taylor was brand new on the job as basketball coach at his alma mater when he went out through Ohio in spring 1959 and rounded up an epochal class: Jerry Lucas of Middletown. John Havlicek of Bridgeport. Mel Nowell of Columbus. Gary Gearhart of Lima. Bob Knight of Orrville. When that class first met with their young coach in an Ohio State locker room or dorm, in that little group were four future Naismith Basketball Hall of Famers: Lucas, Havlicek, Knight, and Fred Taylor.

Taylor, before Knight, introduced the fast-breaking Big Ten to the concept of looking for a good shot while running and winning. The conference record for team shooting for a league season was 43.1 percent, till that first Taylor class checked in with years of 49.7, 49.5, and 49.0.

The league's individual shooting record for a season was 53.8 percent till Lucas had consecutive seasons of 65.6, 61.2, and 67.8.

But defense was the phase of the game where Taylor sought particular improvement early in his first year with The Class. After hearing Pete Newell, coach of 1959 NCAA champion California, talk about his team defensive concepts at a summer clinic and taking notes, Taylor sent an assistant to get more direct information from Newell even after the 1959–60 season was underway. That season ended with Ohio State employing some of Newell's ideas and beating his California team in the national championship game, 75–55. "That really impressed me," Knight said later. "What Pete gave us helped us beat his team for the national championship, and he never regretted it at all."

Those were the concepts that a top off-the-bench player on those Ohio State powerhouses took with him into coaching. He also took Taylor's ever-available counsel, there even when the two were rivals in the same league. And Taylor had no stronger supporter than Knight, who was bitter when Taylor was pushed out as coach in, of all years, Knight's pinnacle season at Indiana, 1975–76. That regular season closed with Ohio State at Indiana, and in pregame Knight gave Taylor the celebration send-off—pregame on-court recognition—that hadn't come back at Columbus. Then, of course, that unbeaten national-championship team gave him a beating, too, 96–67. In the ceremony, Taylor had noted the cheers he received and told the crowd that he hadn't always been treated that kindly in previous Bloomington visits. "Just wait till the game starts," a voice rang out from the stands. "I know," Taylor said. "That's why I'm stalling."

Also from that recruiting roundup, Knight got two close lifetime friends: Havlicek and Gearhart. Each was there for many of his biggest games over the years.

Along the way, Taylor had died. Long before, Knight had led in getting Taylor elected to the Hall of Fame, was there the night he was inducted, was there when he was in his final hospital days, and when a campus street was named in his memory. The disciplined, consistent success of the Taylor program at Ohio State was among the major reasons athletic director Bill Orwig chose to give young Bob Knight, at 30, his chance to coach at Indiana, and Bob more than paid that back.

As a coach on his own, Knight virtually adopted Newell, who himself got out of coaching quite young, at 45, after leading maybe the best amateur team in US basketball history—Oscar Robertson, Jerry West, Jerry Lucas, Terry Dischinger, Walt Bellamy—to the Olympic gold medal at Rome in 1960.

The Knight-Newell relationship kicked into a higher gear the summer of '73. Knight, a master defender looking to create an offense most difficult to stop, concluded the answer to his quest was no organized offense at all: freelancing. So, he sought to maintain a form of order but incorporate as much freelance freedom as possible—to make defenses their own enemy, to "read" the defensive man and defensive team's response to each movement of player and ball and react in a way taking advantage of that response. "Read and react" were the key words. He sprawled on the floor of his living room, diagramming his new plays on three-by-five note cards covering every possible situation.[2]

Newell's particular expertise on offensive spacing was what got him into the fun—two of the twentieth century's best basketball minds taking on a new challenge.

It became Knight's "passing game," and it was sprung onto Big Ten and national defenses at just the time when Knight was bringing along a perfect team to execute and exploit it. In the 1974–75 and 1975–76 seasons, Knight's Indiana teams went 63–1, completing two straight unbeaten regular seasons—the only pair of those by a Big Ten school since the NCAA tournament began in 1939. It was essentially the same team—Quinn Buckner and Bobby Wilkerson, two big, strong, athletic guards who keyed the defense by regularly taking opposing backcourts out of their own offense before they got it started; and Scott May and Kent Benson, a dynamic forward-center combination that scored, rebounded, and played defense. The fifth starter in '74–75 was Steve Green, Knight's first Indiana recruit and a deadly six foot seven

---

2. More than 40 years later on an ESPN "Game Day" telecast from Lawrence, Kansas, where the University of Kansas had just paid big money to get the original copy of James Naismith's first basketball rules for display in its basketball museum, commentator and former Duke star Jay Bilas was asked what historic basketball treasure he would most like to have. His quick response was those note cards Bob Knight used to draw up his revolutionary new offense.

shooter; in '75–76, it was Tom Abernethy, also six foot seven, not the shooter Green was but a better defender, rebounder, and passer. The '75 team was No. 1-ranked when it lost May to a broken arm in late February and, its defense more compromised than its offense by that loss, fell to Kentucky in the NCAA tournament quarterfinals. The '76 team didn't lose to anybody.

The national hallmark of that '76 team was defense. I've always felt its truly unique weapon was at the other end of the court—my choice as the best passing team I've ever seen. The "passing game" that evolved from that summer of three-by-five cards and the blended minds of Knight and Newell was perfect for that team.

Newell lived in California, frequented Hawaii, occasioned Japan, occupied himself with the NBA game as an adviser to San Francisco (later Golden State) Warriors owner Franklin Mieuli, but always maintained tight contact with Knight and Indiana. He didn't come out to Bloomington often—usually once a season, to catch two or three games—but his intimacy with the team was such that players considered him virtually part of the coaching staff. In those days, telephone contact between Knight and Newell was constant, no game undiscussed before and after. Game films, then tapes were shipped out for study and analysis. More even than Taylor, Newell became Knight's basketball father in terms of respect and counsel involving the game both revered. They matched well physically, each six foot three or six four. Each seemed taller than people face-to-face with them for the first time expected, especially the more TV-carried Knight. The public usually saw him on the sidelines in among players much bigger, making him seem of average height. Average there, in a word that averaged about six foot five, was not the average you would approach on the street. Newell was more soft-spoken, though he could flash hot, too. Their commonest bond was deep respect and fondness, and their love of basketball as a profound object of mystery and unreachable—but tantalizing—perfection.

By the 1974–75 season, the one that introduced Indiana to No. 1 national stature for the first time under Knight, Newell had become a virtual assistant coach in exile. He was the key part of a ploy Knight used with only that one team: taped messages played for them before or after a practice in a hushed locker room, or in a hotel room on a road trip, tapes cut by leading people in sports—usually made especially for them and aimed strictly at them: the 1974–75 Hoosiers.

The leadoff tape in the series was the one *not* made for that group. Vince Lombardi died four years before that 1974–75 season began, but he was an all-sports prototype for what Knight was trying to inculcate in his cerebral team. He banked on those players to make the connection between what Lombardi had said to his great Packers teams and what Knight wanted for his team. A Lombardi tape played in preseason to a roomful of players and coaches said:

> Perfection is very elusive. In striving for perfection, however, I think you do accomplish things that you might not accomplish if you did not have that urge.

And, several minutes later it wound up:

> With every fiber in my body, I've got to try to make you the best player that I can make you. And I'll try. And I'll try. And if I don't succeed the first day, I'll try it again. And I'll try it again. You've got to give everything that you have in you in order to stop the play if you're on defense or to make the play go if you're on the offense, because this may be the one play in the whole ball game which can cause the winning or the losing of the entire game.

It set a tone that continued with a message from Lombardi's pro basketball equivalent, Red Auerbach, which was directed at this Hoosier team. And Auerbach's Boston Celtics leader—Knight's close friend and Ohio State teammate, John Havlicek—spoke player to player in his taped message:

> You have to motivate yourself through pride. Over the years, I have pushed myself mentally. I have pushed myself physically. A lot of people say, "John Havlicek never gets tired." Well, I get tired. It's just a matter of pushing myself. I say to myself, "He's as tired as I am; who's going to win the mental battle?"

Pete Newell coached his last game in 1960, his success period basically bordered by a surprise 1949 NIT championship with San Francisco and a 1959 NCAA championship with California—which earned him the 1960 Olympic coaching berth and his most noted triumph at Rome. The brevity of his career made it difficult for Knight to lobby him into the Basketball Hall of Fame. It's at least mildly galling to Knight that the man he considers the best pure basketball coach in history had to go into the Hall in the category of "contributor," but he's in or—count on it—Knight would have never accepted his own entrance a few years later.

Fred Taylor to Knight always was "Coach," never Fred or anything that could in any way be considered less respectful. Pete was Pete, and Knight to Newell was Bobby, not Bob—also the name Taylor always used, from Knight's high school and Buckeye days. John Havlicek sometimes calls him by another name: "Dragon." That dates from early in their college days when Knight wove a tale for his new basketball pals of his high school days in a motorcycle gang known as "The Dragons," which worked till the unreality of gangs in his countrified, population-7,000 hometown of Orrville sank in on them.

Knight is a master of the impromptu tall tale. Once he left a Bloomington doctor wide-eyed for a four-hour car ride after talk of Knight's military days came up. The doctor had said sarcastically, "I'll *bet* a jock like you really saw rough stuff," and Knight in believable anger shot back with story after story after story of his harrowing action—all verbally plagiarized in memory from the range of books he devoured in every unoccupied minute while traveling. At the end of that evening, the chagrined doctor said, "I am *really* sorry, Bob. I had no idea you went through all that." And he never heard otherwise.

On a car ride from LaGuardia Airport to Manhattan with silver-haired IU athletic director Ralph Floyd along, Knight convinced his cabbie—who had innocently asked as a conversation opener, "What are you fellas doing in town?"—that Floyd was the commissioner of a new senior baseball league that was about to be announced, with Joe DiMaggio, Ted Williams, Stan Musial—all the old greats coming back to play, a la golf's Senior tour. Our route passed by Central Park, and Knight told the cabbie the New York franchise's stadium was going to be built right there. How gabby that cabbie was and how many future passengers heard that inside report, who knows?

≈

Road games for Bob Knight—even "road games" that were part of the Final Four—were treated as much alike as Knight could make them: a final full practice at Assembly Hall the afternoon before the game, bus ride with the team from the arena to Bloomington Airport about five miles west of town, flight (by university aircraft, unless the trip was so long it necessitated something bigger) to the game site, then bus ride straight to the arena for a half hour or so of shooting.

That game-eve dinner was where a lot of those people in Bob's galaxy came into mine. Almost always he ate in a place different from where his team went, partly to give them—and him—space. Frequently, he and I, the team trainer (Bob Young through 1981, Tim Garl after) and commonly a few assistant coaches or others in the small traveling party were joined for dinner by a regional friend of Bob's, sometimes several—fishing buddies, coaching friends, a wide, unpredictable assortment that included some celebrities. Before a 1998 NCAA tournament appearance in Washington, columnist George Will joined us. Will grew up in Champaign-Urbana, son of a distinguished University of Illinois professor, and got a degree there. So, America's literate spokesman for late 20th-, early 21st-century conservatives who wrote baseball books about the philosophies of Tony LaRussa and others also was steeped in Big Ten athletics, and the conversation flow with Knight was easy and warm. If politics came up at all, I don't recall, but neither was there on either side an air of stepping down to talk to someone on his limited level. Next day Will came to watch the game, and stayed to extend a hand of congratulations to Knight after an overtime win over Oklahoma.

Minnesota was the annual highlight of such dinners. Way back, Knight formed a friendship with Sid Hartman, a longtime Minneapolis sportswriting legend whose contacts at the top level of professional and collegiate coaching were profound before either major league baseball or the NFL even found the Twin Cities. Sid seemingly knew 'em all and had a direct line to every one of them: Vince Lombardi, Billy Martin, *all.* Lombardi treated Sid like a brother; Knight became Sid's favorite adopted nephew. Every trip into Minneapolis brought a

Sid-arranged night-before Italian dinner spread at Vescio's. Regularly, Vikings coach Bud Grant made it, and the man the public knew as glacial had merry, collegial conversation with the man the public knew as volcanic—straight talk, simple exchanges of experiences that each knew the other would identify with and enjoy. Some had a lot less to do with football (which Knight played in high school) or basketball (Grant won a championship ring playing with the NBA Minneapolis Lakers) than with fishing and hunting, but uncompromising coaching at a championship level was always the common ground.

Sid brought them to Vescio's from baseball (Tommy John, Paul Molitor), football, basketball—a wide array. It was always festive fun.

At other sites, those road trip night-before-the-game dinners sometimes included the home coach. During the time when, as a lead-up to every Indiana-Illinois basketball collision, Chicago newspapers in particular made banner headlines of how much Illinois coach Lou Henson and Knight hated each other, the two frequently picked out a spot to meet for dinner. For a year or two after a particularly hot postgame exchange during which Henson loudly called Knight a "bully," relations had been strained. But the hostility continued in print long after the dinners had resumed. In the meantime, Henson had lost a son, killed in an automobile crash, and only Henson saw the letter of quiet support that his "bitter" Bloomington enemy sent him during those despondent days. Neither bothered to make a public show of renewed friendship, but it carried on through Knight's move to Texas Tech and Henson's to New Mexico State—their teams began regular scheduling, and the dinners continued. In both camps, loyalists ridiculed the other coach. Privately, Knight always said Henson's teams were as well prepared for Indiana games as were any opponent on the schedule, and Henson just as privately acknowledged regularly studying tapes and films to see how Knight-prepared defenses attacked Big Ten teams that the Illini were about to play.

The public dislike between Knight and Bill Musselman, whose Minnesota coaching tenure started the same year Knight's did at Indiana, was much more genuine and long-lasting. They grew up in the same high school class of '58 about ten miles apart in northeastern Ohio, Knight at Orrville, Musselman at Wooster—Wooster a much bigger town and high school than Orrville but the two towns and schools still had a bitter athletic rivalry that covered all sports. Both Knight and Musselman—aware of each other from Little League age up—played them all: Knight an end, the shorter Musselman an outstanding fullback in football; Knight an infielder, Musselman a catcher in baseball; both best known as good, all-round basketball players, Knight a higher scorer, unsurprisingly much bigger Wooster winning most of the games. The Big Ten coaching debut for each was Indiana at Minnesota January 8, 1972—the first time they had been coaching opponents. The rivalry might have had a chance to be friendly, until Knight arrived in Minneapolis the night before the game to read a St. Paul *Pioneer-Press* story quoting Musselman as knowing his Gophers would win because Knight's "a loser"—his evidence their high school competition. It was a quote he later strongly denied ever making, fabricated by a writer to make his pregame story stronger, Musselman insisted to me in private. But, it was hanging in the air when, before a record Williams Arena crowd, 19,121, Knight and Indiana did lose in their first meeting, 52–51. It was particularly painful because the Hoosiers led 51–46 entering the final minutes. This one time the attempted freeze cracked a couple of times and the Gophers squeezed through—on a one-and-one free-throw conversion with 17 seconds left, and a basket-defending fast-break stave-off by Musselman's best inherited player, future Olympic center Jim Brewer.

Two months later, Minnesota was Big Ten champion. On paper at least, reversal of that one-point conference opener would have lifted third-place finisher Indiana into a title share. Along the way, Minnesota had won a brawl-scarred game over Ohio State and Fred Taylor, Indiana had clouted Minnesota 61–42 in the rematch at IU, and IU had given Minnesota its standings separation from Ohio State by beating Taylor and the Buckeyes on the next-last Saturday of the year. Postgame, Knight considered the irony of his first coaching victory over his coach and alma mater, and the Minnesota/Musselman-benefiting ramifications of that victory, and said with a bitter shake of the head, "Isn't that the shits?"

For subsequent years, the two coaches' teams met in annual tension. Sid Hartman took it on himself to ease the relationship and eventually did get the two to exchange a thawing, out-of-the-spotlight pregame handshake in the bowels of Williams Arena one night. When Knight's career was reaching an early peak with his No. 1-ranked 1974–75 team, clouds were gathering above Musselman, who got out of Minnesota ahead of the NCAA posse (which claimed more than a hundred rules violations in putting the school on probation) by taking an NBA job. It was the embattled, criticized Musselman that Knight, the recruiting purist, reached out to befriend. Years later Musselman visited Bloomington a time or two, and the two were open pals—well, not smarmily open—in the last years before Musselman's shocking death in September 2000, when both were 59.

Through their ups and downs, Musselman was always open to my pregame calls, his end of the conversation frequently friendly, in a teasingly cynical way. While their war was still on, Indiana won a Saturday night game at Minneapolis, I stayed in the arena to do my writing, and well after midnight I went outside to catch a cab to the airport for a red-eye flight home. Musselman pulled up, rolled a window down and said, "Knight leave you behind?" When he heard my purpose, he said, "Forget the cab. I'll take you out." And he went an hour totally out of his way to do me a favor—and share a laugh-spiced chat that included more serious things like, "How's he *really* doing? Everything OK?" It was one other illustration of how different public and private relationships were.

Some of Knight's closest coaching friends he rarely or never played. Don Donoher, one of America's best under-the-radar coaches for a long time at Dayton, was one. Bob Boyd, who had great teams at Southern Cal overshadowed into unnotice by greater ones at UCLA, was another. Donoher was on his 1984 US Olympic staff. Both became people I grew to know as friends—and likely, on my own, would not have. The Knight link opened many doors of that sort. To Al McGuire, who never wasted time learning names, I was "Bloomington." Once he was doing an Indiana game, tip-off a half hour away, and he called out to me, "Hey, Bloomington, could you sit down over here and fill me in a little on some of these guys?" For Al, that was "in-depth" preparation, and he made it work well. His working companion with him that day and for a long time at CBS, Dick Enberg, captured every essence of Al in a one-man "play" he wrote and got into production in 2010 (*COACH: The Untold Story of College Basketball Legend Al McGuire*). Enberg thought he was headed for a coaching-teaching career before he got his sports-broadcasting start as an IU graduate student, doing Branch McCracken "Hurryin' Hoosier" radio broadcasts as his first step toward rare dual induction as a media representative in both the Baseball Hall of Fame at Cooperstown and the Basketball Hall of Fame at Springfield, Massachusetts.

The only reason Indiana and UTEP (Texas-El Paso) had regular basketball games was the friendship that Knight had with rustic coach Don Haskins. Without it I'm sure I wouldn't have had the colorful week-of-the-game phone conversations Haskins—a taciturn Marlboro Man, a perfect fit in El Paso—always afforded me, replete with dry-humor tales of his fishing trips with Knight.

Gene Keady at Purdue, Jud Heathcote at Michigan State, Johnny Orr at Michigan were Big Ten contemporaries who sparred competitively while sharing friendships with Knight, and always were open to phone conversations with me that provided quotes for a game preview. In early 1992, Indiana won something rare in the intense Purdue series, a blow-out, at Bloomington in the teams' first meeting. Weeks later I called Keady before the West Lafayette rematch, and he came on the phone ready:

"*Yeah! Bob Hammel!*

"I've been *waiting* for you.

"I want to tell you about those 'great' Indiana fans. On our trip home from that game down there, an Indianapolis car passed our bus and a guy in the car *mooned* me. Right there in broad daylight! What do you say about *that*?"

Gene's tone clearly was faux angry. I laughed, faux sympathetically, and said:

"Uh, Gene, you know how that first game came out [106–65]?"

"Course I do. Why?"

"Are you *sure* that was an *IU* fan?"

He laughed, said, "Come to think of it, you may be right," and we had our pregame talk.[3]

Roy Williams ultimately left Smith and North Carolina to take the coaching job at Kansas—before moving back to North Carolina and winning a couple of national championships. While at Kansas, he made an in-season visit to Bloomington to sit in on a Knight practice. That gave me a good interview/column and a new friendship, which led to before-game phone interview conversations when he and Knight worked out a four-season match-up with their Kansas and Indiana teams. He was still at Kansas when I retired from sportswriting in 1996, and the people who put on a retirement roast for me invited him to send a comment. He did in the form of a letter to me. Williams roasted a bit: "I think truly the joke is on everyone else, because you have been able to handle such an ordinary skill and make money while you were doing it." And he added: "I can tell you what I think your greatest accomplishment is: perhaps 95 percent of the basketball coaches in America feel a sense of trust with you, and I think that is an unbelievable statistic. Maybe some of them feel that trust because they know of your relationship with Coach Knight and think you are a 'little wacko' like the rest of us."

Which is another way of saying what I've been trying to say: it did open doors.

One night Bob, his assistants, and I gathered at a South Bend restaurant the night before an Indiana-Notre Dame game. Frequently Notre

---

3. File this under Who Saw That Coming? Through the 1980s and '90s, there was no hotter college basketball rivalry than Indiana and Purdue, because of the fiery, combative coaches it matched up: Bob Knight and Gene Keady. In that 20 years, each won fourteen times on his home court and six times against loud and fierce opposition in the road arena. "The Chair" game was in there; so was one where both had a technical foul in the first two minutes. Fans were sure they hated each other, which made it an in-state shock when, years later, the two appeared onstage together before big crowds at major venues in Indianapolis, Carmel, Fort Wayne (where in May a mostly red-wearing crowd sang "Happy Birthday" to Keady), and West Lafayette (where black-and-gold was the dominant color and the October crowd actually sang "Happy Birthday, Dear Bobby").

Dame coach Digger Phelps joined us—a relationship that went back to when both were in their 20s, Knight at Army and Phelps a high school coach when they first met. Digger then became head coach at Fordham, and their one Army-Fordham match-up came the last year before their simultaneous moves to Indiana and Notre Dame. Digger's team had one of Fordham's best basketball seasons ever (26–3, advancing to the Elite Eight before losing to eventual runner-up Villanova.) The Army-Fordham meeting was at the end of Knight's only losing season at Army (11–13). The outmanned Cadets fought Fordham to the end, but at a time-out in the final seconds, Knight—a long way from giving up on that game—looked up from his huddle to see Phelps there with a hand out: "My team's going to carry me off the floor after the game, Bobby, I just wanted to do the handshake now." Knight suggested where Digger could stick his handshake. But theirs was a friendship that knew no breaking points, and Digger was a frequent game-eve dinner companion.

On this game eve in South Bend, Bob had booked a surprise guest: Notre Dame law professor Michael Blakey, who came uniquely backgrounded on the Kennedy Assassination, a favorite Knight discussion topic. Bob and I were in opposite camps on that one: I agreed with the Warren Commission finding, that assassin Lee Harvey Oswald acted alone. Bob didn't. He liked the gangland theory: that Chicago mobster Sammy Giancana set it up in revenge against JFK and the Kennedys for (1) pressure on the gangs led by Attorney General Robert Kennedy and (2) revenge for the president's dalliances with Giancana's girlfriend, Judith Exxner.

And Blakey? Prior to taking his Notre Dame professorship, he was general counsel for the House Subcommittee Investigation of Assassinations, chaired by Representative Louis Stokes of Ohio. Knight outlined to Blakey my primary reason for accepting the one-gunman theory: that Bobby Kennedy, as Attorney General, was so embittered by the death of his brother and so ruthless when tracking down enemies that if he had any doubt about the commission's findings, he'd have pursued the tiniest shred of contrary evidence. And Bobby had never voiced any disagreement. Blakey's dismissal of that line of argument: when the commission was meeting, Bobby Kennedy was walking around almost comatose, temporarily mentally destroyed by the monumental upheaval in his life.

Blakey told how his subcommittee brought in and heard every conceivable witness—those who had testified to the commission and others for whom some sort of link was found or alleged. After long weeks, the Stokes Commission reached its final day expecting to, in effect, ratify the Warren Commission's conclusion. That last day a radio recording was entered into evidence. Reverberating sounds from the firing of the shots were found on a motorcycle policeman's radio, then recorded and preserved. Placing the policeman precisely where he was said to be, the recording indicated there had to have been four shots fired, not three—hence, two gunmen, not one; Warren's group was wrong. Later, months after Blakey talked with us, the policeman's precise position was corrected, and that changed the conclusion: An echo effect removed, there *were* just three shots; at the very least, the Warren Commission wasn't disproved. But that night, the location error hadn't surfaced and Blakey was convinced there was another gunman. He leaned toward Knight's Giancana theory. It was an edifying evening— quiet, respectful, interesting debate back and forth. Just another night before a game.

Commonly called Hank then, Henry Iba ruled post–World War II college basketball from his spot as king of the Cowboys of Oklahoma A&M. He brought a toughness to the coaching game while becoming the first to win two straight NCAA championships, doing it in 1945 and '46 with one of the first great Goliaths of the college sport, Bob Kurland. "Hank" fit Iba well, but he was always "Mr. Iba"—*always*—to the rugged young men who carried out his tough playing style. Many of them went into coaching, and some succeeded almost on a level with him. Hank Iba might be the only man leather-faced, hard-eyed Don Haskins ever addressed as Mister.

The Bob Knight reverence for older people in general, particularly older men he respected in basketball, was present when he brought Iba into the Bloomington orbit—but never as Hank, rarely even as Mr. Iba. To Bob he was unfailingly Henry—I sensed he felt "Mr. Iba" belonged to his former players and "Hank" didn't feel sufficiently respectful, so he chose his own form of deference. The two were warm friends, especially after Iba was the 1972 US Olympic team coach and Knight, at 31 in his first year at Indiana, was invited to be on the coaching staff at the US trials. Knight snapped up the opportunity, honored. As part of the player selection procedure, Knight was given an eight-man team to coach in game competition. One morning he showed up to coach his trials team wearing a striped official's shirt, just for the humor of it. Iba saw none, and let Knight know. But the two basketball minds meshed, in direct coaching roles there and in off-duty conversations, and a deep and long friendship followed.

The summer of 1985, Knight took the returning players from his 1984–85 team on a basketball trip around the world. The Hoosiers were invited to represent the US in a four-team round-robin tournament in Japan, in with national teams from Japan, the Soviet Union, and the Netherlands. Another US college team or two had previously made that trip, going to Japan and returning after the eight-game competition there. Knight looked at the jaunt and thought, *Why go and come back the same way, why not go the other way home from Japan and circle the earth?* So, after their tournament commitments had taken them all through Japan, he took his Indiana team into China for three games, to Hong Kong for a respite, then on a long transoceanic flight into Europe to the old Yugoslavia for three games and to Finland for three more. It was a fantastic exposure to world culture. Hiroshima and Nagasaki were among the Japan-assigned game sites, on the 40th anniversary year of the atomic bombs, Hiroshima on the Fourth of July. The Great Wall, Tiananmen Square, and the Ming Tombs were stops made on the China swing. Hong Kong, which had just begun its countdown to becoming part of China, stood out as an oasis of New York-ish high-rises as the traveling Hoosiers arrived via bullet train after passing through rural terraced fields that could have been 17th-century China.

The trip lasted 37 days, just over five weeks. It was a physical test even for the fit 20-year-old athletes. Among others in the traveling party were two men much older. Iba was 81; Everett Dean, 87. Dean, IU's first All-American player and first Big Ten–championship coach, won an NCAA title in 1942 at Stanford, in 1985 was retired and back in Indiana, a Knight friend and supporter. Dean's daughters were not keen on their father's going, but Knight was insistent. On the trip also was IU athletic director Ralph Floyd. Never mentioned by Knight was the common denominator among Iba, Dean, and Floyd: each's wife had died just a few months before. That was at the core of Knight's determination: that none would spend the summer in sad loneliness. Instead, each thrived on the renewed kinship with basketball and with kids. And each of the octogenarian coaches lived another seven or so years, with fresh memories of a fabulous summer.

Clair Bee and Joe Lapchick were legends of the basketball coaching past who were intertwined with much-younger Bob Knight, but only Bee made it into the Bloomington orbit.

Both came into Knight's life during his six years as head coach at Army. He sought them out, visited each at his home. They offered different first-hand perspectives on college basketball's most scarring era. As coach at Long Island University, Bee had built the college game's dominant program before there was such a thing as a national tournament. Lapchick was the coach at St. John's when first New York, then all college basketball, was jolted by the point-shaving scandals of the early 1950s. Some of Bee's key players were implicated in the gambling scandal, and LIU never again was a power. Lapchick's program largely escaped major embarrassment, but Lapchick put together a scrapbook of how the scandal unfolded and made an annual point of showing the scrapbook to his subsequent teams. Both Bee and Lapchick developed a fondness for Knight, the ever-inquisitive young coach at West Point, just up the Hudson for Lapchick in New York, much closer to home for Bee in retirement in the Upstate New York Catskills. Knight courted the counsel of both; decades later he could cite Lapchick's house number ("3 Wendover Road, Yonkers"). After Lapchick's death in 1970, it was Knight to whom Lapchick's widow eventually entrusted that point-shaving era scrapbook.

Bee survived till 1983, and by then Knight was in Bloomington and Bee had been there a few times—as well as on the other end of a lot of telephone calls from Knight—some just to keep in touch, others genuinely seeking advice. In Knight's best season, 1975–76, he brought

Bee—just short of his 80th birthday, near blind, frail, bent by age but sharp of mind—to Bloomington to see his team play. The names— May, Buckner, Benson—were not new to Bee. He had followed them for three years, however he could.

In 1972 Buckner was a football-basketball phenomenon who had come straight from high school to start every game as a free safety- punt returner on Indiana's football team, getting some all-conference mention. A day after football ended, he was suited up at Assembly Hall playing in a Sunday afternoon basketball team scrimmage, with play- ers he was not just on court with for the first time but, for the most part, actually meeting. Three days later, Bee got a late-Wednesday af- ternoon phone call from Knight, who had just completed a practice. His season opener with Harvard just three days away, Knight faced a dilemma brand new to him. "Coach," he said, "I've got a teamful of kids who have been busting their asses for six weeks now, but if I start my best lineup Saturday, it will include a guy who just joined us Sunday." Then start him, Bee's advice ran—the only thing you owe those other players is that they know you're starting your best combination to win the game. He did start Buckner, and a career of incomparable leader- ship was launched—historically, even portentously. It started with the tip-off: future CBS TV commentator James Brown, an outstanding basketball center for Harvard, controlled it toward a teammate, who had the ball in his hands for just a flash before freshman Buckner stole it—his first entry into the box score a credited steal one second into his college career.

In the 1974–75 season, Bee kept track by television—as well as he could with greatly impaired vision, his insights sharpened by periodic phone reports from the coach—as Knight's Indiana program rose to the top nationally. Then came the injury to All-American May, and a season-shattering tournament loss to Kentucky. Within a few days, the bottomed-out Knight got a 105-word letter from the Catskills:

> Take a deep breath. Get your bearings. Set your sights on even greater
> heights and start all over again.
>   The young man, the leader, rebounds swiftly from adversity . . .
> strengthened by the very blow that cut him down. Now he knows the
> rough spots that pit the roads and the quicksand that lies so innocently

nearby. He knows because he has fought his way up that path of agony—almost to the very top.

Then, suddenly, refreshed by the driving desire that has always inspired young leaders, he grasps the new challenge with eager hands and races for the starting line.

He will be back.

It was therapeutic at the time, prescient about the future. The young man did reset his sights, did bring his new team surging back. It was a polished machine that was coughing just a bit with about a month of the 1975–76 season left when Bee was brought to Bloomington. The '74–75 team from very early on had blown everyone away, regularly taking a death grip by halftime and never easing off. Midway through '75–76, the Hoosiers trailed in a game at halftime for the first time in a year and a half, then did again, and again. Knight wasn't happy with the trend. The night Bee was there, a home game against a good Minnesota team, it happened again. Bee's calm counsel essentially said, "So what?" He claimed he actually liked to be behind at the half because then his players listened better. Knight never grew to like being behind, period, and he groused unhappily after that 76–64 win. But, his postgame remarks one game later after another pull-away win over Iowa showed Bee's counsel had sunk in.

> We've been talking about how we can't do this and we don't do that. I saw it mentioned in a local paper how often we've been behind at the half lately. But it seems like we're always ahead at the end. I feel very proud of these kids. They've done some things that no other team in the history of the Big Ten has done. They've had to play a lot of good basketball in a tough conference.

The sailing was much, much smoother the rest of the way, and Bee was there to see the last four tournament victories.

It wasn't coincidence that Knight's second of his two sons—born six months before Knight left West Point for Bloomington—bears the name of Patrick (Bob's father) Clair Knight.

And Lapchick? The night that Indiana won the 1979 NIT championship—the night that Knight achieved with an Indiana team what had been his highest dream in four turned-back attempts with his Army teams at Madison Square Garden—Knight showed more pure glee than after any other tournament championship. "We've won the NIT!" he exulted more than once in the postgame melee. Once the trophy was in hand, he headed straight to courtside where he exchanged victory hugs with Mrs. Barbara Lapchick, his guest at the event, which her late husband had won a record four times.

Maybe more than any of the other men in athletics who became his closest friends, Bo Schembechler could have been Bob Knight's brother. The two were German tough, Northeastern Ohio raised, bright, brusque, tough, driven, focused, profane, witty . . . with a love of laughter, at the right times. Sometimes even the . . . wrong?

For Knight's 50th birthday, a fund-raiser roast in Indianapolis brought in many who could needle the "honored" guest. Schembechler would have been one, but he couldn't make it so I was charged by event planners with getting a taped zinger from him. Bo was out of coaching, the president of the Detroit Tigers at the time. I called his office there, he knew why, but he came on in loud, gruff form—no "Hi, Bob," no "How you doin'?" just in words that came out briskly Schembechler-clipped:

"In my *present* job, I don't *have* to talk to the goddamn press, so I *don't* talk to the goddamn press, now *what* the *hell* do *you* want?"

And we both laughed.

Bo joined Bob and me for an eve-of-the-game dinner on IU basketball trips to Ann Arbor a few times. In 1979, Indiana's football team had played at Michigan. Bo regularly hammered Indiana, but this day an Indiana team that went on to score the school's first bowl win in just its second bowl game ever played his team hard. With a late touchdown drive and extra point, Indiana pulled even 21–21 with only a minute left. It was a wild last minute. Michigan prolonged it with an illegal "fumble" that went out of bounds—actually a 20-yard intentional heave after a tackle near the middle of the field, improperly stopping the clock and allowing one more play—then won it on a last-second touchdown pass to All-American Anthony Carter. The game-winning thunderbolt touched off a frenzied on-field celebration, still a classic moment even in that storied stadium, players burying the frightened Carter under a wild pile while fans spilled from the stands onto the field.

At Ann Arbor close to 20 years later, at one of those night-before road basketball dinners, Bo couldn't hold a question back any longer. With no lead-up, his eyes zeroed in on me across the table and said, "*You* were there—tell me one thing: Why did he *do* it?" ("He" was Indiana football coach Lee Corso, and "it" was, after the touchdown, kick a tying extra point rather than try to run or pass for a two-point conversion that could have won).

Before I could answer he painted the picture:

"He had a chance to beat Meeshigan—to beat *Meeshigan*—and the son of a bitch *kicked* the extra point to tie? *Why?*"

"For one thing," I said, "Tim Clifford [the IU quarterback who would have handled any two-point play] got hurt on the touchdown play—took a hard hit on his right shoulder; I'm not sure he *could* have run a two-point play.

"But the big thing was Indiana hadn't been to a bowl game for 12 years, and I'm sure Lee thought a tie at Michigan would look good on the resume at bowl-selection time. Rather than risk everything going for a win, I think he *was* playing for a tie."

Bo couldn't fathom that. He shook his head. "He coulda beat *Meeshigan!*" he said one more time. "*Jeeezus!*"

(PS—That 1979 IU team did go to a bowl, the Holiday at San Diego, and there Corso, Big Ten MVP Clifford and all delivered Indiana's first bowl victory ever: 38–37 over heavily favored, unbeaten Brigham Young.)

Michigan had a fund-raiser on one of Bo's birthdays, after he'd retired from coaching and joined the Tigers. It was on a winter Sunday afternoon, and among the speakers brought in were Penn State football coach Joe Paterno and Knight—in the middle of a basketball season, a time when only a Bo could have been given such Knight time. I went along, and when it was Knight's turn onstage, there he came wearing Bo's usual sideline attire: a navy blue Michigan sweatshirt, huge sunglasses, and a Michigan baseball cap. Wife Millie spotted Knight's

approach first, grabbed Bo's shoulder, and spun him that direction saying, "Oh, Bo, look at this!" Slouching his shoulders as he walked in the
intense Schembechler style, Knight rattled off Bo-isms as he strode
slowly across the stage. "Jeeezus Christ," Knight-Bo muttered, "I've got
guys on my team who can't play worth a shit and I'm payin' 'em tons
of money and we're losin' games—*damn*, you'd think I was coachin'
football at Illinois."

It went over much, much bigger in that Michigan audience that night
than—after word got around—it did at Illinois, where the school was
still recovering from being on the brink of Big Ten expulsion for foot-
ball-recruiting laxities under coach Mike White. The Big Ten office,
which has rules against intrafraternity insults, officially didn't chuckle,
either. Didn't need to. There had been more than enough of those at
Bo's party.

Knight and Schembechler first met when Bob was a student at Ohio
State and Bo was an assistant on Woody Hayes's Buckeye football staff.
The Ohio high school baseball tournament championship finals were
at Ohio State, and Knight went to a session with buddy John Havlicek.
They were watching a game when Schembechler came up from behind
and said loudly, "This reminds me of the time Schembechler and Nara-
gon [future major league catcher Hal] carried Barberton to the state
tournament and . . ."

Knight's hometown of Orrville was close enough to Barberton that
he knew of that state tournament, so in salty irreverence he interrupted,
"You mean the time when you came in as a relief pitcher and you got
beat . . ."

The two were naturals for each other.

John Havlicek and Knight were together lots of days during their
Ohio State basketball years.

Havlicek was the developing star. Nowhere near so celebrated as
classmate Jerry Lucas when their careers started, Havlicek didn't start
their first college game but did every one after it and blossomed game by
game. Never a first-team consensus All-America, he was second-team
his senior year. He was the first-round draft pick of the NBA-champion

Boston Celtics, but even that meant seven players were taken before him. He was the one with legendry ahead. Nobody picked ahead of him and none of his touted and talented Buckeye teammates, including Lucas, had the NBA career Hall of Famer Havlicek did—Knight a friend and a fan soaking in every achievement, every significant honor.

On the evening of May 10, 1974, I was driving as he and I headed home from an out-of-town trip. Knight fished around on the car radio till he picked up Game 6 of the NBA championship series. The underdog Celtics entered the game leading Milwaukee 3–2, with a chance to clinch in this game at Boston Garden—a loss meaning they'd have to play the decisive seventh game at Milwaukee. Game 6 still is a playoff classic: a double overtime that Havlicek—now 34 and a venerated ancient warrior—dominated for Boston and young, fresh, superlative Kareem Abdul-Jabbar for Milwaukee. Knight intensely wanted a Celtics win, but his passion was personal: for Havlicek through the agonizing final seconds, one-point leads swinging back and forth. Then it was overtime. The second overtime, we were on the edge of Bloomington and we pulled over to the berm so he could hear more clearly and put his full coaching self to work. With 7 seconds left, Havlicek's basket— giving him a game-high 36 points—nudged the Celtics in front, the championship teasingly close.

Time out.

Under pro rules, that meant the Bucks would pass the ball in from the side, in their frontcourt. Knight had a radio in front of him but saw— saw—Milwaukee's Oscar Robertson holding the ball on the sideline, looking for a target, a specific target: Kareem Abdul-Jabbar. *"Don't let him come to the ball!"* Knight screamed into the radio, as into the game as he would have been if coaching from the sidelines. *"Don't let him get the sky-hook!"*

Dave Cowens, the burly Celtics center who had the body and defensive savvy to do what Knight wanted, had just fouled out. The radio voice said:

"Kareem comes to the pass at the top of the key, rolls to the baseline and..."

Abdul-Jabbar arched his signature hook shot from 15 feet out, over the Celtic defender, and Milwaukee won.

A dead hand went out and silenced the radio, and there were seconds with no sound, Knight's face in his hands. Long seconds. I drove on, and he was disconsolate—for his friend. "He would have been remembered forever for this game," he said in soft agony. "He would have been MVP."

Darned if the Celtics didn't come back two days later and win the seventh game in Milwaukee, and old John Havlicek *was* the finals MVP. And what Havlicek and Abdul-Jabbar did that special Game 6 *is* remembered forever.

It worked the other way, too. Havlicek just as ardently always knew what Knight's teams were doing, what they were playing for, how they came out. There were always phone calls, of congratulations at high times, of consolation when needed. Havlicek squeezed an opening into the Celtics' schedule to be at St. Louis and talk to Knight's Indiana team at his first Final Four appearance in 1973. Did it again when they won everything at Philadelphia in 1976. And—by then retired—at Philadelphia in '81, and at New Orleans in '87.

In the middle of the holidays in December 2006, Knight had brought all college basketball eyes onto an arena not used to such attention: United Center at Texas Tech. If Knight's Red Raiders beat UNLV on Thursday, December 28, it would give him 880 career victories and the major-college men's basketball record. The afternoon of the game, Havlicek—and Gary Gearhart, and a classmate who was the student manager of those great Buckeye teams, Eddie Gottlieb—came in from different points but arrived on the same shuttle flight from Dallas at Lubbock airport. There was a car to greet them. Knight was the driver, poking a hole in his always regimented Game Day schedule to be there for his friends. They went to a barbecue place for a light afternoon meal and some needling, some chatting. They separated when time to play came and reconvened afterward in Knight's private quarters just off the court. In between, UNLV spoiled everything and won. The record, the celebrating, didn't come off that night.

Havlicek and all the others had commitments that would take them away before the next chance (four days later, on New Year's afternoon against New Mexico). The loss hanging in the air like a black cloud, nevertheless the travelers went out with Knight for a postgame meal.

Conversation was not gloomy—nor was it close to the celebration that it would have been, a lot just left unsaid. The next morning, Knight took Havlicek to breakfast, drove him to the airport, and their parting was hard. At curbside at the airport, Havlicek's luggage out of the trunk and ready for him to carry to his flight, Knight steeled himself and semi-choked out an apology, for—by friendship—bringing Havlicek across most of the continent, fruitlessly. Havlicek was as close to choking as Knight, telling him he was *glad* he had been there, and that he would be just as glad—wherever he was—when that record did come, as he knew it would. It happened in that New Mexico game, by a breathless 70–68, a 3-point Lobo shot in the air at the buzzer missing by not very much. ESPN and Dick Vitale carried that game live across the land, to Havlicek wherever he was and to everybody else. It was a weekend for nostalgists, for the record book, and for close friends.

Bill Parcells, a part of our wild Washington trip, was another achiever whom Knight followed as the kind of fan only a friend can be. That relationship started when, during Knight's six years as head basketball coach at Army, Parcells was a young assistant coach on the football staff there headed by Tom Cahill, his New Jersey high school football coach. Parcells, who had played high school basketball under a friend of Knight's, Mickey Corcoran, became almost a volunteer assistant to Knight in their years together at West Point—attending practices, sitting on the bench during games, traveling with the team to some road games. One of those road nights, Parcells sat with Knight through a contentious finish in a hostile arena. After the game, a tough Army loss, Knight walked with his team toward the locker room, his head down and mind locked into the game. As he was leaving the court through a portal, a man leaned over a rail and swung and missed with a punch that Knight never noticed. Parcells, walking right behind, saw it and delivered a punch of his own, smack into the face of the hothead, and walked right on. A little time passed. After Knight had finished talking to his team and the press, Parcells said, "Uh, Bobby," pulled him aside, and told him what had happened. By then, outside the locker room door, the fan was claiming assault and police were gathering. The Army team left with Parcells disguised in a priest's apparel —who knows where it came from?—unspotted, and the budding career of a future football Hall of Fame coach survived.

Their developing careers divided them, but Parcells and Knight maintained close contact. Parcells left West Point in 1970 for what became assistant coaching roles at Florida State, Vanderbilt, and Texas Tech. In 1978, Parcells began his head coaching career at Air Force, then moved into the NFL as a Giants assistant. In 1983, when Knight already had two NCAA championships logged at Indiana, Parcells became the Giants' head coach. In 1986–87, the Giants won Super Bowl XXI—two months before Knight won his third NCAA championship at New Orleans. Parcells repeated with the Giants four years later, and Knight frequently made September and October trips to go through Game Day and stand behind the bench area during Giants—or, later, Dallas Cowboys—games.

Through those NFL years, Parcells was a regular visitor to Bloomington, especially in February when the NFL annually held its scouting combine in Indianapolis. That usually was the occasion for a night out at Bloomington's most noted steakhouse, Little Zagreb. Parcells' young assistant coach, Bill Belichick, came along a time or two, at least once so did New York radio personality Mike Francesca. But the table conversation was all Knight and Parcells, some of it serious coaching stuff, more laugh-filled story-telling, usually from their West Point days. Belichick previewed his later-signature tight-lipped persona by saying almost nothing, attentive but basically joining Francesca and me in listening.

Baseball manager Tony LaRussa showed up in Bloomington in late October 1990, momentarily down, manager of the Oakland team that had just powered its way to the American League championship but shockingly got swept in the World Series by the Reds. A few weeks later, Knight spoke in Chicago, Tony was there, and—I'm not sure whose idea it was—Tony wound up coming to Bloomington with Bob on a university plane. It was a brief touchdown; they then rode with the team and the rest of us on that same plane to Fort Wayne for a preseason intrasquad exhibition game. LaRussa's explanation for his extemporaneous adventure: he wanted to observe the inside of how Bob Knight operated leading up to a game, travel and all; during a game; and afterward.

A close, lasting friendship came out of that. I wasn't privy to many top-level coaches or managers in such circumstances, but among those I did see, Tony came closest to Knight in the emotional bottoming-out he plunged into after defeat—*every* defeat. In the summer of 2003, LaRussa was managing the St. Louis Cardinals. Knight spoke at a Green Bay Packers event in Milwaukee, then flew to St. Louis to meet me for a two-day stopover we had arranged that included two Cardinals night games—sandwiched around a lunchtime visit Knight wanted to make to an ailing special friend, Jimmy Russo (fig. 4.2). Jimmy, by then in his 80s, had been labeled baseball's "Super Scout" when his advance work before the 1966 Baltimore Orioles' shocking World Series sweep of the Sandy Koufax–Don Drysdale Dodgers got cover treatment from *Sports Illustrated*. Like me he was a Huntington, Indiana, native—we collaborated on my first as-told-to autobiography, *Super Scout*. He had adopted IU basketball under Knight as his off-season passion, regularly making a December trip to Bloomington to catch a couple of games and practices. It was Jimmy who, at spring training one year, introduced Knight to Ted Williams, launching that friendship that took two fly fishermen to waters here, there, and everywhere, Russia included.

It was a timely visit; Jimmy hadn't been out of his home for weeks, but that day he chose the lunch spot and reveled in matching memories with Knight. That winter he died, his the lead obituary in that day's *New York Times* section.

And the baseball part of the trip? The first night went fine; Bob's pal Tony's Cardinals won (figs. 4.3, 4.4). The second night, they didn't. The Phillies' Jim Thome, on his way to 2018 Hall of Fame induction, was the reason. A Peoria native, Thome was a Knight-IU basketball fan himself—came to Bloomington for a game one night with his dad and two brothers, each of them massively built, renowned softball sluggers back home but as genial as Big Jim over pizza and stroms with Knight after a Hoosier win. This night, Thome hit two home runs, the second a game winner in extra innings.

4.2. Jimmy Russo—"Super Scout" intent at the ballpark, even in retirement.

LaRussa had arranged in advance to go to dinner after the game with Knight at former Cardinal Mike Shannon's restaurant. Thome happened to go there, too, his table close. Cardinals trainer Barry Weinberg, an Indiana University graduate who did some student training with Knight's basketball team in the coach's early Bloomington years, came with LaRussa, surprised that the ultracompetitive manager he knew well would go anywhere socially after a lost game. It was a labored dinner, LaRussa doing his best to be hospitable to Knight but in no mood to break bread cheerfully with a man who had just beaten him—amiable as Thome is, as much of a Knight friend as LaRussa

4.3. Cardinals manager Tony LaRussa in his office with "adviser" Bob Knight.

4.4. Behind the batting cage, Bob Knight and longtime Cardinals legend Red Schoendienst.

is. Nothing ugly happened, but Tony was clearly uncomfortable, and uncharacteristically quiet. I drove Bob to the airport the next morning and remarked that I couldn't believe how one loss could so devastate a man whose team plays 162 times every season. Bob just stared at me, shocked that I couldn't understand Tony's depression, 162 games or not. Soulmates.

In 1992, when his very good Indiana team let a Big Ten championship slip away with a late-season shooting slump, Bob saw no tournament hope for the team and accepted a late-offered afternoon speaking engagement in Phoenix on the Monday of Final Four week. Surprise! By that Monday his Indiana team had come back together so spectacularly well that it was in the Final Four, matched against favored defending champion Duke. It was spring break on campus, so the team practiced with him Monday morning, was lined up for film-watching time in the afternoon to reassemble that evening, and Bob talked me into flying with him by private jet to Phoenix for his talk. With a two-hour time difference between Bloomington and Phoenix, we got there early enough that we first swung by the A's spring-training camp in Phoenix. It was morning, activities hadn't started yet, so Knight and LaRussa stood on the edge of the outfield grass on an idle diamond, swapping conversation and needles. All of a sudden, from the A's dugout came a shout. "Hey, Knight! Take a chair!" And a wooden chair came flying from the dugout 120 feet away, to within a few feet of Knight and LaRussa—surely a world-record chair throw in obvious parody of Knight's more infamous toss seven years before. In the distant dugout, grinning, was a man strong enough to make the heave: future record-breaking slugger Mark McGwire. (The interrupted practice time didn't hurt Knight's team. That Saturday, the beautifully prepared Hoosiers made one of the most lamented efforts in IU history, putting Duke into a stunning, deep hole early before suddenly accumulated foul trouble took one Hoosier after another out—a Knight-career-high four fouling out by game's end—and the Blue Devils got through, 81–78. Ever after, with some subsequent fortification, game official Ted Valentine's name has been anathema in Hoosierland.)

After LaRussa left Oakland to manage the St. Louis Cardinals, a trade reunited him with McGwire. Through his record year, controversial later with his feat drug tainted but wildly popular at the time, McGwire had frequent conversations with Knight. McGwire gave him the bat he used to hit one of his milestone homers.

Knight and LaRussa remained so close they could argue hotly, even break off relationships for a while, but still be friends. Somewhere in their conversing, an unconventional baseball idea was hatched, its fatherhood somewhat in question. During the epic McGwire–Sammy Sosa home run chase of 1996, Knight frequented Busch Stadium and LaRussa's office adjacent to the team's clubhouse, often at other times talked to him on the phone. As McGwire headed unstoppably toward his ultimate record 70 home runs (to Sosa's 66), LaRussa acknowledged wrestling with how to make those home runs more valuable: how to get more people on base in front of McGwire. With no one on base, McGwire that year rarely saw a good pitch, walks frequent. Even one man on base when he came up made it different, and more valuable for LaRussa when McGwire's homers were for two, three, or four runs—not solo. I'm an American League fan. I mentioned once to Knight that in that league, with a designated hitter eliminating the pitcher from the batting order, the ninth hitter was often not the weakest hitter on the team but a good on-base man, preferably fast, a virtual second leadoff man tasked with getting on base ahead of the power hitters to come. Knight reasoned out loud: "Why couldn't they do that in the National League? Who says the pitcher has to bat ninth?" Soon thereafter, LaRussa was the talk of baseball because—though history showed times when it had been done before—Tony alone among 1990s peers moved his pitcher up to eighth in the order and after the first inning always had two good base-reaching threats at ninth and leadoff ahead of third hitter McGuire. The kindest of LaRussa's immediate critics screamed "Sacrilege! It's just, just not *right* that anybody but the pitcher bats last—it's *humiliating* to a regular-lineup guy to hit ninth." Those purists/critics rejoiced every time a Cardinals pitcher batting eighth came up with a scoring opportunity and made the final out of the inning. But there were at least as many times when the two "leadoff" guys batting consecutively started things rolling toward an attractive situation for McGwire, exactly the intent of the change.

It was a tactic solely identified with LaRussa until 2015, when American League veteran Joe Maddon of the Cubs and others reintroduced the pitcher-batting-eighth idea in the National League. *Sports Illustrated* writer and MLB Network commentator Tim Kurkjian in addressing the resurfaced approach said he understood the idea really started with a college basketball coach: Knight. Whatever. LaRussa obviously deserves primary credit (or blame). Even if Knight and he did discuss it, Tony was the only one who could actually implement it, and he did—*then* some others, most notably Maddon. And whatever the purists' disdain for outside-the-box thinking in a by-the-book sport, *I* think—for the unusual McGwire situation—it was ingenious.

Proximity made the boy Bob Knight a Cleveland Indians fan, his native Orrville an easy car ride away. The Indians were strong then, winning the 1948 World Series (when Knight, about to turn 8, was a second grader) and going 110–44 to get in it again in 1954 (14, eighth grade). Geography—his coaching job in Bloomington—similarly gave him attachment to the best baseball team of the mid-1970s, the "Big Red Machine" at Cincinnati. In '75 and '76, when the Reds won World Championships, Knight had his own Big Red Machine going at its best in IU basketball. Hospitality worked both ways. Winter nights Reds players and executives frequented Hoosier games at Assembly Hall. Summer nights Knight had no problem getting tickets in the sold-out ballpark, primarily thanks to Reds publicity director Jim Ferguson, who had covered Knight's Ohio State teams as a Dayton sportswriter and made Knight a regular in the Reds' stands and clubhouse. Knight developed friendships with manager Sparky Anderson, successor John McNamara, and all the Hall of Fame–caliber stars of that storied era—Johnny Bench, Pete Rose, Joe Morgan, Tony Perez, the whole brilliant group. In the 1976–77 basketball season, Knight's Indiana team struggled without its graduated champions and—no NCAA tournament to prepare for—in March he headed for Florida and joined the twice-World Series-champion Reds in spring training. Marquette and North Carolina played for the 1977 NCAA championship. The day of the game, Reds players massed around Knight looking for inside information: Who's going to win? Both coaches involved, Al McGuire of Marquette and Dean Smith of North Carolina, were close Knight friends, but he had no hesitation: "Has to be Carolina," he said. Marquette won. Next morning, when Knight arrived for the Reds' workout, he was barraged from the dugout with baseballs, gloves, all sorts of debris, including verbal. A good possibility: a dollar or two had gone down the drain with their inside information, from the most virulently antigambling coach in sports.

Bench was closest to Knight among the Reds stars. It cost him once: Johnny took some buckshot in his butt from a Knight friend's stray shot in a fall bird-hunting outing near Bloomington. Still, Johnny was a frequent guest at IU basketball games, and in retirement he was there when the '87 Hoosiers won the national championship at New Orleans. Bench—who named his son Robert (only he knows if there was a Knight touch to that)—was the one of the Big Red Machine group Knight always gave all-time esteem: the best catcher ever, he maintained. He loved a supportive stat that I gave him from my own box-score perusings: in postseason games for his full career, Bench—known for his slugging and run production and brilliant catching skills, everything but his running speed—stole more bases than opponents stole on him. You can look it up.

Book Five

FRIENDSHIPS AND RELATIONSHIPS

WHAT HOWARD HOUGHTON WAS TO ME AT MY CAREER START, what Perry Stewart was in enabling its apex, a non-newspaperman named Bill Cook was in its twilight: a door opener, totally without any initiative or instigation by me.

I was just about to turn 70, still writing a Sunday *Herald-Times* op-ed column and operating out of the basement "lair" Michael Koryta described in this book's preface, when two things happened:

1. Bill Cook, who with wife Gayle started a medical device manufacturing company in Bloomington, had in 30-some years grown that two-person, spare-bedroom operation into a global giant that made him the richest man in Indiana. I always planned in my retirement years to do some biographies. Bill Cook's was my No. 1 target—I didn't have any idea how that shoestring-to-colossus thing happened or even who this Bill Cook was, so I was pretty sure most of Bloomington didn't, either. Before I did anything to initiate something, in late-September 2006, Bill reached out to me and asked if I would be interested in doing such a book. Bingo!

2. To facilitate the interviewing and research essential for such a project, Bill gave me an office in his company's world-head-quarters building, a considerable step up from my *Herald-Times* "office." I loved that weekly column, even that lair, and figured I could do both book and column and shuttle back and forth between offices, till I went to lunch with editor Bob Zaltsberg one November day. We're good, longtime friends; where we ate was close, so after eating I took him to the Cook building and showed him the office. From a chair across the desk from

5.1. Bill Cook and Bob Hammel—book partners (Cook, Inc. photo arrangement by Mike Galimore).

me, the exact spot where Bill Cook was sitting almost daily for tape-recorded conversations that were the heart of *The Bill Cook Story—Ready, Fire, Aim,* Zaltsberg carried out the I'm sure unpleasant job of telling me I would have to move out of the newspaper location because the *Herald-Times* needed that basement space. I could keep submitting a weekly column if I wanted but payment—$250 a week for it and some semi-volunteer editing work—would cease as of January 1.

It ceased sooner; a few days after our conversation, I moved out Thanksgiving weekend and left a farewell column behind.

Bill Cook kept me too fascinated and too busy for that abrupt farewell to journalism to carry any remorse. And a decade later I still have that Cook office, never an employee but a convinced devotee of that Cook culture after being immersed in it (fig. 5.1).

Writing the book took about seven months. Production took some more, so it was early 2008 when it came out—to, I must say, exceptionally generous coverage by Zaltsberg and his *H-T* staff, particularly reviewer-interviewer Rebecca Troyer.

5.2. As a byproduct of working out of a Cook, Inc. office to do a biography of company founder Bill Cook, fitness advocate Cook signed me into workout membership that opened valued friendships with Cook architect George Ridgway and "coach" Grace Cissell—with T-shirts that united us in "Grace's Breakfast Club."

The "Ready, Fire, Aim" part of the title was Bill Cook's idea. That was his operating style: Don't waste time getting a job done. Plan it ("Ready"), launch it ("Fire"), and if adjustments are needed, make them ("Aim"). In the health business, of course that "Ready" part included more than due diligence regarding planning and testing. Just no tarrying.

I had a lot of terminology to learn (I still have my well-thumbed paperback 500-page *Dictionary of Medical Terms*) in those almost daily 30-to-40-minute interview sessions—really, conversations—with him, a tape recorder in between us (fig. 5.2). My hunch was right. There *was* an astonishing story in what Bill and Gayle Cook had done, what they were, what they were leaving as their legacy to Bloomington, to Indiana, to his boyhood hometown of Canton, Illinois, to their world. They lived as simply as billionaires as they did when their bank account was several zeroes short of that, when early-days business was so sparse they celebrated each incoming sales check by going out with infant son Carl for a McDonald's "dinner." Carl eventually succeeded his dad and continued the Cook company culture, including a uniquely personal brand of tailored philanthropy that touched lots of fields but carried the Cook stamp best in restoring treasured buildings. Restoration came with one insistence: the work wouldn't just preserve the building's beauty but must restore it to its original function. Downtown Canton and downtown Bloomington are two glorious examples. More spectacular ones are the luxury hotels a mile apart in back-roads southwestern Indiana, at West Baden and French Lick. Those magnificent hotels were world-class centers of splendor when they went up as bitter rivals around 1900 but, like the tiny communities around them, almost desolate and near collapse when the Cooks put a half-billion dollars into their restoration—not preservation, *restoration*, because they are the centers of a thriving resort now in those revived, spirited twin towns.

The book came out in 2008; Bill was 80 when he died of congestive heart failure in 2011. A few years later Gayle called me, noting that Bill lived almost four years after the last writing on his biography, four Bill Cook years, which means highly productive. "Could you add a couple of chapters to the book to cover those years and make it a full biography?" she suggested. I started in on a remake, quickly saw those four years deserved much more than two chapters, learned some significant other things about the illness that cost him his life, about his final days, and more, and the result was *The Bill Cook Story II—The Re-Visionary* (fig. 5.3), that last word not to be confused with revisionist, as in history rewriters and distorters. It described a man—and his wife—gifted in visualizing how decayed relics could be rejuvenated and revived.

I learned of Bill's death late on a Friday afternoon while riding in a car toward a dinner appointment in Indianapolis. The next day, Julie and I and all in the Cook orbit had been scheduled to attend the opening and dedication of his last restoration project: of the deteriorated, storied Central Avenue Methodist Church—"Old Centrum"—just north of downtown Indianapolis. Bill and Gayle, and a guest group that happened to include Indiana governor Mitch Daniels, the Saturday before had attended the first event in the "new" church, a wedding. Bill made one last pre-dedication inspection tour on Tuesday, then, with every intention to be there for the gala Saturday, entered Bloomington Hospital for weekly treatment on Thursday, and died on Friday.

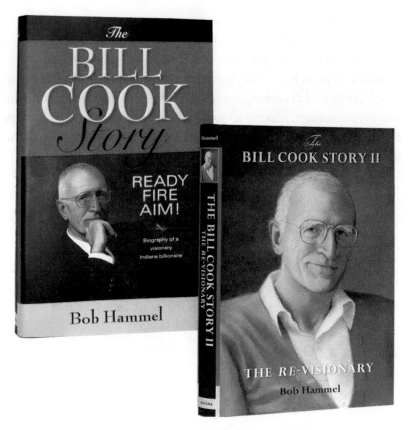

5.3. The biography, plus, of an entrepreneur extraordinaire (Indiana University Press books).

Of course his death stunned me. But even then, even while feeling shocked and despondent, I couldn't suppress a smile—at how all those typical Bill Cook make-every-day-count hurry-up elements of his final days reminded me of the classic William Cullen Bryant poem *Thanatopsis*, and primarily its closing stanza, on how best to approach impending death:

> So live, that when thy summons comes to join
> The innumerable caravan, which moves
> To that mysterious realm, where each shall take
> His chamber in the silent halls of death,
> Thou go not, like the quarry-slave at night,
> Scourged to his dungeon . . .

Those schoolboy-memorized lines juxtaposed so perfectly with Bill's final days that I ran through them in my mind and thought, "Boy, he sure *didn't* go like a quarry slave, cowering in any dungeon . . ."

That was years before Gayle's call . . . before I wrote *Bill Cook II* in which Gayle told of coming home to find Bill had died there while she was, on his request, picking up some relatives arriving for the next-day dedication . . . years before I wrote in that book her memory of how she found his lifeless body when she got home that late afternoon:

> Bill was upstairs, lying on the couch. He had taken a shower, put a robe on, and lay down on the couch. He wasn't trying to call 9-1-1, he didn't fall down on the floor, he just took a nap.

And, alone, he died.

Not till long after the book was published did I on a whim pull out *Thanatopsis* and read on beyond the lines familiar to me, on to the closing ones that say, rather, how the poet felt death *should* be met:

> . . . but, sustained and soothed
> By an unfaltering trust, approach thy grave,
> Like one who wraps the drapery of his couch
> About him, and lies down to pleasant dreams.

Almost exactly 200 years before, Bryant recommended exactly what Bill Cook did. Gayle was convinced Bill knew his time had come—not through any eerie prescience but his own studied knowledge of how the human body works. Like the doctor he had once aspired to be, he knew, with his heart problems, what had happened to him in that last-minute "routine" hospital stop—a sudden decline in low blood pressure recovery—meant death was close. He accepted it in Bryant-recommended peace, and Gayle's description coincided with the poet's even to the word "couch."

More telling about Bill Cook, though, was how well his life fit the first part, the one that starts "So live . . ."

Those years with Bill Cook are the final example of how, throughout my 65-year professional life, sheer luck dealt me a continuingly lucky and winning hand.

Luckier, I've asked myself, in people met or in events covered? People I got to know who were world-famous for their achievements and brilliance—or my exposure to history that my education and credentials in no way qualified me for?

I claim both. Great fortune squared.

But of the two, the people were my favorite.

I always was inclined to like, and to empathize with, coaches I covered, especially some. Maybe having a brother as a coach contributed to that, but it was evident much earlier.

The Bob Knight of my early years was the last basketball coach I covered at Huntington High School. Bob Straight was as tall as Knight, as demanding as Knight, as inclined—even determined—as Knight not to go the popular route toward high-scoring, up-and-down play but to win by insisting his teams took nothing but good shots at one end of the court and minimized those at the other. I left Huntington in 1963, and right through to his death at 92 in November 2018, Bob Straight was one of my closest friends. A Hammond native and fellow Chicago White Sox fan, he and I—and frequently one or both of my brothers —for many summers picked out one or two midweek afternoon Sox games and went. His and my accumulating age finally ended that, but we picked a great denouement—July 23, 2009, when the Sox' Mark Buehrle pitched the ultimate baseball rarity: a perfect game (fig. 5.4).

Bob Straight was also one great high school coach, the greatest in my own ranking. He coached the best Huntington team ever (27–2 and state runner-up in 1964) and the best Huntington basketball era. I was there when he went into the Indiana Basketball Hall of Fame, and when the floor today's Vikings play on formally became Bob Straight Court.

Bob Knight knew of Straight and his Huntington program before Knight arrived in Indiana. In his earliest days as IU coach, Knight engaged Straight as an early Indiana high school coaching link and reliable talent evaluator. The two became great friends. Straight rarely made it to Bloomington but regularly went to much-closer West Lafayette when IU played at Purdue. There and everywhere else, Knight always stayed in a locker room during pregame warmups, emerging just before

5.4. Bob Straight, with brother Bill Hammel at Mark Buehrle's perfect game in 2009.

the tipoff. At Purdue, Straight would spend the last pregame half hour secluded with Knight, talking, then walk with him through the doors out onto and across the Mackey Arena court. Stride for stride they'd walk toward the IU bench, and of course lusty boos accompanied them. Once Knight looked over to Straight en route and said, "What the hell did you *do* to piss these people off so much?"

There's a powerful bonding experience in the day-to-day business of putting out a newspaper. That's my best explanation for how close four of us from four different towns became over a period that spanned 50 years and never really ended. Tom Schumaker—"Jack"—was one

5.5. My lifelong friends from many, many newsroom combinations—Skip Hess, Jeff Smithburn, and Tom "Jack" Schumaker.

of them, Jeff Smithburn and Skip Hess the others (fig. 5.5). Each of us worked together in about every possible combination at Wabash, Kokomo, and/or Bloomington. Skip's entry into the business, straight out of the army, was as the first person I ever hired: to assist me in sports at Kokomo. He succeeded me there when I left for Indianapolis and later went to the Indianapolis *News* himself, then into the Indiana Journalism Hall of Fame for his reporting skills. Tom was the best user of talent I've ever seen, not exploitatively but as a newsroom concertmeister. A splendid writer and reporter himself, he was unmatched at coaxing or cajoling outstanding work from his staff. Jeff, intelligent and devilishly witty, didn't stay in newspapers long, finding a better payoff in Price Waterhouse accounting. A genuinely gifted writer, he had something of a blog before such a cyberthing existed—irreverent, merciless, wonderful. Those three words, with "laugh-filled" and "noisy" added, pretty much described our get-togethers: one or two a year for maybe 25 years, until Skip retired to Florida. Our last time together was probably our best behaved: at Skip's Hall of Fame induction ceremony in 2012. Correspondence among us, sometimes indelicate, never stopped.

≈

Newspapering introduced me to some other Bloomington-area people as high in their own fields as anyone I covered.

One of my duties after sports retirement was heading up planning for expanding our Sunday edition after the parent Schurz chain through newspaper purchases extended our Sunday circulation into nearby Martinsville and Mooresville. My first expansion venture was planning and weekly delivering a Views editorial section. I set out to engage 13 regional writers to do one column every three months on whatever topic they wished. I aimed very high—among them IU history professor Robert Ferrell, who had written several books on Harry Truman and other presidents; James Alexander Thom, the best novelist-historian I know of, in Jim's case particularly on the Lewis and Clark expansion era and Native American–US relationships; Dennis Reardon, an extraordinary playwright and IU professor with Broadway credits; and Janos Starker, a spectacularly gifted, world-acclaimed cellist who wouldn't seem to fit in a writing group.

Cellist Starker definitely did fit, as a columnist neither miscast nor a happenstance choice. As he often did with people brilliantly successful in other fields, Bob Knight invited Janos to speak to one of his basketball teams. I listened in and was struck by how this man of no real basketball knowledge—with words, not his performing artistry—grasped and held full attention of his young listeners, among them All-American Isiah Thomas. I wrote about it, so when I wrote to invite him to join the new venture, Janos knew me, knew I was serious, and to my delight accepted enthusiastically. He submitted some extraordinary columns, a few of which appeared later in his autobiography.

Moreover, in appreciation of the opportunity he gave my wife Julie and me a night that went way past extraordinary. He invited us and two other couples to have dinner with him and wife Rae at their Bloomington home. That was exquisite, as was the conversation. But nothing in my life's experience compares with what followed: the true definition of chamber music, Janos on his cello and retired IU School of Music Dean Charles Webb accompanying on piano.

The blessings of Bloomington . . .

≈

The resident saint of Bloomington when I was a student, when I came back as a newspaperman, and long before and after either point in time, was the school's 25-year president and virtual forever president, Herman B Wells.

Anyone with Indiana University familiarity knows of Dr. Wells' eminence, his impact, his unimaginable personal identification with everything and everyone around him.

That included even a local sportswriter. Never did I get an award or a recognition without arrival within a day or two of a congratulatory note from Herman. Those are a treasured collection. At the 1996 roast marking my retirement, he distinguished it incomparably just by coming, then in his follow-up note that time apologized for having to leave early—as if at 93 any kind of explanation was needed. That note is among my preserved Hermanisms.

Once, when America was about to attack Iraq, I used my sports column to deplore the idea, to object to sending the kind of young men I was used to covering to fight and inevitably die in a war I considered over oil, over wealth. Herman's note that time was more personal than any, most treasured of all.

An IU professor before Herman Wells became president (1938) and after his death (2000) became one of my favorite Sunday op-ed interviews.

I knew of Henry Remak formally as Professor Remak, but mostly as Henry. Fondly. Respectfully. Henry Remak's son Bruce worked for me during his student years. I knew and liked another son, Ron. For decades I'd heard raves about Henry as an IU teacher, a lecturer. It wasn't until 2004 that one day I thought of him in column terms: Henry's 88 and still lecturing—is there anybody else like that at IU? At any college?

No, I decided after an afternoon conversation with him at a quiet Bloomington restaurant with a tape recorder whirring between us. We talked of his own education and background, of the challenge and the fun an octogenarian has in teaching today's kids, of the day a teenaged student told him his was his favorite class and, pressed, explained it wasn't because of content or lecture quality, "You remind me of my grandpa!"

Mostly though, that afternoon this professor of comparative literature taught me comparative history.

He was a boy who grew up Jewish, in Berlin, in the years that elevated Adolf Hitler to dictatorship. That emboldened me as a superior American to ask him to explain my greatest enigma of the twentieth century: How did his country—so universally admired for its sophisticated culture and its standing in public education—let that happen?

It could happen here, he said. In 2004.

Henry was born in Berlin in 1916, when his father, a World War I railroad engineer with the German army, was in France. The war's end, Germany's defeat, heavy reparations demanded by England and France—that created the chaotic Germany of infant Henry's first memories. "Right after the war was over, 1918, there was a civil war. The new republican government, run by moderate socialists, was opposed by the Communists. There was shooting in the streets. My brother—I was 3, he was 4—and I had a playroom, facing the streets. My dad came in and said very quietly, 'You'd better play in the bedroom. There's too much shooting in the streets.' I never forgot that.

"Then there was inflation. When I was 7, my father gave me money and sent me to the bank to get some change. The bank teller had a big bowl filled with money and said, 'Help yourself.'

"But then the government stabilized and Germany had five very successful years of the Weimar Republic."

Then: the Great Depression—everywhere. Hardship, unemployment, desperation . . .

And in 1933: Hitler.

There Henry's reminiscing became personal. Analytical. Philosophical.

"Most people have a good childhood and a good adolescence, they don't have responsibilities, and the real adventure starts when they are on their own. With me, it was the other way around. My most dramatic and existential times came before I was 20."

Most dramatic of all was being a young Jew in Berlin and watching Hitler come to power . . . not by revolution but by the ballot box . . . in accord with Germany's constitution, stretched a bit—then a lot. "It could happen here . . ."

So, Henry, how did it happen in Germany?

He keyed his explanation around a word I'd never heard associated with Hitler. Patience. And timing—a cunning sense of when to seize new ground and when to pull back a little, and wait. In a Germany so desperate for self-worth, a brazen new leader seemed of little risk. In a nation that had gone through so much and now was starving, witness Henry Remak recalled Hitler promising "'I will get you jobs.' Very, very smart." That promise, woven in among his Super Race and viciously antisemitic ravings and his speaking magnetism, in 1933 won his Nazi party more seats in the German parliament than any other party, not a majority but an edge. And a wedge.

Henry recalled, "On January 30, 1933, I was skating on a lake in Berlin when my father came waving a newspaper that said Hitler had become chancellor. My father was an intelligent man, and he said, 'That is the thing to do. The way to fight radicalism, like the Nazis, is to bring them into a coalition government.'" To pass legislation and govern, he reasoned, Hitler and the Nazis would have to work with moderates to get majority votes. "What my father didn't realize," Henry started, "was . . ."

All Adolf Hitler needed was a foothold. Quickly, he turned marginal control into dictatorship—at home, then with growing aggressiveness outside his borders. He won the election flaunting his flaming antisemitism, and he put it into action immediately against Jewish merchants and citizenry. But for a while Berlin and even some German Jews saw his Nazi government as brutal and rights-trampling but endurable, so much so, witness Henry Remak recalled, that "in 1935, some of our German Jewish friends, who had emigrated, came back to Germany." In 1936, he said, Jews there "were still thinking, 'It can't get much worse.'" They terribly underestimated Hitler's evil, and his cunning. "Hitler was waiting for something that would justify a more radical thing," Henry said. "In December 1938, a Polish Jew shot and killed a German diplomat in Paris—exactly what he was waiting for. That's when he rounded up all Jewish men under 60." In horror, Henry Remak said, Berlin Jews watched Hitler's brown-shirted thugs do their arresting "very quietly," at 2 in the morning, not smashing down doors, not terrorizing neighborhoods. Henry remembered it as evil, shrewdly cloaked—"the cleverness: coming at night, at 2 o'clock, no noise . . . being nasty to Jews but keeping them well enough that they could use them."

Henry saw the intent of those 1930s roundups as extortion, not extermination, and expulsion of those arrested Jews and their families— "ethnic cleansing," in Nazi terms, but short of slaughter. "Hitler wanted their businesses and their money, and to get them to leave Germany." The wealthiest obviously didn't want to leave, thus forfeiting their money and property to the Nazis, "but if you have a choice of being in a concentration camp or getting out, you'll sell everything you have," Henry said.

Those who didn't went to concentration camps brutal but different from the ones with gas ovens at Auschwitz and Dachau that the word "Holocaust" and its six million victims were to symbolize, Henry said. "People today don't know that he waited with the Holocaust until there was a war."

As close as the western world was watching World War II play out, the first that most citizens of the Allied nations knew of what really was happening at Nazi concentration camps came when, as war in Europe was ending in April 1945, American and allied troops went in to Dachau, Auschwitz and others to free captive Jews and found walking skeletons, and those furnaces. Before he reached 30, Henry Remak watched his beloved country go from ballot-box choice to Hitler's Third Reich: twelve years of cold, contrived, and calculated evil that patiently followed a plan, nationally and internationally.

Again, Henry. How?

"Hitler," the patient uberprofessor began, "was very smart. In every meeting with the French or the British, he won. He said, 'The last thing I am going to do is the occupation of Austria.' Well, the French and British thought, 'after all the Austrians *are* German-speaking . . .'

"Same with Poland. He was diabolic, but very, very smart."

By late 1936, Henry was watching it all from afar: from safety in the United States, from Bloomington. But he knew the terror. "My father was in a concentration camp. He owned a factory. They let him out to run it because they needed the precision parts his factory produced.

Then they took the factory for much less than it was worth." In 1939, his father and the rest of Henry's family made it out, to America.

Henry died at 92 in 2009, a year or two after finally retiring from his beloved classroom. That day of our interview in 2004, he said,

"I was lucky. So much is just luck. What is *not* luck is how you cope with a situation. For me, good German that I still feel that I am, strongly influenced by German culture, I became an outcast because of my religion. Totally unexpected."

So was his life in Indiana. His father lived out his American years in California, but Henry merrily recalled a Bloomington visit John Hans Remak made.

"He said, 'Henry, you are really in a racket. You do between 8 and 5 what you love to do: teaching literature, teaching students, being in a stimulating atmosphere, on a very attractive campus, in a town where you don't waste any time getting around—and you get paid for it.'

"I must say he had a point."

I am not really a jazz fan. I analyze my own love of music as best triggered by familiarity, by recognition. I didn't initially care for Elvis, or the Beatles—or, earlier, for Frank Sinatra and Glenn Miller, Rodgers and Hammerstein—till I had heard their songs enough times that I could anticipate and more richly savor particular phases. Jazz is the antithesis: improvisation, not repetition—artistic takeoffs that jar my expectations.

But I went to a lot of Bloomington jazz concerts because one of my favorite people was the late IU jazz professor, writer, performer, Hall of Famer David Baker (fig. 5.6).

David and I once talked of collaborating on a biography, to be based more on his growing-up years in Indianapolis and his profound grasp of the world around him than his music itself. We taped some preparatory interviews toward that, and his stories were golden:

. . . of spending winter nights in his early teens with his like-minded peers listening from the cold streets outside to some of America's greatest jazz artists, among them homegrown Indianapolis stars Wes Montgomery, Slide Hampton et al . . .of his own big-band experiences

5.6. David Baker—jazz professor, writer, performer, Hall of Famer.
Photo courtesy of Indiana University Archives.

under Stan Kenton, Count Basie, and Lionel Hampton . . .of making *Billboard*'s cover as upcoming young artist of the year.

. . . of how wrong I was in presuming mixed bands meant music was way ahead of America in integration, that even at Carnegie Hall white musicians entered one door, blacks another . . . how mixed bands south of the Mason-Dixon lines played separately: all-white performers for some numbers, all-black for others . . . and even in the North, whites stayed in hotels and black band members each kept a book on African American families who would have a room for them.

. . . of how movies well into the 1950s were so race conscious regarding love scenes that when Louie Armstrong on film sang "Jeepers creepers, where'd you get those peepers," he had to sing it to a horse.

. . . of how as a boy in Indianapolis he had to walk his younger sister Shirley to school, and—though the two adored each other to their last days on earth—he insisted she stay a few feet behind him so potential girlfriends wouldn't think he already had one . . . how once when he and Shirley arrived home and their stepmother had left them pieces of cake, he grabbed the much bigger one and, left the smaller, Shirley cried . . . and from there the dialogue went:

"Whatcha *cryin'* about?"

"You took the *big* piece."

"What would *you* have done?"

"*I'd* have taken the smaller one."

"Then *whatcha cryin'* about?"

It would have been a terrific book—and a wonderful experience.

In three stunning days in spring 2018, because of a fall that caused fatal brain injuries, we of Bloomington lost former IU football coach Bill Mallory. In that dark time while he hovered near death in those final hours, thoughts like that—of a book that could have and should have been done—flitted in and out among other memories for me. This was a Hall of Fame coach who paid for his loyalty to Indiana University by—while vastly exceeding in on-field success any recent predecessor or successor—losing enough games to drop him below the Hall of Fame's unrealistic winning-percentage requirements.

That didn't keep Bill Mallory from being a Hall of Fame human being. He and wife Ellie were the Bloomington couple closest to Julie and me while the four of us passed astoundingly similar milestones. Julie and Bill were a few years apart in age but their birthdays (Bill's May 30, Julie's June 3) were so close the four of us would always work a dinner in for combined celebration; Ellie and I were born a day apart in October, so that was another time for us to go out; we were married eight days apart, June 14 and June 22, 1958, and somewhere within June 2018 was to be a special time together: our 60th anniversaries. Bill died five days short of his birthday, so those times together didn't happen. But at his Celebration of Life in Bloomington, the turnout included hundreds of his former IU, Miami, Colorado, and Northern Illinois players and their families, and lots of others. We had company in loving the Mallorys.

Modern thinking shaped by contemporary history to the contrary, I prize—unapologetically and still—the familiarity I had with Penn State football coaching legend Joe Paterno.

I didn't hear about or read about Joe, I met Joe. I *knew* Joe. I *liked* Joe and especially liked interviewing him, talking with him.

I mused about that when recently I ran across in my files Paterno comments from some time we talked in 1994—nothing momentous, just pertinent and thought provoking. It was just after Penn State joined the Big Ten and the subject of people who had changed college football came up. And here was this man of the 1990s weighing in on Army's "Touchdown Twins" of the '40s, All-Americans/Heisman Trophy winners Felix "Doc" Blanchard and Glenn Davis—on how he actually saw them play, how as unquestionably great as they were they didn't really qualify as people who changed football.

"My high school coach took me up to the Polo Grounds to watch them play Duke. I think they beat Duke 19–0 and Blanchard hit the second or third play from scrimmage and ran the whole distance."

But . . .

"That Army team was just a matter that all the great athletes were located in one place, and they were playing against people who weren't as great as they were. That's not to say that Davis and Blanchard were not great players. They were. But what they were doing was not different from what anybody else was doing at that time. They just happened to be better.

"I think the people who changed football were the Big Eight in '68 and '69, when they put those kids with super speed at the wideout positions, the Mel Grays, with the big backs and tremendous offensive lines, John Riggins on that Kansas team . . . and maybe Minnesota a little bit prior to that, when they started everybody bringing up those great black athletes from the South. They changed everybody's thinking about how you play."

He got uncomfortable only when—inevitably, because this was a man in his 70s doing a young man's job—the subject of retirement came up. *His* retirement—is it getting close?

"I really *enjoy* coaching," he demurred. And, given that, simply because of age he should quit?

"What am I going to do? There's nothing else I can think of that I would like doing as much, so why should I get out? I don't want to retire and play golf every day.

"I *really* enjoy game days. I don't know what I'd do if I had to sit in the stands on a Saturday.

"I like to be *involved* in the games. I like to see young kids come in, see them grow up and hopefully be a little better after they get out of here than they were when they came in. It has really been fun for me.

"I even enjoy recruiting. I like being with people.

"And I'm *healthy*. I haven't had any problems. I can be on the practice field three and a half hours and it's fun.

"If I could figure out something I would feel would be productive, and I'd enjoy it—I could get up in the morning and look forward to getting something done—I probably would start to think about it. But right now I'm not even thinking about it."

He never got to make that retirement decision. A fast-moving world took that choice away from him, and then he died.

Yes, there were horrendous and heinous wrongs that had direct links to his program. Please don't try to tell me Joe Paterno had any real concept of what was going on with a trusted assistant, who was molesting—criminally and cruelly and repeatedly—young boys. Tell me Joe certainly should have known, some way or another, and I'll agree, just as I agree that for all of Bob Knight's professional and personal virtues, uncontrolled temper too often eroded his pluses with an ogre's ugliness. I see frequent parallels between the reigns and falls, the achievements and the stumbles, of Julius Caesar and Bob Knight in Marc Antony's funeral speech. But I'll also inject an additional persuasion: that the Joe Paternos and Bob Knights who genuinely tried to build solid, I'd even use the word pure, college athletic programs paid a much higher price in media vitriol when they stumbled than did the outright cheaters and charlatans who don't even pretend a student-athlete concept and carry on blithely and triumphantly, not just tolerated but revered.

By the time he came into the Bob Knight–Bloomington orbit, David Halberstam already was a big part of America's social conscience. Already written by then were several books establishing Halberstam's eminence, among them

- *The Best and the Brightest,* one of the first scathing insights into the Vietnam war;
- *The Children,* his account as a young *New York Times* reporter of covering and sometimes accompanying the imperiled kids known as Freedom Riders outside and Outside Agitators inside the bitter and brutal '60s South;
- *The Powers That Be,* an inside look at the American press during tumultuous times.

The Knight-Halberstam relationship began when Halberstam set out to write his second sports book, *The Summer of '49.* It covered the fabled post–World War II pennant race that established Joe DiMaggio as the Archetype Winner and Ted Williams as the supertalented Ultimate Loser in a morality myth whose shaping had much to do with the dominance of the New York press. Halberstam, a New Yorker, wanted to play it down the middle with his study of the 1949 pennant race and to do so needed access to Williams—though he never got the same to DiMaggio. He heard that Knight might be able to supply a contact and called to ask. Knight called Williams and told him, "This is a good guy."

That proved enough—Halberstam, surprised to be granted interview time, tucked this into the book's acknowledgments: "Robert Montgomery Knight was valuable serving as Ted Williams's press aid."

Their meeting came when, in the winter of 1984–85, Halberstam agreed to do a story on Indiana's passion for basketball for a special "Portrait of America" *Esquire* magazine edition. Halberstam called Knight, explained his assignment, and Knight told him IU basketball wasn't what he was after, Indiana high school basketball was the soul of the state, and invited him to come out and go with him to a game. It was the year that *Hoosiers*, the magic movie capturing the dreamy romance of Indiana's high school tournament, was just out and wowing the land. The movie fictionalized little Milan's run to the 1954 state championship—the only true replication the film's Jimmy Chitwood standing with ball in hand for long seconds in a tie game before going one-on-one on a cleared-out court to get and hit the championship-winning jump shot at the buzzer, exactly as Bobby Plump did to gain Hoosier immortality for him and his Milan team.

In inviting Halberstam, Knight knew one of the most colorful subsequent Milanish stories was going on very close to Bloomington. L&M, a four-year high school of just 132 total enrollment (Milan had 128 in 1954), had two six-foot-five players who wound up on Big Ten rosters (Jeff Oliphant on Knight's at IU, Tony Patterson at Purdue)—bright kids who became lawyers, excellent shooters whose team was very good. In a state that at the time didn't differentiate between small and large schools, even in its in-season polls and rankings, L&M was in its second year of being a regular in the state-ranked Top 10, sometimes Top 5, a definite Final Four, even state championship threat. In his 2,000-word *Esquire* story, Halberstam described the L&M game Knight took him to, the crowd, and his ride to and from the game in Knight's car: "We rode through the night, a few friends of his, two assistant coaches and two writers."

Hey! . . . "two writers" . . . parallel mention of me with David Halberstam, *by* David Halberstam!

Might be—shoot, *has* to be—the best professional compliment I ever had.

5.7. In a Bloomington appearance a month before his death in an auto wreck, author David Halberstam signs a book for me (Bloomington *Herald-Times* photo by Jeremy Hogan).

After the game that night, we found a late-night Bloomington sandwich stop. The conversation centered on Halberstam's books, and Washington, and opinions—David's unhesitant and informed, inside knowledge on a wide range of topical subjects.

He returned other times, and in April 2007 he was back for some Indiana University speaking appearances (fig. 5.7). One was to the Bloomington Press Club, and I was there as a member. On entering the room, he saw me, walked over, and grabbed me in a hug. In his talk he explained the hug: "Bob and I are veterans of The Battle of Bob Knight." His last book, *The Coldest Winter*, an analysis of the Korean Conflict, was about to come out. Clearly, he loved it, especially loved what it did to give proper tribute to General Matthew Ridgway and the opposite to General Douglas MacArthur. A few weeks later he was dead, at 73 killed in a traffic accident while at Cal Berkeley on another university speaking appearance. My op-ed column that Sunday began with a description of my library at home, particularly the floor-to-ceiling shelves at each end of it: "My real, my inner me." The top row of those shelves

> is book after book—sixteen of them—by a giant we said goodbye to in Bloomington, without knowing it, in the middle of March. David Halberstam died at 73 in a San Francisco auto crash April 23, five weeks to the day after he gave a new bloom to Bloomington on the last of what he acknowledged to be several visits he had made to our little town. His trips always were purposeful. One or two helped supply the key section on Indiana University professor/sex researcher Alfred C. Kinsey in Halberstam's book, *The Fifties.*

In the column I mentioned his relationship with Knight, including Halberstam's using him as an interview subject—'Tell me about coaching Michael Jordan on the 1984 Olympic team'" (for Halberstam's Jordan book, *Playing for Keeps*).

As their relationship developed, Knight graduated to what Halberstam laughingly called his agent, the friend whose recommendation to *his* friends opened for Halberstam doors impenetrable for almost every other author-writer: to Ted Williams (for *Summer of '49*), to Bill Belichick (for *The Education of a Coach*).

The column continued:

> In his Bloomington appearances in March, Halberstam talked of *The Coldest Winter,* his new book about to come out, on the Korean War—his best book, he considered it. He talked to other groups, but he was in town to speak to Indiana University students, spreading a gospel rarely heard anymore: that the profession of journalism isn't dead, that it's wide open to people whose vision and perspective equal their writing talent. They heard it from a man who before he was 30 had gone into physically dangerous areas, who in print had dared to assess authority coolly and objectively, whether that authority was as repulsive as the KKK or as suave as JFK. His was an inspiring message.
>
> The trip that cost him his life was another step in the same mission, to other young students whom he hoped to inspire and no doubt did.
>
> The night I heard of his death, I glanced at that top shelf again, that row of Halberstam books. The day he was here, I mentioned to him that *The Children*—his close-up view of the unusually young people who bled and died in peace-ing Jim Crow to death—was my favorite of all his books. "That's my wife's favorite, too," he said. In the repose of gloom

the night of his death, I pulled *The Children* down and skimmed slowly through it. Then I started waiting for the new book, *his* favorite, to come out.

I served for 25 years as Midwest chairman of the Heisman Trophy selection committee. It was a distinct honor that carried with it annual invitations to the awards announcement ceremony and the banquet, which—because it is in early December and basketball is always in high gear by then—I was able to accept only a few times.

Still, Heisman trips introduced me to some outstanding people, even to history.

For a long time, the announcement program and the follow-up awards dinner were in the Downtown Athletic Club's headquarters building in the New York area called "The Battery"—the Statue of Liberty, Staten Island ferry, Ellis Island all close. So, too, were the World Trade Center's Twin Towers, so close that the horrors of 9/11/2001 eventually made the DAC building unusable. But, three months later with trucks still removing debris from Ground Zero, it still was the housing base for the 2001 Heisman announcement.

Julie and I went that year because Bloomington-raised Florida star Rex Grossman was the year's consensus All-America quarterback and a Heisman contender (he finished second, should have won, but that's not the point here). The presentation banquet was downtown, DAC guests taken there in limos. Julie and I happened to be paired in one with Rex's coach, Steve Spurrier, and his wife, Jerri. Steve couldn't have been more conversational—we talked some about Rex, but he also knew Indiana basketball names current and past and asked lots of Bob Knight questions. And this man of irreverent quips that sometimes zinged people in my profession on that ride made some personal history. I was 65 at the time, and southern gentleman Steve in our back-and-forth conversing was the first college football coach to address me as Mr. Hammel. (For the record: The first college basketball coach was Stan Van Gundy, then of Wisconsin, later of the NBA. I'm not sure there ever was a second in either group.)

≈

5.8. Frank and Mildred Eliscu—the artist behind the Heisman pose.

Another Heisman trip opened an unlikely but treasured relationship for Julie and me with Frank and Mildred Eliscu (fig. 5.8). Julie and I arrived early at a 1995 Heisman-weekend luncheon, sat down at a table for four, expecting to be joined by a man we both liked, Maury White. Before Maury arrived, a Heisman official brought over a silver-haired couple and asked if they could join us in the two unoccupied seats. Our situation with Maury was unarranged, so of course we welcomed them, but I'll have to admit unenthusiastically. Frank, about 80, was wearing a sports coat that flashy doesn't begin to describe. I didn't say but thought: "Must be a New York zillionaire who bought his way into the Heisman elite . . . this will be thrilling." Turned out I was wrong on everything but the term I used in jest. Frank Eliscu turned out to be a genuinely thrilling man to know.

As a Depression Era art student just out of Pratt Institute in his hometown New York, young Frank submitted the requisite three prospective sketches and beat out an all-star field to be the Downtown Athletic Club's choice to design the Heisman Trophy—the annual award that dates to 1936 and honors the man voted college football's best player: maybe the most recognized individual trophy in American sports. Frank went on to become an esteemed sculptor, among his works the massive Cascade of Books display at the Library of Congress in Washington.

Julie and I followed that luncheon talk with a couple of visits to the Eliscus' Sarasota home, where walls were adorned with some of his works and with tools of his trade that went back to the Etruscans, or close. Frank, by then well into 80s, was still working beautiful wonders in his home studio. My last trip there had a purpose. I was an officer with the Football Writers Association of America when some in the organization clamored for overt FWAA action to get better Heisman-voter consideration of defensive players. True, offensive players dominate it—recently quarterbacks, 2017 winner Baker Mayfield of Oklahoma the fifteenth in the 2000s. Before that, the Heisman went more frequently to running backs, a la the straight-arm, side-stepping pose of the athlete in the Eliscu statue. But, any FWAA step to influence Heisman voting was intolerable for both Heisman and FWAA people.

At the time, Charlotte was celebrating landing an NFL franchise, and the Charlotte Touchdown Club hoped to get national visibility by teaming with the FWAA in giving a major college football award annually.

In the FWAA hierarchy, a light went on: how about, in effect, a "Defensive Heisman"—the first college football Defensive Player of the Year Award?

Up to then, there had been positional awards—best lineman, best linebacker, best defensive back—but not recognition of the best player on that side of the ball. The FWAA created it, the Charlotte club adopted it, and we had an award (which ultimately took on the name of Bronko Nagurski, the Minnesota legend who in football's one-platoon days achieved something never duplicated: he was named 1929 All-American at *two* of the eleven positions, at tackle, which he played on defense, and fullback, his offensive role).

We had an award, but no trophy.

I remembered Frank had told me the sketch that became the trophy was not his personal favorite of his three submitted. He described another, of a tackler flowing into contact with a running ball-carrier. Straight from Charlotte I went on to Sarasota to see if 60 years later that sketch was still around, and the man who designed the Heisman Trophy could also be the creator of the Defensive Heisman. I asked. At work on a project, he smiled, set his tools down, walked to a filing cabinet, opened the third drawer down, fingered his way past manila folders to near the back and extracted one. Still silent, he handed it to me for my own reading, opened to a back page. It was the original contract with the Downtown Athletic Club. One paragraph near the end specified that the artist selected would never do another football trophy. There's a good chance only Frank knew of that. He had outlived everyone else involved. But he was too much a man of honor even to ask if maybe the statute of limitations on that agreement had expired. So Charlotte got another sculptor and a magnificent trophy, but what a neat "twin" that new award might have been.

Both the Football Writers' group and its other collegiate version, the US Basketball Writers Association, were invaluable to me in circumventing the presumed handicaps of small-town sports coverage. They and another group in which I was active, the National Sportscasters and Sportswriters Association headquartered then in Salisbury, North Carolina, gave me fraternity and friendship with some of those bluebloods I had known only by stature. Even before that World Series–eve press banquet at St. Louis in 1964, when I was still in Huntington I had attended a Football Writers' breakfast at the Hotel Sherman the week of the 1962 College All-Star football game in Chicago and heard live a classic Vince Lombardi talk. I saw a lot of big-name guys in my profession there, too, but didn't know—and wasn't known by—any of them.

Involvement in those writers' groups changed that. Furman Bisher of Atlanta went for me from a *Sporting News* bylined giant to a first-name friend. Joe Falls of Detroit was another; consummate Southern gentlemen Fred Russell of Nashville and Will Grimsley of Associated

Press two of many others. Will had been retired for about a year when I was nearing my own exit from sports, and I set up a breakfast meeting with him at Salisbury one April to ask, "Tell me, what am I going to miss the most?" This pleasant man of bushy white eyebrows and total unpretension paused over his sunny-side-up eggs to think for a second before saying, "I can't say I really *miss* anything... except... every now and then something happens that I'd like to comment on, and I can't." Years into my own retirement, I consider Will a prophet.

The major-league events my newspaper let me cover led to other unlikely friendships. At my second Olympics at Montreal in 1976, mutual coverage interests helped me form one with an Olympic rookie from the Milwaukee *Journal*, Bill Dwyre, who was one big job change away from becoming a national leader in sports coverage and in journalistic ethics. As sports editor of the Los Angeles *Times*, Bill's daily section during the 1984 Olympics was such a thorough and vital coverage Bible that he and the *Times* deserved a Pulitzer, which didn't come. Our particular link was Tracy Dodds, who worked with me at the *Herald-Telephone* while getting her degree at IU and then was the first woman on the sports staff at the Milwaukee *Journal*. When Dwyre left there to become the *Times* sports editor, he eventually brought in Tracy, and in '84 she headed the *Times*' encyclopedic Olympic swimming coverage (fig. 5.9).

At the 1996 Associated Press Sports Editors' convention at Cleveland, a few weeks before the Atlanta Olympics, Dwyre chaired a session on experiences of Olympic veterans who were at the convention. He let me speak for smaller papers, and I "thanked" him by telling of maybe my most—ornery?—Olympic memory. At Montreal in 1976, Bill and I began almost every day sharing breakfast in the press cafeteria. Even by then his zeal for lifting sportswriters out of the payola days when sports editors and writers commonly accepted gifts from event promoters was so nationally known, respected, and followed that I couldn't resist a daily gig. The hosts at Montreal offered writers a new souvenir each morning, ours for simply signing our name. Bill, of course, scorned them, but every morning for three and a half weeks before sitting down to my bacon and eggs with him I signed for my "prize" and laid it on the table for him to sneer at.

5.9. 1996 Curt Gowdy Award winners at Naismith Basketball Hall of Fame—
Dick Enberg and Bob Hammel with Gowdy (photo by Jane Priest).

The last morning Bill's exasperation finally spilled out and he said, "Doesn't it bother you, even a little bit, that a guy behind a window in Montreal knows that Bob Hammel is on the take?"

"No," I said, "not a bit.

"Because I've been signing in every morning as Bill Dwyre."

Salisbury and the NSSA also provided significant opportunities for me. NSSA for years was designated by the US Olympic Committee to, by membership vote, pick new inductees for the US Olympic Hall of Fame. Representing the organization at the 1989 Olympic Sports Festival at Oklahoma City when that year's selections were inducted, I spent two delightful hours at a shopping center interviewing and just chatting with boxer George Foreman in between his autograph requests at an advertised appearance.

The gold-medal 1980 US hockey team was also an '89 inductee, represented by one of the team's stars, Bill Cleary. Bill, whose outstanding playing career got him the on-ice "acting" role of Ryan O'Neal in the movie "Love Story," by '89 had completed a career as one of college hockey's great coaches at Harvard and become the school's athletic director. Meeting him at Oklahoma City gave me the only hockey columns I ever wrote in Bloomington—interesting thoughts from a coach whose sport was being raided by the pros years before they plundered college basketball. That was good, but better was the friendship formed. Within a year, Julie and I spent some vacation time in Boston and were Bill's guests for dinner at the Harvard Club and premium seats with him at a Red Sox game in Fenway Park.

I'm pretty sure Bill Veeck never would have recognized my name, but the genius of this baseball executive exemplar was that he made time for nonentities like me, in conversation across a desk or table gave each one of us his colorful, insightful opinions, and even listened to ours.

Over the years, I had four or five individual interview sessions with him, while representing small-circulation newspapers from areas unlikely to net him ten ticket sales a year.

Two times with him in particular stand out.

The night of June 11, 1981, Veeck had every reason to be upbeat: his White Sox team was in legitimate pennant contention and had just delighted a big Thursday crowd by beating the Veeck-despised Yankees. Veeck had every reason but one. Harold Baines caught Willie Randolph's fly ball with the tying run on third to end the 3–2 Sox victory. And baseball stopped.

The game's first protracted work stoppage shut down major league baseball for two months, wiping out 713 games. And still that night Veeck, heartsick, sat down in Comiskey Park's Bard's Room at a table with a few of us, quaffed some beers, and let that heart bleed openly.

This was the Veeck who in June 1959 responded to that same writer's nervy invitation to speak to maybe a hundred people at a small-town men's church group in Huntington, Indiana—150 miles from old Comiskey. Veeck arrived in a chartered plane, opened his talk by saying how happy he was with his present team—"Usually, we're mathematically eliminated by Mother's Day"—and, without accepting a penny for his appearance or expenses, left behind a charmed and bedazzled group, That team he joked about—Looey Aparicio, Nellie Fox, a fast, exciting bunch—ended a 40-year post–Black Sox Scandal dry spell by winning the American League pennant. Lost the World Series to the Dodgers, yes, but a pennant finally flew in Chicago!

This was the Veeck who as July opened in 1977 was on a magic-carpet ride with a team in preseason picked to be dismal. Veeck operated with baseball's shortest shoestring and the free-agent era was about to begin, dooming the money-short. That economic inevitability everyone knew, but not much more in the last year as baseball entered totally uncharted waters. Like French Marshal Foch in World War I ("My center is giving way, my right is retreating, situation excellent, I am attacking"), Veeck attacked. With a "Rent-a-Player" scheme, he traded great young players (e.g., Hall of Famer Rich Gossage and a similarly hard-throwing young relief star Terry Forster) for stars likely to leave their present team in end-of-the-year free agency. Shazam! Sluggers Richie Zisk (Pirates) and Oscar Gamble (Yankees) led into surprise pennant contention a zany group. "The South Side Hitmen" they called them, defensive misfits and maybe the worst baserunning team but guys who could clout the baseball. And they won games.

July 4 is the date when baseball gets serious, when unpredicted division leaders take on credibility. Minnesota, an established power of the day, arrived July 1 for a four-game, Friday-to-Sunday series, leading the Sox by a game. Somehow the Cubs, also always underdogs, were leading their division, too, and on Monday, July 4, they were playing a doubleheader with star-loaded Montreal at Wrigley Field. Maligned and pitied Chicago all of a sudden was baseball's hot spot. Pizazz was unbounded. Rod Carew of the Twins came to town flirting with a .400 season, *Time* magazine's coverboy that week. A Big Ten colleague of mine, Bob Markus, in a Chicago *Tribune* story, cited all the newspapers from around the country in town to cover this firecracker of a weekend, and right in there with the biggies he included the Bloomington *Herald-Telephone*. (Yeah, I did clip and save; Perry Stewart would have, too.)

Friday night, Comiskey was electric—filled and loud. First time up, Zisk homered, then hit another to seal the win that jumped the Sox into the division lead.

The Saturday game was barely fourteen hours later, starting at 1:30. I had an appointment for a pregame interview with Veeck. I was there well before noon, but Veeck wasn't—he was at a downtown luncheon marking the thirtieth anniversary of his breaking the American League's color line by bringing Larry Doby into Cleveland. I sat, I waited, and game time neared. I figured at best I'd get a hurried comment or two. Even that seemed optimistic when Veeck arrived, rushed into his office, and genial Sox press director Don Unferth of the Sox asked if I could do the interview while he snarfed his lunch. Expecting I'd have maybe five fast minutes, I accepted them gratefully. I was, after all, from the Bloomington *Herald-Telephone.*

I jumped right in trying to recapture the Norman Rockwellish scene the night before: when the crowd—abuzz all night, over the top with the Zisk homers—was so enchanted when the game ended with the Sox in first place that almost nobody left. For a *long* time—a long, merry, jubilant time. The stands stayed full and loud, particularly the celebrants just outside the open end of the press box from where Veeck through the game and afterward had kept a lively conversation going with fans outside.

Veeck's face brightened as he recaptured the moment:

> "It *was* kind of a magic night," he said, eyes filling at the memory. "It was a happy crowd. They came in that way. They, too, sensed something different. An hour after the game, people were still sitting here because they didn't want to break the spell. My wife, my sons and I—we felt it. We didn't want to go home, either.
>
> "It was like that song from *My Fair Lady*: 'I Could Have Danced All Night' . . . or 'Why Can't This Night Go On Forever.'
>
> " . . . I often think in song titles."

And so we talked, of this team, of free agency, of his optimism that his "Hit Men" could keep slugging and—who knows!—maybe even win. He talked of the years before when, after he won a World Series at Cleveland (1948) and a pennant with the White Sox (1959), a combination of bad health and limited finances forced him out of baseball, confined to a chair on the outskirts of Baltimore. It had to hurt a baseball man, exiled from baseball, I posited. But, no, it didn't, the unsinkable one insisted.

> There was a certain amount of nostalgia at times, like opening day of spring training. But I wasn't vegetating. I spoke on college campuses from coast to coast, 20 a year. That's a great way to keep track of what's going on.
>
> I had the enjoyment of watching my kids water ski for the first time off a dock, of seeing my daughters overcome problems and difficulties and win equitation championships. I wrote some books, did a column, finished some furniture, restored some junk, had a greenhouse and propagated azaleas. I got to read five books a week. I went to ball games, maybe 50 a year.

But, boy, was it clear he was glad to be back—and winning.

> This is a time when there is a rediscovery of the joys of baseball. Roger Angell says all the things I feel but he says them so much more beautifully than I can. It *is* "a game to be savored." It is one of the most unchanging things in a society that is firmly based on quicksand. In this confused and confusing world, here is some stability. During the '60s and '70s we got to thinking our society was speed, action and violence. Our national sports were ones that typified those—football, basketball, hockey and mugging. I may have those in the wrong order.
>
> But baseball is a game of romance and nostalgia. Fans say, "Hey, that catch is like Gionfriddo's," or "I was there when Nicholson hit it on the roof."

And Bill Veeck?

> I'm a traditionalist with no regard for tradition. That's why I took the AstroTurf out [to go back to a grass infield]. That's why I put the name back on the park [Comiskey Park, after previous owners junked the club owner–stadium builder's name for "White Sox Park"]. He [Charles Comiskey] was the fellow who built this park in 1910. It took some conviction to do that in 1910. He's entitled to have his name on it till it falls down.

It was flowing so beautifully, but on the brink of game time, *I* was the one who suggested we end the interview so he could see the game. It was worth seeing. Journeyman first baseman Jim Spencer drove in eight runs that day and the Sox solidified their league lead. With the stadium nearly full the next day, the Sox swept the doubleheader and the series, and—wow!—a runaway loomed. I sent in a two-column series on Comiskey happenings, then completed the writing duties by going to Wrigley and watching the Expos sweep the Cubs, a humiliating 19–3 in one game. Still, on July 4 both Chicago teams were in first place.

The Cubs died first. Then, alas, George Brett and the Kansas City Royals were just better than the Sox and eventually won out, as better teams tend to do in baseball's long season. That winter, free agency and skyrocketing salaries entered the game and the Veecks and Charlie Finleys, with their imaginations and derring-do and stretched-thin budgets, had to leave it. And soon Comiskey Park and what it said about respecting the past was gone and the first of a series of corporations bought its name onto the replacement ballpark. And player salaries soon were a couple of digits beyond Veeck's biggest White Sox payroll. Gone was a precious, and fairly recent, time—the highlight of which to me were those July 1977 moments with Bill Veeck, when I could have danced all night.

So it was that when he died at 71 January 2, 1986, I pulled out those notebooks from '77 and '81 and talked of the club owner who really was just a fan, and a lovable one. Some dancer, too—not with his feet, but his eyes, and his wonderful baseball insight.

D. Wayne Lukas, who trains horses for a living, a good living, was another luminary Bob Knight brought into my orbit. Until contemporary Bob Baffert passed him in spring 2018, Lukas's horses had won more Triple Crown races than anybody's, including four Kentucky Derbies. He was the first trainer to top $100 million in career purse winnings. Before all that started, he was an assistant basketball coach at his alma mater, Wisconsin—he and future Michigan coach Johnny Orr assistants under John Erickson, during the days when Knight was on the Ohio State teams that dominated the Big Ten. In three championship years, those Buckeyes lost two league games. One was to Wisconsin—after, Knight always reminded Lukas, Ohio State already had clinched that year's Big Ten title.

It was after Lukas's more familiar career had taken shape that he and Knight met—through Pete Newell, "a complete, degenerate race-tracker," Lukas fondly called Newell. "I had followed Bob's career closely. I knew he and Pete were good friends, and I said, 'Pete, let's get Bob, and get together.'" That came at the 1988 Kentucky Derby, and Knight helped root new-friend Lukas's first Derby winner, Winning Colors, home. "That was Bob's first Derby," Lukas said. "Pete told me, 'I've seen Bobby in a lot of situations. and I've never seen him as excited as he was when Winning Colors hit the finish line.' It was just a great moment for me, and to share it with him was special because we have become good friends."

It was the first of several Derbies at which Knight was Lukas's guest, and a few times Lukas reshapedhis year-round work demands to get to Bloomington for a dinner, or a game, or a practice. "I miss this a lot," the only trainer in both the thoroughbred and quarterhorse racing halls of fame said one of those times.

The Knight-Lukas friendship took on a new dimension in fall 1993. Lukas's son, Jeff, virtually a copartner in the training operation, tried to corral a runaway prize horse after a workout and was gravely injured. Within a few hours, Knight was in telephone contact with Lukas at Jeff's bedside, contact repeated often over the harrowing next several weeks—long, fearful, agonizing days that crept by like a slow metronome for Lukas, who rarely left his son. "They thought they had lost him twice," Lukas said. His skull fractured, Jeff Lukas was comatose for four weeks. He survived.

Just before Christmas 1993, Knight became a horse owner. Gogarty, a six-year-old Irish horse, was Lukas's pick for him: "I just said, 'Bob, this is a damned good deal. Just send me a check." Gogarty *was* a good buy: he earned more than he ate, before Lukas amicably divested his investor.

As rich as my sports-coverage memories are, they are not regret free. I was always aware those great young athletes I was covering were kids—somebody's son or daughter, somebody's grandchild. And still...

My 40 years of covering sports were over, but—on Thanksgiving weekend of 1998—I was still involved as analyst alongside play-by-play legend Don Fischer on radio broadcasts of Indiana University basketball. To start a new year in that role, I was on a plane with my wife Julie and daughter Jane, headed for Hawaii, on a Sunday. The basketball team was already in Maui, but I stayed behind to watch the football team end its season against Purdue.

I had extra duty on that flight. Antwaan Randle El, a rookie quarterback, already had emerged as an exciting, exceptional football player. Beyond that, the Cubs drafted him in baseball, and he was so good in basketball he had Bob Knight's permission to join that team when football ended. Antwaan was on that Hawaii-bound plane—not seated at the back with the three of us but about midplane, where I could watch him. That was part of my assignment; Antwaan had never made a flight that included a switch of planes, as this did, and he was told I'd be along in case he had any confusion. We met for the first time in the Indianapolis airport just before takeoff; I went to all the football games, marveled at his superlative play, but had no coverage role with the team, thus no personal familiarity with him.

The day before, Antwaan had taken a terrible pounding from rival Purdue, on the scoreboard (52–7) and on the field. Like every game, he handled the ball on every play and took a hit on most of them. As a passer, a runner, or a dazzling executioner of an option play that was a lightning-quick pitch-or-keep decision for him to make, every play usually ended for him with a jarring tackle—in possession of the ball or not. After a day like that and a drubbing by the Hoosiers' biggest rival, he had every reason to be sore head to toe, to be down, wanting to catch some sleep, to avoid conversation, even at the risk of seeming impolite.

But that wasn't the young man I watched. The plane included dozens of other IU fans, headed for the Maui Classic. All seemed aware he was aboard. He was in an aisle seat, so there were few moments in the long flight when someone wasn't at his side making conversation, getting an autograph, taking pictures—and I couldn't believe his patience, his amicable tolerance, his never-fading smile. *This*, I thought, *is a remarkable young man.*

The switch in planes came at Honolulu, where we left our big 727, got our baggage, and eventually boarded a much smaller commuter craft to make the hop to Maui.

It was during that stopover that the four of us got together. For the first time, Antwaan opened his team-issued bag, pulled out and took an almost disbelieving look at the brand-new white Indiana basketball uniform he would be wearing. Carefully, he lifted jersey and pants, neatly folded together, out of the bag. With a child's Christmas-morning look in his eyes and grin on his face, he ran a hand gently, caressingly, up the back of the uniform he was seeing for the first time—and my two ladies fell in love. This was college athletics at its storybook best.

Antwaan played basketball just that one year but football for four years that no one with IU loyalty ever will forget. Game in, game out, dependably every Saturday for four full seasons, he was the most spectacular player ever to wear an Indiana uniform. "Ever" exceeds my qualifications—I'll limit it to the 70 years that I have seen Indiana football teams. Never, *anyone* like him.

A sportswriting friend of mine from Chicago, Skip Myslenski of the *Tribune,* came to Bloomington to cover the IU-Northwestern game Antwaan's senior season. At pregame lunch, Skip—obviously alert to Antwaan's Chicago background—asked, "What's so special about this kid?" I said, "All I can tell you is I promise you he'll do something today that you have never seen on a football field before. I don't know what it will be, but there'll be something."

His senior collegiate year was the only one he returned punts, at which he later excelled with the NFL Steelers. This day, in the first half, he retreated to catch a high Northwestern punt, disdained a fair catch, and bolted straight upfield, as punt returners are taught to do. But, this time after a couple of steps he stopped, looked to his right and—option-quarterback style—fired a lateral pass a good twenty yards to a teammate coming up the sidelines. It worked for twenty extra yards. Never did it before, never again—but that was Antwaan. In his press-box chair several seats to my left, Skip Myslenski leaned back, looked toward me, and with a grin and a nod said, "I see what you mean."

Bill Mallory was out of coaching by then, his last fourteen seasons at Indiana. He was at Colorado when Oklahoma had a dazzling string of great option quarterbacks (Thomas Lott, J. C. Watts). "Randle El,"

Mallory said firmly, "is the best I've *ever* seen." In an Indiana victory over Minnesota, he passed for more than 200 yards and ran for more than 200—the only 200–200 game in more than a hundred years of Big Ten football. In a game at Cincinnati he ran for a touchdown, passed for one, and caught a pass for one—an Indiana first if not Big Ten. He made every play breathtaking, the threat of a Houdini escape always present. He was four years of excitement, of thrills.

And 20 years later, a Super Bowl star wealthy after free-agency but his career over, he opened up to a news reporter about the price he had paid for all of our onlooking fun. He told of trouble walking down stairs, of memory problems. The movie *Concussion* had just come out, nailing the sport of football with responsibility for causing brain damage that traumatically affected the lives—and assumably caused the eventual deaths—of many players, some of them stars and some not. Those, of course, would have been the iceberg tips for oceans of lesser-knowns who played the same game, took the same hits, and paid the same price.

So where are we, in the middle of the twenty-first century's second decade, with this game that America calls its favorite—this game that I have loved, have written about, have thrilled to for a lifetime?

Do we—*can* we—change it? Save it? Outlaw it?

A learned man vilified in *Concussion* as an enabler in football hierarchy's refusal to accept mounting evidence of the game's risks, Dr. Joseph Maroon once also wore an Indiana football uniform. As "Little Joe" Maroon, he rivaled even Antwaan in gutsiness, a terribly undersized (five foot seven, 160) tailback who was the leading rusher (364 yards, two touchdowns) on the underwhelming Hoosier team of 1960 (1–8, the only victory over Marquette, which after that year dropped football). It was the only season he lettered before moving on to medical school and a career that won him national, even international acclaim as a neurologist and recognition from his alma mater (from its 500,000 alumni, IU in 2011 gave Maroon one of its five Distinguished Alumnus awards). Google his biography and read:

> Dr. Maroon has been the team neurosurgeon for the Pittsburgh
> Steelers since 1981, and is Medical Director of the World Wrestling
> Entertainment (WWE). He has successfully performed surgery on
> numerous professional football players and other elite athletes with

potentially career-ending neck and spine injuries. Notably, he safely returned most to their high level of athletic performance.

Dr. Maroon is highly invested in the prevention and treatment of concussions in high school, college and professional sports, specifically football. While working with the Steelers in the early 1990s, the lack of an objective, reliable instrument to evaluate concussion symptoms became very apparent to Dr. Maroon. To fill this void, he and Dr. Mark Lovell developed an easy to administer, 20-minute-long test to assess presence and severity of concussion symptoms [which] has become the world-wide standard tool to assess sports-related concussions, and has been used on over 4.5 million athletes. In 1994, Dr. Maroon joined the National Football League's mild Traumatic Brain Injury Committee as concussion expert. This committee, which in 2007 was renamed National Football League's Head, Neck and Spine Committee, is still in place.

This is the team doctor/executive/spokesman, identified by name and played in the movie by actor Arliss Howard, who comes across there as a shill for the National Football League . . . as bullying the question-asking neurologist (lead actor Will Smith) not physically but contemptuously for the audacity of his challenging so majestic an entity as the NFL, and the very sport of football. Sorry, moviemakers, that one scene I have trouble buying. But I do wonder where this man of such superior intellect is on this question of moral justification for survival of the sport he loves?

And somewhere in the middle of that tense confrontation are you and I. Where *do* we go with this? *Will* we, *can* we accept a less violent game, a safer game? *Will* we, *can* we as mothers and dads continue to put our kids in helmets and on football fields? *Will* we, *can* we as fans not to mention sportswriters continue to admire "great" hits, or accept a game without them?

I'm over 80. It's not going to be my decision to make.

But I think of the times I sat thrilled in a press box watching Antwaan Randle El take hits, and avoid hits, and run and pass and score and . . .

All the time I was feeling thrilled, he was accumulating the body damage that led him in retirement to say if he had it to do all over again, he wouldn't have played football.

I confess to feeling really, really guilty.

I hear the fitting strains of Bob Hope's "Thanks For The Memory" as I near the door, and under their charm wanting to get there by tapping into my most remembered high school Shakespeare quote, from *Macbeth*:

> Tomorrow, and tomorrow, and tomorrow,
> creeps in this petty pace from day to day . . .

It's unwise to rewrite the Bard, but my review of my fortune runs more to

> Yesterday, and yesterday, and yesterday,
> raced at a merry pace from thrill to thrill . . .

I actually did think over the years of tapping that *Macbeth* lament for a memoir title, maybe going on to lines four and five:

> And all our yesterdays have guided fools their way to dusty death.

To come up with the title
All Our Yesterdays . . .
Or going farther into the passage for

> Life's but a walking shadow, a poor player
> That struts and frets his hour upon the stage,
> And then is heard no more. It is a tale
> Told by an idiot, full of sound and fury,
> Signifying nothing.

Which could have given me
Tales of an Idiiot
Or
Walking Shadows
But not
Sound and Fury
Faulkner already stole that.
C'est la vie.
Mine.

Acknowledgments

THIS SECTION OF A BOOK NORMALLY IS IN ESSENCE A THANK you to many who were vital in preparation and production of a book, in this case the names of editors David Miller and Carol McGillivray and overall chief Gary Dunham at the top of the Indiana University Press list.

But, what I'm most eager, maybe even desperate, to acknowledge is how so many people who were close to me and major figures in my writing career were shorted in the editing, bobtailing, tightening process that cut a planned manuscript roughly in half.

So many people . . . so many friends . . . so many memories . . . so many precious times.

These pages are full of them, based on them, but so much was left out. My son, Rick, was with me and around me in many of those moments and knew of their importance to me—so why, he kept prodding, is this not in there, or that?

After one quick but quite observant trip through the near-final manuscript he insisted:

1. "You've *got* to say more about that 1967 IU Rose Bowl season, and the colorful characters on that team, and Coach [John]

Pont—that's when Bloomington first really got to know you. And Coach [Bill] Mallory, and Anthony [Thompson] . . ."

2. "There's not nearly enough about Doc [Counsilman] and how fantastic those swimmers and those teams were—how much he and those years did for you. And Hobie [Billingsley] and all those great divers."

3. "You know IU people are probably going to care the most about your basketball years. Hey, I'm one of them. I'd like to see more about Quinn [Buckner] and Scott [May] and Isiah [Thomas] and Landon [Turner] and Randy [Wittman] and Steve [Alford] and Calbert [Cheaney] and Damon [Bailey]—*all* of those guys and teams. And Coach Bell [track coach Sam], and [Olympians] Jim Spivey, Dave Volz, Bob Kennedy. I know you had to assign soccer to someone else, but you can't just leave out how great a job Jerry Yeagley did."

Dr. Richard Hammel, who has an MPH (for master of public health) behind his name along with his MD, is quite accomplished and distinguished in his field. He hasn't met a lot of editors, who rarely ask for more in their zealous pursuit of words and paragraphs and pages to cut.

Which doesn't make Rick wrong. For now, genuine acknowledgment should be made of the people whose steadfast insistence as well as encouragement eventually wore down my own reluctance that had been stiffened by wife Julie's early and very realistic reaction to suggestions of a memoir: "Who would read *that*?"

I've often said to others thinking about writing their own life story: "*Do* it! By all *means*, do it! If no one reads it but your grandkids, they'll know you better—know what in your life was significant to you."

Turned out even Rick and his sister, Jane—and probably, too, their mother—learned things about me they didn't know. I hope among those things is how much the back-and-forth love within our family was the biggest thing of all to me.

As Michael Koryta says in his preface, he and our frequent lunch partner, the late Indiana University history professor George Juergens, were among the prods who now face accessory responsibility for the finished product—Michael much more than George because he took on the professional task of editing and pruning and challenging and criticizing. Too gentle, yes, that could be charged, but within the bounds of friendship his bites and barks were effective.

Lunchtime in retirement started for me with two outstanding IU professors, Bill Wiggins and Larry Onesti, great partners in their own retirement—the chemistry in our get-togethers as terrific as our backgrounds were different. Wiggins, an ordained minister and an outstanding African American educator who played on three state basketball champions at Louisville Central; Onesti an Italian Catholic and leader in Northwestern's late-1950s surge under Ara Parseghian, then an undersized pro linebacker whose real stardom was as a geography professor; and me: a no-degree nonathlete raised in and fond of what was labeled a "sundown town." About the only thing we weren't was Hispanic, so Bill naturally tagged us "Three Amigos." And I lived to mourn the passing of both.

My brother, Bill, and Spyridon "Strats" Stratigos, two other weekly lunch companions in my senior years, also contributed encouragement, sometimes disguised as borderline abuse but never unappreciated. Despite our 16-year age gap, Bill is the closest thing to a twin I have—not identical but fraternal. Our similarity of thinking, of political and against-the-grain ideological leanings is uncanny for two brothers who really never lived together—by the time he was old enough to be influenced in any way by a much-older brother, I was out of the house and married. Even our voices must sound similar to others, though not to us. As an IU undergraduate on his way to a law degree, he was in our part-time sportswriting corps, and very good. Law paid better.

I was in a couple of other remarkable breakfast groups, Mallory in both and retired congressman Lee Hamilton in one. A lot of terrific people were. Bloomington is an edifying place to eat.

Before retirement, I had a lot of entertaining lunches with a sports giant who dropped in my newspaper office one afternoon, and both of our lives got better. Neither I nor the sports world knew anything of Jeff Sagarin then. New in town, his visit was to introduce himself and the idea he had: in the dawning of the computer age, to take opinion out of rating sports teams and let their results speak for themselves. This was 1977. Math-based sports ratings had long since been marketed. But not by a Jeff Sagarin, not by a man prestigious MIT twice has profiled in its own publications, not by a mind that moves a layman like me to use the word "genius"—the Einstein kind.

Jeff's roots were in New Rochelle, New York, his upbringing modest. He brained his way to MIT and ultimately followed college friend Wayne Winston to Bloomington, where Wayne was an IU professor. Jeff had no such job, just an idea that already had given him introduction to one of America's top sports editors: Dave Smith of the Boston *Globe*, the first newspaper to use Sagarin ratings. Jeff's process requires game scores, *all* game scores, so gaining access to our wire-service score lists was why Jeff looked me up. We talked of his plans, I wrote a column headlined "His computer rates the teams," he let us use his college football and basketball rankings for something like $5 a week, and the Sagarin rocket was launched. Soon *USA Today* found Jeff's numbers as compelling as I had, and overnight Sagarin became a name that sports followers by the millions grew to know but almost nobody could pronounce (try SAG-uh-rin, not sa-GARE-un or the more common and worse SARE-uh-gun). Forty years later Jeff still subjects his systems to constant review and refinement, and his field of coverage has expanded to include almost everything in sports—except horseracing, which makes me wonder how much of that sport's unpredictability is equine and how much human, as in manipulations. He even has a more plausible computer-based political redistricting system than gerrymandering Congress has.

At the *Herald-Telephone*, we supplied Jeff with a fellow traveler down Stats Road: my chief aide, John Harrell. The two of them made our pages sing with varied use of Jeff's numbers, extended just for us at first into Indiana high school basketball, eventually women's sports, plus all the pro games and players Jeff's data graded. And John and I added a lifelong friend, a quirky one, but brilliant. Both John and I, largely because of his diligence at continually seeking improvement, consider him peerless in a crowded field. So do the millions for whom "Sagarin" is that field's standard.

John Harrell, who came along just as I was leaving Huntington, was the best of the many great staff additions I made in Bloomington. My goodness, we had some talent on our staffs. The first outsider I added was Bob Getz, straight out of the Army with no newspaper background at all but a passion and gift for writing. His first weekend with us I assigned him to a high school football game; he warned me, "I'm from Winamac [a small northwest Indiana town]. I don't know anything about football." I realized he wasn't kidding when his first story referred to the area past the goal line as the "in-zone." But, he was a marvelous writer and went on to become revered in Wichita, Kansas, as the local columnist for the *Wichita Eagle*.

A key in putting our staff together during crosstown competition days was bringing back one who had left us, Rex Kirts. Perry Stewart had to be talked into that one, because he was on record against taking any "defectors" back. "Give me a reason why I should with Kirts," he said. I told him, "I'll give you two: it will help us and hurt them." And it did, especially in strong high school coverage that, even in a college town, was vital.

My first hiring of any kind was Greg Dawson, who caught my attention during my first Bloomington basketball season with a letter to the sports editor that read so well he could bolster our short part-time staff. The letter was signed Gary Vance, junior, Bloomington High School. The school was across the street from the *H-T*. I called athletic director Bill Frohliger, who said yes, he knew Gary Vance, and agreed to tell him I'd like to talk to him after school. About 4 o'clock, a high school–age kid showed up, I said, "Hi, Gary," but he corrected me: "I'm not Gary Vance, I'm Greg Dawson, but I wrote the letter." He wrote it, didn't have the nerve to put his own name on it but had enough to use a friend's and mail it. Well-written fraud must appeal to me; I hired him and called him my Clifford Irving while benefiting from his great natural talent, and a 50-year friendship.

He came as close as the son of two college professors could to emulating my collegiate performance. He did a little time at Oberlin College, then pretty much skipped the rest of school and became terrific—as a columnist with the *Herald-Telephone*, a TV columnist with the Boston

Herald, a general columnist and reporter on the Boca Raton, Florida, *News* under Tom Schumaker, stints back in Bloomington and at the Indianapolis *Star* before settling at the Orlando *Tribune.* Late in all that, he wrote a book called *Hidden in the Spotlight,* the fantastic story of his mother's life—her escape as a teen-aged Jewish piano prodigy from the Nazis in the Ukraine. You think you've read all the chilling Holocaust stories you want to read. Read this one, and a follow-up, *Judgment Before Nuremberg,* the by-product of Greg's research into Ukrainian records for facts about his mother and her Nazi-executed family. Other Dawson books have followed, all excellent.

Greg is representative of the extraordinary part-time employees, most of them IU related, who kept coming to us through the years. Included are two women who became nationally known journalists. Tracy Dodds went from us to Milwaukee, then to Los Angeles, then to be the first woman sports editor at a major Texas daily, the Austin *American-Citizen.* While at Austin, she was president of the Associated Press Sports Editors, a Bill Dwyre–inspired organization that made "sports journalism" not an oxymoron. Tracy and another IU student who started in sports with us in Bloomington, Kristin Huckshorn, were among the early leaders in formation of American Women in Sports Media—Kristin one of the four founders. AWSM—an *awesome* acronym—gives an annual Pioneer Award to one member, a list that amounts to its Hall of Fame. Two of that award's first eight recipients were Tracy and Kristin, whose journalism resume included the San Jose *Mercury News,* New York *Times,* and ESPN.

Rick Bozich, on his way to the US Basketball Writers Association Hall of Fame in a career highlighted by his years with the Louisville *Courier-Journal,* is one of our alumni. At our paper, Rick's job was half sports, half news. Louisville used him better.

The biggest national sports media name to get his start on our staff is TV headliner Jason Whitlock. Jason's days as a lineman at Ball State weren't far behind him when he met editor Bob Zaltsberg at a job fair and signed on for part-time work. Within a few short years, he was lead sports columnist at the Ann Arbor *News,* then at the Kansas City *Star,* on his way to national TV eminence as not just a major black voice in American sports but a major voice, in sports and more.

Jason and Tracy are in the Indiana Sportswriters and Broadcast-ers Association. Kristin should join them soon. And there was the day when Andy Graham of our staff was inducted into that Hall of Fame, completing what surely is precedent setting. Andy joined John Harrell, Rex Kirts, Lynn Houser, and me in it. That was our entire full-time sports staff at one point, indicating a statewide respect for what we were doing in Bloomington—the most meaningful of compliments for all of us.

One key colleague who never was on a newspaper with me had an exceptional impact on my life. In the 1972–73 IU basketball season, an early 6–0 jump in the Big Ten got young coach Bob Knight and his program spotlighted by *Sports Illustrated*, which sent writer Pat Putnam and photographer Rich Clarkson to do a feature. Clarkson, whose first prominence came as a photographer for his hometown Topeka, Kansas, *Capital-Journal*, already by '73 was one of the top stars in sports photog-raphy, and he meshed quickly with Knight—to an almost unaccount-able, but lifetime, degree.

So it was that as the 1974–75 powerhouse Indiana team began to emerge, Clarkson came up with a suggestion for a book he and I could do on the season. Knight agreed to go along, and I would be the writer. The night before Indiana was to play a game at Northwestern, the three of us went to a suburban Chicago high school game, then met in a Greek restaurant in Evanston. There was no negotiation, just planning; the book was coproperty of Rich and me, and Bob agreed to make his play-ers available and to open his locker room to Clarkson—as he never had to anyone else, including me. The book obviously featured him, ultimately was titled *Knight with the Hoosiers*, but he never got a dime from it.

In mid-conversation the waitress called our attention to a man sit-ting alone in the restaurant's bar. "That's the Northwestern president (Robert Strotz)—his wife is out of town, he's by himself, he heard you talking about tomorrow's game, and he'd like to buy you a drink." Nei-ther Bob nor I ever drank anything beyond a Coke, but of course we invited him over.

We all presumed he knew who Knight was, till conversation showed us he didn't, way too far along for introductions. President Strotz, understandably no sports fan, at a distance had heard us talk fondly of the Northwestern basketball coach, Tex Winter, whom we all knew and liked. He couldn't have been more amiable—nor Knight, who bit his tongue but didn't react to: "I know we don't have much chance tomorrow. That Indiana team I hear is a bunch of pros." His farewell line was, "I think we all agree that we might not win tomorrow but we won't be outcoached." Getting out the door before exploding into laughter was tough.

The next year, John Pont, IU's 1967 Rose Bowl coach and then Northwestern athletic director, brought president Strotz back to dine with us: same place, same game-eve situation, no more identity confusion, great time all around.

By then, *Knight with the Hoosiers* had come out, the first of 10 books I did while at the *Herald-Times*. And the first of two team-ups with Clarkson for me: in 1996, after Bob's 25th year as IU coach, we coauthored *Silver Knight*, one of the most beautifully illustrated (with Clarkson's signature pictures) sports books ever. Rich, honored by the NCAA when he photographed his 50th Final Four, also contributed considerably to other books I did, including the cover shot for Bob's autobiography, *Knight: My Story*. In 2009–10, when IU opened Cook Hall, named for chief donor Bill Cook—a basketball practice building that included a two-story basketball museum, Clarkson's action pictures from all those years of covering Knight teams gave the displays their richest illustration.

For all the time I took from their coaching husbands, several wives were special friends of both Julie and me—Karen Knight, Ellie Mallory, and Marge Counsilman matchless, and Fran Bell, Sandy Pont, so many through the years.

All those were among the people vital to my career—way up at the top Perry Stewart and Bob Knight, and the man who gave me a starting chance, Howard Houghton, with a few others up there very close. I hope all are properly recognized in these pages. It's those who are not whom son Rick had in mind, and that list is long. Acknowledged or unacknowledged, they have my thanks.